KOREAN CULTURAL HERITAGE

Volume IV

Traditional Lifestyles

Korea Foundation

한국국제교류재단

FOREWORD

The Korea Foundation is pleased to present Traditional Lifestyles, the fourth volume in its Korean Cultural Heritage series, which was launched to foster a better understanding of Korean Studies abroad.

Since the publication of the first volume in this series, Fine Arts, in 1994, the Foundation has published three additional volumes: Thought and Religions (vol. 2), Performing Arts (vol. 3) and now Traditional Lifestyles (vol. 4). Each volume features in-depth and high-caliber articles written by scholars and specialists from various fields of Korean art and culture.

Traditional Lifestyles examines traditional Korean life in regard to such aspects as clothing, food, housing, family systems and rites of passage. It also includes information about Korea's regional traditions and folk culture. A wealth of photographs supplements the text, helping traditional Korean life and culture come alive for the reader.

We hope that this volume, like the past three volumes in the series, will serve as a useful resource for Korean studies scholars as well as for general readers interested in learning about Korean culture.

We are especially grateful for the dedicated efforts of those who made the publication of this volume possible.

Joungwon Kim
President
The Korea Foundation

KOREANA

KOREAN CULTURAL HERITAGE

Volume IV

Traditional Lifestyles

Copyright ©1997 by
The Korea Foundation

This book is mainly a compilation of articles published in KOREANA from its inaugural edition in 1987 through 1997 and the third of a series on Korean culture. Some articles have been added or edited for style and space.

Publisher/ Editor
Joungwon Kim

Art Director
Park Seung-u

Copy Editor
Julie Pickering

Layout & Design
Art Space Korea, Seoul

All photographs, except where otherwise indicated, are the property of Art Space Korea, Seoul.

Printed in December 1997 by Samsung Moonhwa Printing Co, Seoul

Price: US$40.00 (₩30,000)

ISBN 89-860-9013-9

CONTENTS

Food and Drink

Appendices

INTRODUCTION

Our survey of Korean lifestyles begins with Professor Kang Shin-pyo's article on traditional life. Kang considers the basis of Korean culture and customs: the relationship between the individual and the community; the Korean concept of nature; Korea's syncretistic religious and philosophical tradition; and the importance of family throughout Korean history.

Korea's topography, climate and geopolitical circumstances have combined to create a culture in which the collective has taken precedence over the individual. Traditional life revolved around the agricultural cycle. The agrarian lifestyle required cooperation and the sharing of labor. During the busy planting and harvesting seasons, neighbors pooled their labor and tools. When the work was done, they celebrated their good fortune and performed rites, which expressed their veneration of nature and ancestors who brought them into this world.

Indigenous folk beliefs, shamanism, Buddhism and Confucianism all developed in response to the traditional concern for natural phenomena and the order of nature. Agrarian life required dedication to community and family. As Kang explains, the nation was an extension of the family. Confucianism, which originated in China, was embraced by the Korean people and further developed, making Korea, in many ways, the most Confucian society in the world.

The father-son relationship was the fundamental bond in Korean society. Respect for one's parents and, by extension, loyalty to the nation were the guiding principles of Korean life, clearly evident in rites of passage, architecture, clothing, even in Korean food.

Professor Kang closes with the observation that urbanization and the opening of Korean society to the outside world have disrupted traditional lifestyles. As Koreans move from their native villages and join the modern work force, individual interests and needs often overshadow the interests of the group. The years ahead will tell whether the traditional commitment to collective harmony will have a place in modern Korea.

Traditional Life in Korea

Kang Shin-pyo

Koreans often use the word *uri*, which means "we" or "us," when English speakers would use "me" or "mine." Why is this? Don't Koreans differentiate between the individual and the collective? Or is it because the individual and the collective cannot be separated in Korean culture? This issue provides an important clue to the understanding of Korean life.

The word uri is said to have come from *ult'ari*, the wall around a house. This wall, made of clay or wood, establishes a living space for a family. Those who live within this boundary are called uri, without distinguishing between individuals. They live together through hardships and joy. One becomes uri by birth or by being neighbors. In other words, uri is a living community.

Traditional Korean life was based on agriculture, which required the sharing of labor. Many people pooled their resources—labor and tools—when planting, weeding and harvesting. Everyone worked, rested and played together. The year was divided into a busy period and a slow period. Everyone in the village worked together and rested together as the seasons changed.

Life revolved around the cycle of nature. Koreans had no choice but to accept what nature handed them. No one thought of trying to dominate or control nature. Farming followed the four seasons. Water was provided by heaven. Too much rain meant floods; too little meant drought. These were great concerns but neither flood nor drought was under human control. Natural disasters were accepted as heaven's punishments. The king was thought to have done something wrong to deserve such punishment. He bathed and donned clean clothes to pray for forgiveness. For their part, villagers performed rites pray-ing for rain. Various rituals were developed as expressions of their devotion, combining elements from indigenous folk beliefs, shamanism, Buddhism and Confucianism.

This accommodation to the natural order as a way of finding stability was applied to social life as well. Living together in a community required dedication to the community and mutual adjustment. The family was the basis of life. It is no coincidence that the Korean word for "nation," *kukka*, contains the ideograph *ka*, meaning "family." The nation is an extension of the family. This concept is shared by Korea, Japan and China, the East Asian cultures that use Chinese characters in their writing systems. While the three cultures are linguistically distinct, they have used the same Chinese characters for the past 1,500 years. China was the center of the East Asian world order. The common use of Chinese characters allowed the Chinese worldview to dominate those of its neighbors. The Chinese system laid the foundation for every aspect of life, including politics, economics, society, culture and religion. For this reason, many clues to everyday Korean life can be found in comparisons with lifestyles in China and Japan.

In particular, it is no exaggeration to say that the Chinese public order formed the foundation for the Korean public order. In many ways, the Confucian system is stronger in Korea than in China, where it originated. In Korea, various Confucian attributes, including ancestor veneration, strict family hierarchy and family rituals remain strong. During the Chosŏn Dynasty, political leaders sought to govern according to Chinese Confucian ideology. They were scholar-bureaucrats who studied and practiced Confucian ideology and philosophy.

The Chinese public order was not limited

Traditional life revolved around nature.
The changing seasons brought new tasks such as the replacement of
thatch roofs and long-cherished rites and festivals.
At right is a thatch-roofed house in Koch'ang, Chŏllanam-do province.

Traditional folk belief and imported philosophies such as Confucianism have been intertwined since early times. A spirit post (above); clan elders bowing to ancestral tablets (opposite).

to Confucianism, however. Before the introduction of Confucianism, Buddhism, which also came to Korea through China, influenced the Korean worldview for 1,000 years during the Three Kingdoms and Unified Shilla periods and the Koryŏ Dynasty. Throughout Korean history, it normally took 300 years for a foreign idea to merge with native thought and become part of everyday life. Syncretism of native and foreign beliefs has been a frequent occurrence. Folk beliefs, shamanism, Buddhism and Confucianism remain intertwined today.

On the other hand, once introduced to Korea, foreign religious thoughts remained true to their prototypes in many ways. As mentioned before, the Confucian prototype is better preserved in Korea than in China. Shamanism and Buddhism have also maintained many of their original characteristics in Korea. Relatively speaking, foreign elements exist in parallel with preexisting elements.

Perhaps this is the context in which we can best understand the boom in Christian belief since liberation from Japanese colonial rule in 1945 and the Korean War (1950-1953). In Korea, Christian prayer meetings held at the crack of dawn draw larger crowds than in other countries. These early morning gatherings are comparable to the folk practice of *pison* in which old women rise at dawn to pray before a bowl of freshly drawn well water, and to dawn chanting sessions held in Buddhist temples. Researchers have also pointed to the shamanic fervor of Korea's Christians.

A recent study shows that Confucian values occupy the depths of Korean Christians' consciousness. On the surface, Christianity, introduced from abroad, may dominate, but deep in the Christians' psyche, the ethic of filial piety remains central.

In traditional Korean society, the most important human relationship was between father and son. From it grew other relationships, between monarch and subjects, husband and wife, old and young, and between friends. Thus an understanding of the father-son relationship sheds light on traditional life in general. It also extends to relationships between parents and all their children. In these relationships, filial piety is the guiding principle.

According to sociologist Choi Jae-seok, filial piety is a one-sided relationship. Of all relationships involving respect, respect for parents is the most important and fundamental. Filial piety is the foundation of morality and benevolence, and therefore is the source of all behavior and the guiding principle of human

life. It is also the basic ethical relationship. Clearly Chinese Confucian principles run deep in Korean culture.

But what does filial piety mean?

First, it refers to respect for one's parents. Children should respect their parents and follow their parents' wishes in attitude and behavior. Children should never do anything without first seeking their parents' advice and permission. And without parental consent, they should not act. This norm applies not only in their relationships with their own parents but also in relations with senior relatives, neighbors and members of society.

Second, children should care for their parents. They should recognize their parents' desires, even when unexpressed, and make sure their parents' wishes are realized. Material

The Korean word for "we," uri, is thought to derive from ult'ari, the wall around a house. Those within the wall share their lives. They live together at work and at play.

needs—clothing, food and housing—should also be satisfied. Children owe their lives and upbringing to their parents, and as adults they are obligated to support and wait upon them.

Third, children should do everything possible to give their parents peace of mind. They should try to provide pleasure to their parents and never go against their wishes. Abiding by parents' wishes means inheriting and practicing what one's parents have failed to achieve themselves. Children should enjoy what their parents have enjoyed, they should respect what their parents have respected, they should be friendly with the people their parents have been friendly with. And when parents pass away, filial piety is practiced again in the form of funeral rituals and ancestral memorial rites.

Fourth, carrying on the family line is essen-

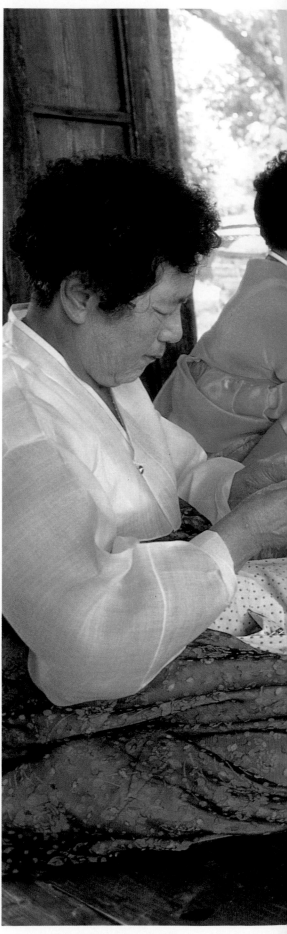

tial to filial piety. The Korean family system is patrilineal. For a son, the most important filial act is marrying and producing a son of his own. In the olden days, women who did not bear sons were expelled from the household or a concubine was taken in to produce a male heir. Sometimes a boy was adopted from the man's brothers. This is quite different from the Japanese custom, where the ability to carry on the family business was as important as bloodline in the adoption of male heirs.

The systems of inheritance in Korea, China and Japan are quite different. In traditional China, family property and ritual obligations in ancestral memorial rites were distributed equally among sons. Family headship was not handed down to one son in particular. In Japan, both birth sons and adopted sons inherit property along with ritual obligations in ancestral memorial rites. The family does not continue through bloodlines, but through the person who inherits the family line.

In Korea, on the other hand, the eldest son inherits the most property and family headship. In return he pays most of the expenses for ancestral memorial rites. Roger and Dawnhee Yim Janelli have noted that because Korean parents divide property while they are still alive, there are fewer disputes over the division of property than in China. (Roger L. Janelli and Dawnhee Yim Janelli, *Ancestor Worship and Korean Society* [Stanford, California: Stanford University Press, 1982], pp. 104-105.)

Filial piety was the behavioral norm of traditional Korean life and has remained at the foundation of the Korean consciousness throughout the transformation from agrarian to industrial society and from rural to urban life. Even today, Koreans address strangers in the street as grandfather, grandmother, uncle or aunt, depending on their age. They are treated as family members, though they are not blood relations. Major conglomerates refer to their employees as "family." In the workplace, filial piety is expressed as loyalty to the head of the company or union boss. While loyalty to nation (*chung*) and filial piety (*hyo*) are different concepts, in action they are quite similar.

Farm utensils stored under the eaves of an earthen house symbolize the importance of work in everyday home life.

From this perspective, the nature and unique characteristics of traditional Korean life are apparent. First, an individual cannot exist as a separate being. All Koreans are identified as a member of a group. In fact, only as a member of a family is one's identity confirmed. The family belongs to a clan, to the same bloodline and to the same surname. It is also confirmed through regional ties. Individuals are often categorized as natives of the Kyŏngsang region, the Chŏlla region, or sometimes as members of a certain workplace. Hence the use of the term uri forms the basis of community life.

Second is the hierarchical order of human relations. The fundamental patrilineal relationship develops along generational lines according to which the leaders rule and the younger generation obeys. In traditional society, a class order dividing the *yangban* elite from the common people was also part of this strict hierarchical consciousness. Bureaucrats monopolized wealth and status, which were reflected in their clothing, food and housing. Honorific forms of address born in this hierarchical tradition live on today. They may serve to perpetuate and re-create a hierarchical mind set.

Lastly, throughout history, Koreans have placed the highest value on community cooperation and harmony, just as they have valued harmony with nature. In a society where an individual could not survive alone and individual existence was not recognized, community-centered life may have required loyalty and filial piety within a strict hierarchy. Children and subordinates were expected to serve the interests and desires of parents and other elders, even when their wishes were not explicit. Community harmony depended on an almost telepathic understanding of each other's needs and desires. In other words, the community came before the individual.

Today, urbanization and the introduction of Western lifestyles have disrupted the traditional Korean lifestyle. The individual is taking precedence over the group, and people are beginning to express their own opinions. Equality is overpowering the traditional hierarchical order. Conflict is more common than collective harmony. In fact, some people embrace conflict as a strategy. As Koreans pass through the industrialization stage, traditional lifestyles are entering a transitional period. We must wait and see how society changes, but we can be certain that traditional culture will be re-created over and over again in the depths of the Korean consciousness. ◆

RITES OF PASSAGE AND FAMILIAL BONDS

The family system forms the foundation of Korea's traditional culture. As Professor Lee Kwang-kyu points out in the first article of this section, we must understand the Korean family system in order to understand Korean culture. Korea's patriarchal family system derives from the country's agrarian roots and the adoption of Confucianism as the state philosophy centuries ago. As Lee shows, the family is the unit of production and consumption, a venue for education and a religious forum in which rites of passage and the veneration of ancestors take place.

Marriage and procreation were essential tasks in traditional society. Marriage was not simply a union of two individuals; it marked the joining of two families in the perpetuation of stability and tradition. Professor Park Hye-in offers a brief history of wedding customs in early Korea as well as a detailed description of the traditional ceremony performed in Chosŏn society.

Chang Chul-soo considers funeral rites, which in Korea serve as a means of coping with grief, marking the passage of a generation, confirming family values and traditions, and facilitating social inheritance. Chang compares Korean funeral practices with those of China, noting important similarities and differences.

Ancestral rites, the focus of Kim Yong-duk's contribution, serve to confirm family ties and the hierarchical status quo. They express gratitude to ancestors and strengthen ties among living family members. Kim describes the many types of ancestral rites performed in Korea, their history and function.

Chung Seung-mo focuses on clan genealogies, or *chokpo*. He explains how these records of family history and accomplishments underpin clan cohesion and reinforce family hierarchies. His article offers us a history of clan record keeping and describes the many functions of clan genealogies.

Korea's Family System and Rites of Passage

Lee Kwang-kyu

o understand Korean culture one must understand the Korean family system. Many East Asian countries including China revered Confucianism and promoted a patriarchal system, but Korea placed an especially strong emphasis on the family. Why was family so important to Koreans in traditional society and what was the nature of the Korean family system? These questions can be answered from a historical and economic perspective. Korea adopted Confucianism as the state philosophy from the beginning of the Chosŏn Dynasty. Confucianism is a philosophy that emphasizes the importance of familial relations but it could also be called a religion that places the highest value on the family. From ancient times, Koreans have cultivated rice, and the family has been the basic farming unit. The family is a unit of production and consumption. In Confucianism the family was the unit by which education was achieved. Individuals were educated within the family. When a family was stable and enlightened, the nation was stable and enlightened. Confucianism emphasized rites of passage such as coming-of-age ceremonies, marriage, funerals and ancestral rites as specific means of educating the family. Now let us consider how the family system worked and what role was played by rites of passage in traditional society.

The Korean family system is basically a patriarchy in which the eldest male of the oldest surviving generation is the family head. Among his privileges are the right to act as family representative, the right to supervise family members, the right to manage family property and the right to perform *chesa*,

Confucian rituals paying homage to ancestors.

The family head has the authority to represent the entire family at village assemblies or clan meetings. He must also assume moral responsibility for other family members. When a family member commits a wrongdoing, the entire family, not the individual, is held responsible. Gifts and money offered in congratulations or condolence to other families are made in the name of the family head. He also assumes responsibility for educating all members of the family to their full potential.

The Korean system of inheritance vividly illustrates the structure of the family system. The inheritance is divided unevenly among offspring with the oldest son receiving the largest share. If a father with three sons owns 13 parcels of rice paddy, six parcels are given to the oldest son and the rest are divided between the other two sons. The oldest son inherits most because he lives with and cares for his parents after marriage, performs ancestral rites and entertains guests of the family. After marriage, younger sons live at home temporarily, then establish separate households. Only the oldest son and his family continue to live with the parents. This family structure—several generations living together under one roof but with only one married couple per generation—is called a "stem" family structure. While it may include three or even four generations, the stem family is unique because it includes only one married couple from each generation.

A stem family can be perpetuated with only one son. Thus, the traditional desire for many sons derived not from the need to preserve the family structure but to secure more

Regular ancestral memorial rites bring families together in common purpose.
Here male members of a clan share a meal following an ancestral memorial rite.

The coming-of-age ceremony, kyerye for girls (above) and kwallye for boys (opposite), marked a young person's readiness for marriage and the responsibilities of adulthood.

manpower. The status of the oldest son who carries on the family line and that of younger sons who merely exist as reserves are quite different. The oldest son is the successor to the patriarch while the younger sons are simply reserve forces.

The oldest son's household, which is comprised of his wife and children as well as his parents, is referred to as *k'ŭnjip*, literally "the big house." The younger sons may live at home temporarily after they marry, but they eventually establish their own households. The concept of the main family and branch fami-

lies developed out of this tradition. The timing and conditions of the younger sons' establishment of a separate household after marriage varied according to local customs, historical circumstances and family conditions. In the past, younger sons branched out after a period of ten years, but in more recent times they have established separate households immediately upon marriage. The period spent together with family elders is meant to help the new daughter-in-law familiarize herself with the customs of her husband's family.

When younger sons establish their own households, they receive a portion of the family assets in accordance with the traditional inheritance system. Parents with adequate means usually provide them with their own house to live in. Poorer families provide a rice kettle, and the extremely poor offer a spoon and a pair of chopsticks. Traditionally, "family" meant sharing meals from one rice kettle. The gift of a rice kettle or a spoon and chopsticks symbolized the establishment of a separate household.

Younger sons who receive property from their parents and move into their own homes are, in social terms, creating an independent family unit. There is no need for this new family to subordinate itself to the main family, or *k'ŭnjip*, where the oldest son lives. However, a newly created branch family has no ancestral spirits of its own. Members of branch families must go to the *k'ŭnjip* to attend ancestral rites for their parents or grandparents. Thus, while branch families are independent in economic and social terms, they are subordinate to the main family in religious aspects.

Ancestral rites are an essential element in the definition of family relations. The gathering of siblings to perform ancestral rites for a parent is called *yijong*. The gathering of descendants of a common grandparent, thus a gathering of cousins, as well as siblings, is called *chojong*. The gathering of descendants of a great-grandparent is called *chŭng chojong*. The gathering of descendants of a great-great-grandparent is referred to as *kochojong* or *tangnae*. Tangnae is the equivalent to *chip-an* in pure Korean, that is, "same family" or "closest kin." Thus, ancestral rites for a common great-great-grandparent gathers what in the West might be considered distant cousins. To Koreans, however, these relatives are part of the extended family.

The most important duty of this extended family or tangnae is the performance of ancestral rites. Spirit tablets (*shinwi*) for ancestors up to the fourth ascending generation are enshrined at household shrines, or *sadang*, and regular rites honoring these ancestors are performed by descendants. These rites are called *sadaebongsa*, "Offerings to Four Generations." Rites performed at the household shrine include *kije*, which is performed on the anniversary of an ancestor's death, and *ch'arye*, which performed on special holidays.

The ancestral tablets of ancestors of the fifth ascending generation and above are buried at the ancestors' graves, and kije is no longer performed. Instead, the entire clan performs *shije*, a "seasonal" rite, once a year in the tenth lunar month at the grave site.

Accordingly, there are three types of ancestral rites: kije, ch'arye and shije. The main purpose of a clan, or *munjung*, is the performance of shije. As such, the Korean clan system was created to perform commemorative rites for paternal ancestors.

Rites of passage are rituals that individuals perform or participate in on important occasions throughout their lives. In Korea these include birth rituals, coming-of-age rituals, marriage rituals, sixtieth birthdays and funerals. These rites of passage are generally personal events as they center around an individual. In some countries, they are performed as communal rituals by a tribe, clan or village. After the introduction of Confucianism, Koreans regarded these rites of passage as a means of educating people and began to perform them within the family. For this reason, they are called *karye*, "family rites." They are also called *sarye*, the "four rites," referring to coming-of-age rituals, marriage rituals, funeral rituals and ancestral rites. The rites differ slightly in accordance with the customs of each family.

The coming-of-age ceremony for young men was called *kwallye*, literally the "hat rite." Its name derived from the fact that a young man's long hair was tied in a topknot and placed in an ornamental headpiece, or *kwan*, for the first time. Young women's hair was tied in a bun at the nape and fastened with an ornamental hairpin, or *pinyŏ*, a sign of womanhood. This ceremony was called *kyerye*, the "hairpin ceremony."

Originally, kwallye was held between the ages of 15 and 20, but due to the prevalence of early marriage, the age was lowered. The ceremony was usually held in the first or fourth lunar month before marriage. Initiates' hair was tied in a double topknot, or *ssangsangtu*, and initiates dressed in a special robe, belt and shoes. The ceremony was presided over by a *pin*, a senior male in the family or community who was of high moral repute. This man was

assisted by someone who was skilled at tying topknots.

In principle, the kyerye was to be held at the age of 15, but most women went through the ceremony on the morning of their wedding. It thus came to be identified as a wed-

ding custom. The ceremony was presided over by a respected woman in the community, *kyebin*, like the male pin, and the initiate's mother. The initiate dressed in a long silk gown, and the kyebin twisted her hair in a bun, fastened it with a long hairpin symbolizing adulthood, and placed a flower-like cap, or *hwagwan*, on her head.

In traditional society, these rituals were generally performed by the ruling *yangban* elite, but they were officially abolished when the government ordered men to cut their hair in the Western style toward the end of the Chosŏn Dynasty.

Weddings were generally in accordance with *Procedures for the Four Ceremonies* (*Sarye p'yŏllam*), a ritual guideline from the late Chosŏn period, but there were slight discrepancies between the guideline's prescriptions and what was actually performed. *Procedures for the Four Ceremonies* outlined four wedding procedures: *ŭihon, napch'ae, napp'ye* and *chinyŏng*. Ŭihon refers to marriage negotiations between two families. Napch'ae involves sending the prospective groom's year, month, day and hour of birth, or *saju*, the "four pillars," to the bride's household. Napp'ye is the delivery of a box containing bridal gifts (*ham*), and finally, ch'inyŏng is the wedding ceremony itself. The *Book of Etiquette* (*Yesŏ*) found in *Procedures for the Four Ceremonies* states that ch'inyŏng is performed at the bridegroom's house. In reality, however, weddings were performed at the home of the bride's family.

Funeral rituals are as complex as traditional weddings. When a person appears near death, he or she is laid on fresh bedding on the warmest spot of the main room's floor. Children are morally obliged to be present at their parent's deathbed. When the death is confirmed, the children begin to keen and one member of the family takes a piece of the deceased person's clothing onto the roof. There he shakes the clothing and calls the deceased's name and the word *pok*, meaning "come back," three times. Then a ritual table honoring the "messengers of death" (*sajasang*) is set up in the courtyard or near the door to the house. The offerings at this table are meant to provide the messengers of death with sustenance and travel expenses as they lead the deceased's spirit to the next world.

The deceased's hands and feet are then bound with cloth, and the body is laid on a narrow wooden board to be placed at the bottom of a coffin. The feet are pressed against the wall. The bereaved members of the family set up a small table holding the spirit tablet and appoint a principal mourner. Other matters, such as whether the death should be declared propitious (usually when the person has died old and rich) before issuing an obituary, are also decided at this time.

Before the body is placed in the coffin, it is washed (*sŭp*) and bound in cloth (*yŏm*). After bathing, the body is dressed in a shroud, and uncooked rice is placed in the mouth together with coins or a piece of jade. The body is then bound and placed in the coffin whereupon the mourners wail in grief.

Once the body is placed in the coffin, family members and other mourners don mourning clothes in accordance with their relationship to the deceased. The donning of proper mourning clothes is called *sŏngbok*. After dressing properly, the family performs the first memorial rite, *sŏngbokje*. After this rite, the official mourning begins. Pallbearers also perform a bier ceremony or entertainment (*nori*), practicing for the following day. The pallbearers show off their individual talents and join the lead singer in song. Afterward, the family of the deceased treat them to a sumptuous feast.

When the coffin is taken from the room, its front end is used to break a gourd dipper. The coffin is then placed on the bier in the courtyard, and a ritual called *pal-inje* is performed. The pal-inje is the final rite performed at home. Offerings of food and drink are placed on a ritual table and the mourners bow before it. This rite signals the deceased's departure.

Next *nojŏnje* or *kŏrije*, literally "road rite," is performed in the street before the bier leaves the village. Female mourners return home after this ritual, and the funeral procession heads to the burial site.

Grave diggers prepare the burial site prior to the funeral procession's arrival. The coffin is lowered into the pit at an auspicious hour. At this time the geomancer calls out the names of people who are not allowed to witness the burial process. The principal mourner, usually the oldest son, scoops up earth with his clothes and throws it onto the coffin. Then the grave

Traditional funerals are occasions for the confirmation and reinforcement of familial and community ties. At right is a scene from a Confucian funeral held by Confucians in Ch'ŏngdo, Kyŏngsangbuk-do province.

diggers cover the coffin with dirt. When the dirt reaches ground level, *p'yŏngt'oje*, the final rite held at graveside, is performed. The eldest son-in-law presides over this ceremony, which features many offerings. Following the rite, the pallbearers and grave diggers share the ritual food and drink, and the mourners return home with the spirit tablet of the deceased.

The mourners set up a table with a portrait or picture of the deceased (*sangch'ŏng*) at home and perform *samuje*, the third rite after death. *Cholgok*, literally the "end of keening" rite, is performed within three months of the death. The following day, the ancestral spirit tablet is enshrined at the household shrine, or *sadang*, in a rite called *puje*.

The first anniversary of a death is called *sosang* and the second *taesang*. *Tamje*, a ritual signaling that the mourners are finally at peace, is held two months after taesang. Then *kilche*, literally the "good" rite, is performed, within three months of taesang or 27 months after the death. Following this rite, the bereaved family members come out of mourning and return to a normal life.

Traditional weddings have largely been replaced by Western-style nuptials because they directly affect the lives of young people, but funeral rituals have changed little over time. The preferences of the younger generation do not affect funeral practices because spirits are involved. The only significant changes have been in modifications of mourning clothes and the acceptance of a one-year mourning period over the traditional three-year period. Today the vast majority of Koreans come out of mourning after the first anniversary of death, or sosang.

A perusal of traditional rites of passage reveals that the Korean family system is a typical patriarchy based on a unique structure called the stem family. The structural principle of the stem family was inherent in Korean society from the beginning. Patriarchal rights were emphasized because traditional Korea was an agrarian economy and the social background emphasized the rights and obligations of the family head.

The Korean family was a unit of production and consumption, a forum for education, and above all else a religious forum dedicated to the veneration of ancestors. Rituals associated with coming-of-age, wedding, funeral and ancestral rites were the specific means for enlightening and educating members of a family. In other words, these rituals were not simply rites of passage. They were ethics in action. ◆

Marriage Customs

Park Hye-in

I n Korea, the phrase *changga kada*, which means "to take a wife," is used to describe a man getting married. The phrase *shijip kada* is applied to women. It literally means "to go to the in-laws' house." In order to get married, a bridegroom goes to the bride's house and spends a set period of time there. This begins on the wedding night following the traditional wedding ritual and can last anywhere from three days to several years. The length of stay is shorter these days, but until the 1950s, it was customary for a bridegroom to spend several years at his bride's family home if circumstances allowed it.

After this stay at her family home, the bride accompanies her new husband to his parents' house. Upon arrival, she formally presents herself to the groom's parents and relatives in a traditional ceremony called *p'yebaek*. After receiving their blessings, she begins work in the kitchen on the morning of the third day, signaling the start of her married life.

Prior to the Chosŏn Dynasty and the embrace of Confucian family etiquette, free encounters between single men and women and romantic love matches were not unusual. Weddings of commoners were quite different from Chinese weddings, which took place at the groom's house. In Korea, weddings of commoners were traditionally held at the bride's house, even after the mid-17th century when the rituals of birth, marriage, funerals and ancestral rites were thoroughly Confucianized. It was also customary for the married couple to remain at the bride's home for a fixed period after the wedding. This custom is attributed to Korea's matri-patrilocal system, which was quite different from China's patriarchal society.

During the Shilla Kingdom, men and women circled a brick pagoda, chanting and praying for good fortune and longevity, at Hongnyunsa Temple in what was then the capital, Sŏrabŏl. The practice, which lasted one week from the eighth day of the fourth lunar month, Buddha's Birthday, was called *pokhoe*, "gathering to wish for good luck." Circling the pagoda deep into the night and reciting Buddhist invocations, young men and women had plenty of opportunities to get to know each other in what could be called a public group date.

In the Koguryŏ Kingdom, men and women often gathered in the evening to sing, dance and participate in a variety of group activities. According to Koguryŏ marriage customs, when a man and woman promised to marry, the woman's parents built a small "son-in-law's house" (*sŏok*) behind their home. It was customary for the prospective son-in-law to come to the gate of the bride's house after sunset, kneel on the ground, announce his name and beg to be allowed to stay. After two or three begging sessions, the parents of the bride finally gave their permission and allowed him to stay in the sŏok. The custom of returning to the groom's parents after saving money and raising children at the bride's home for several years derived from this tradition. The lengthy stay at the bride's home remained a popular custom until Korea was influenced by Western marriage practices.

The Paekche Kingdom gave birth to a legend about a man called Sŏdong who, upon hearing that Princess Sŏnhwa, the third daugh-

The bride and groom share a cup of wine in hapkŭllye,
the third step in the traditional wedding ceremony.

ter of Shilla's King Chinp'yŏng, was an exceptional beauty, shaved his head and went to Shilla's capital of Sŏrabŏl. Sŏdong handed out bolts of hemp to village children, who followed him everywhere. He then composed a children's song and instructed the village children to go around the capital singing it.

> Princess Sŏnhwa has a secret lover,
> Sŏdong whom she brings to her room.

The song spread from street to street and soon reached the palace, where court officials decided to banish the princess to the countryside. As Princess Sŏnhwa headed away from the capital, Sŏdong appeared to propose. It was only then that the princess learned his name and understood how the song came to be circulated. Sŏdong finally returned to Paekche with the princess as his wife.

In traditional society, when a man or woman reached marriageable age, their family began the search for a prospective spouse, discussing marriage through a matchmaker. The matchmaker had to be a person of advanced age, usually a woman who knew the families well. After discussions through a go-between, the groom's family sometimes sent a matchmaker to the bride's family to finalize the marriage, but only after consulting a fortuneteller who could confirm the couple to be a harmonious match. The fortuneteller first examined *saju*, the "Four Pillars" (the year, month, day and hour of birth), of the prospective groom and bride to divine *kunghap*, their mutual compatibility. There are two kinds of kunghap: "inner" kunghap (*sokkunghap*), which divines sexually compatibility, and "outer" kunghap (*kŏtkunghap*), which predicts compatibility in personality. If the two families agreed to the match, the matchmaker was treated to a feast on the wedding day and received a pair of shoes or an outfit of clothes as a gift if the groom's family was wealthy.

The exchange of saju documents symbolized the two families' formal agreement to the marriage. The date and hour of the groom's birth was carefully written with ink at the center of a large piece of white paper folded five or seven times from left to right. The paper was then put in a paper envelope marked "saju." The characters *kŭnbong*, "carefully sealed," were written three times on the outside of the envelope. A stick of bushwood was tied to the envelope with long strands of red and blue thread. This symbolized a solid relationship. The envelope was wrapped in a *pojagi* wrapping cloth, which was blue inside

31

and red outside.

The saju envelope was delivered to the bride's family on a day deemed auspicious by the groom's family. A person whose first child was a son and who enjoyed a happy family life was usually chosen to deliver the envelope. The reception of the envelope by the bride's family was considered an important event, as it signaled the promise of marriage. The bride kept the saju document in her wardrobe for the rest of her life.

After receiving the groom's saju, the bride's family picked an auspicious day for the wedding and informed the groom's family in writing. This letter was folded like the saju document, put in an envelope, wrapped in a blue and red silk pojagi and delivered by a person who had enjoyed good fortune.

On the wedding day, the bridegroom rode on horseback to the bride's house for the marriage ceremony. The procession, called *ch'ohaeng,* the "first visit," was led by the *sanggaek,* usually the father of the groom, his grandfather or an uncle who represented the groom's family. The *hamjin-abi,* who carried the *ham,* a chest of bridal gifts, and several close relatives accompanied them.

The hamjin-abi was selected by the groom's family. He was usually a person who was considered lucky and whose first child was a son. The wedding chest contained a letter of marriage proposal and bridal gifts, which included bolts of blue and red silk for the bride's costumes. Usually there was enough fabric for two *chŏgori* blouses and one skirt, or *ch'ima,* or for two skirts and three chŏgori, all placed in the chest in a deliberate mismatch. The blue silk was wrapped in red paper, and the red silk in blue paper. Other bridal gifts included jewelry, bedding and objects symbolizing the desire for male offspring and happiness. Walnuts, peppers and skeins of blue and red thread symbolized the birth of sons and marital happiness.

To receive the gift chest, the bride's family placed a straw mat in the front courtyard, put up a folding screen, rolled out a woven mat and set up a table laden with steamed rice cakes. Another table holding a piece of dried

The formal "exchange of bows," kyobaerye, *is typical of the highly ritualized wedding ceremony.*

pollack and a bowl of water drawn from the well at daybreak was placed before this table. The chest was placed on the table and a member of the bride's family groped inside without looking. If the person grasped red cloth first, it was believed that the couple's first child would be a girl. Blue cloth symbolized a son. It was also believed that the bride would have a hard time living with her in-laws if the cloth was dark in color and a relatively easy time if it was light. The gift chest was usually received by the bride's parents, her older brother or a female relative with many sons and a history of good luck.

The bride's family prepared for the marriage ceremony and waited for the groom's arrival. The ceremony was called *taerye*, the "great rite," and consisted of three main parts: *chŏn-allye*, *kyobaerye* and *hapkŭllye*. Taerye, as its name signified, was thought to be life's most important ritual. In a house with a large hall, the wedding was held indoors, but generally it was performed in the front courtyard under a tent screened off by curtains.

The ceremony began with the bridegroom's entrance. A village elder chosen for his good fortune and profound knowledge of Chinese characters officiated over the ceremony. The marriage procedures were written in Chinese characters.

An older brother of the bride greeted the bridegroom and led him into the house. The bridegroom knelt before a ritual table, facing north. Then an assistant, who accompanied the groom from his home, handed him a carved wooden goose, which he placed on the table. The bridegroom then rose, lit incense and bowed twice before stepping back. The goose symbolized a happy marriage, because geese mate only once and remain faithful to their mate throughout life. Blue and red threads were woven around the goose's beak and jujubes were strung from the threads. The goose was wrapped in a blue and red pojagi, with the red side facing out. A piece of paper with the Chinese characters kŭnbong, "carefully sealed," was attached to the red knots. The mother of the bride accepted the wooden goose and wrapped it in one of her skirts, which she then placed in the family rice cabinet for safekeeping.

Two candlesticks, several boughs of evergreen trees such as pine and bamboo, chestnuts and jujubes were always placed on the ritual wedding table. Rice, a hen and rooster wrapped in a pojagi, rice cakes, fruit and dried fish or meat were also placed there.

The bridegroom stood before the table, and

33

the wedding proceeded as the bride emerged from her room assisted by servants. She bowed four times with the servants' help, and the bridegroom knelt to receive her bows. Then the bridegroom bowed twice while the bride sat to accept them. This process was called kyobaerye, the "exchange of bows." The bridegroom bowed twice and the bride four times in accordance with the principles of *yin* and *yang*.

A female servant of the bride's family then poured wine into a cup wound with blue and red threads. The bride merely touched the cup to her lips. It was then handed to the groom

A pair of chickens is among the offerings on the ritual wedding table.

from the left. An attendant accepted the cup, brought it to the groom's lips, then placed it on the table. The attendant poured wine into the cup and offered it to the bride from the right. This process was called hapkŭllye, the "sharing of cups." A wine cup made from a split gourd was traditionally used. It was bound with blue and red threads to symbolize unity as a whole.

Hapkŭllye was an important process for it symbolized the joining of bride and groom as one. After these three steps, guests put chestnuts and jujubes from the wedding altar in the groom's pockets to eat in the nuptial chamber. Chestnuts and jujube symbolized the birth of many sons.

After the main wedding rite, the bride-

groom went into a room to change into daily attire prepared by his new in-laws. He then received *k'ŭnsang*, literally the "large table," laden with food and wine prepared by his in-laws for him and the sanggaek. Camellia and peony flowers were placed in the first row of "offerings;" rice cakes, chestnuts, dried persimmon, jujubes and fruit in the second row; sweet pastries in the third; slices of boiled meat and seasoned greens in the fourth; and rice and soup in the last. Usually the groom and sanggaek sampled only a few of the dishes, which were packed and sent to the groom's family who then shared them with relatives and neighbors.

The groom then formally presented himself to the bride's elders. The bride also greeted members of her in-laws' family. The sanggaek usually returned home on the day of the wedding or the following day. Before he departed, the bride honored him with bows, and he presented her with wedding gifts in a process called *shinbu ponda*, literally "viewing the bride."

At nightfall after the guests left, the newlyweds retired to the nuptial chamber prepared at the bride's house. A servant spread the bedding on the floor, set up a folding screen and placed a bowl of water and sweet rice punch in the room. Cotton or rice chaff was placed in the chamber pot, and a sewing box was placed in the room as well. Then a simple table with wine and side dishes was brought in. The bride had to sit quietly, answering the groom's questions in a shy and low voice. He then undressed her and blew out the candle. This was the signal for relatives to punch holes in the window paper and peek inside.

During the groom's stay with his in-laws, the younger members of the bride's family and neighbors played a variety of practical jokes on the groom. This tradition, called "handling of the bridegroom" (*shillang tarugi*), involved asking strange questions and teasing, all meant to ease their sorrow at losing the bride. They sometimes tied a piece of cloth around the bridegroom's ankles and hung him upside down from the ceiling, interrogating him about his intentions toward the bride. When the groom failed to answer properly, they hit him on the bottom of his feet with a stick and demanded wine and food from the bride's family in return for his release. After obtaining the promise of a fine feast from the bride's family, they released him.

The procession that took the bride to her in-laws permanently was called *shinhaeng*. The day was chosen by the groom's family.

Before leaving her parents' home, the bride went to the kitchen and clanged the lid of the rice kettle three times to bid farewell. Two members of the bride's family accompanied the bridal procession. Usually the bride's grandfather, father, brother or uncle followed as a sanggaek, and another relative assisted the bride with her belongings.

The bridegroom rode on horseback, the bride in a palanquin, and the others followed on foot. A blanket decorated with pictures of a tiger or a tiger skin was placed on top of the palanquin to protect the bride. The bride took a wardrobe, a mirror stand, clothes, bedding and a chamber pot as well as food and other dowry items such as clothing for her in-laws and close relatives and traditional socks, pŏsŏn, for distant relatives. Rice cakes, meat, wine, chicken and jujubes strung on thread were also prepared for her new in-laws.

Before the bride entered her in-laws' home, straw was piled at the gate and burned to rid the area of impurities. Family members then threw red beans over her palanquin to drive away evil spirits. When movers set down the palanquin in the yard, the groom opened the door, and the bride headed straight to the nuptial chamber and sat in an auspicious spot.

The bridegroom's family prepared a "large table" laden with food for the bride and her escorts. The leftover food was then sent to the bride's family in large baskets to be shared with relatives and neighbors.

After receiving the ritual meal, the bride presented herself to her in-laws and relatives to receive their blessings in a tradition called hyŏn-gugorye, a rite known as p'yebaek today. Depending on family traditions, the bride first paid her respects at the family shrine where ancestral tablets were enshrined. Hyŏn-gugorye began with the bride preparing a table of rice wine, chicken, chestnuts and jujubes for her in-laws. She presented the table, then bowed and offered them wine. The in-laws tossed jujubes into the bride's skirt and wished her many sons. At this time, the women of the husband's family inspected the gifts brought by the bride. The mother-in-law rubbed a piece of taffy and cautioned them to be quiet and mindful of what they said. The taffy symbolized a closed mouth.

The bride rose early the next morning, dressed immaculately and inquired after the health of her in-laws. She continued to offer these greetings to her in-laws morning and evening until they told her it was no longer necessary. They usually told her to stop after three days. The first morning, the bride pre-pared a table of the food she had brought from her parents' home and bowed to her in-laws in the hall with the door open. She repeated the greeting in the evening. The mother-in-law took the new daughter-in-law with her on visits to relatives to help her familiarize herself with family customs.

The bride actually worked in the kitchen for the first time three days after arriving at her in-laws'. She began work by drawing well water at daybreak and placing it in a bowl. She then prepared her in-laws' breakfast from food and ingredients brought from her parents' home.

After one or two months, or sometimes a year, the bride made her first visit back to her parents' home. On this visit, called kŭnch'in, she was usually accompanied by her husband, who carried rice cakes and wine made from grain harvested since the wedding. The bride's family shared ch'aban—the rice cakes, rice candies and fruit prepared and sent by the in-laws—with their neighbors. Escorted by his brother-in-law or mother-in-law, the groom called on his wife's relatives during this visit, which generally lasted for several days. The relatives sometimes invited the married couple to a meal. The bride's family also prepared food and gifts for their return. Kŭnch'in, a bride's first visit to her old family, marked the completion of the complicated marriage process. ◆

The ham, a chest of bridal gifts, is delivered to the bride's home for her family's approval.

Funeral Rites

Chang Chul-soo

The death of a family member is, in part, an occasion for bequeathing his or her assets and social status to a living person. For this reason, death is especially significant to those with ties to the deceased. Of course, there is a psychological dimension to the sadness caused by the death of a loved one, but social inheritance is a more important factor for it is closely related to the lives of the deceased's survivors. Death was even more significant in agrarian society where people's livelihoods depended on land. Death was an occasion on which social and economic relationships between the deceased and the living were clearly revealed.

A death in the family confirms the rights and duties that have formed between family members over the years. In everyday life these links are not always apparent and can be forgotten. During the Chosŏn Dynasty, which was founded on Neo-Confucian ideals, the relationship between a father and his eldest son was of absolute importance because direct ties of consanguinity were considered paramount. The rights and duties of the eldest son in relation to his parents had priority over all other relationships. The eldest son was required to live with his parents and care for them, and understandably his share of the inheritance was the largest. Not only were the house and land handed down to the eldest son but also the site of the family's ancestral graves. In turn, he was required to perform regular memorial rites for his parents and other ancestors.

Funerals provide an opportunity to clarify familial and village ties and remind family members and neighbors of their obligations and rights.

From this perspective, the rights and duties of the eldest son can be interpreted as repayment for inheritance. However, the ethic of filial piety advocated by Neo-Confucianism is founded on children's gratitude to their parents who gave birth to them and raised them. Supporting elderly parents who can no longer lead an active life is a natural obligation.

Nevertheless, economic relationships based on inheritance or psychological debts arising from parental care enjoyed in childhood are not the sole determinants of the rights and obligation of descendants. To think that they alone determine the attitude of descendants would be overly utilitarian.

At the heart of the relationship between ascendant and descendant are the rights and obligations felt toward the entity that made one's own existence possible. Human birth originates in a limitless, mysterious world. One's being is the accumulated result of countless relationships since the beginning of human existence on earth. In this respect, these rights and duties only truly reveal themselves when one's existence is fully understood. Each person's existence is sacred. The death of the being who gave birth to us is the death of the origin of our own being. Therefore funeral rituals must be solemn. Funeral rituals consist of the various procedures associated with the burial of a social being who has left descendants to carry on the family line. These procedures are followed during the moment of death, the handling of the death and the acceptance of death as a new life.

According to the *Family Rites* of Zhu Xi, the great Chinese Neo-Confucian (1130-1200), the transition from life to death consists of six procedures: *qianju* (*ch'ŏn-gŏ*), the "moving of residence"; *fu* (*bok*), climbing to the roof with the deceased's clothing and calling "fu" (return) three times before returning to the house to cover the body with the clothing; *shoushi* (K. *sushi*), "arranging the corpse"; *yifu* (*yŏkbok*), changing into mourning clothes; *dian* (*chŏn*), setting a simple ceremonial table before the spirit tablet; and *fugao* (*pugo*), the announcement of death. In practice, however, Koreans follow somewhat different procedures: *ch'ohon*, the "calling of the spirit"; *sajasang*, setting a ritual table honoring the "messengers of death"; sushi, yŏkbok, *sangshik*, routine offerings of food to the spirit in the morning and evening, and pugo.

The orthodox Chinese procedures and those of Korea differ in the Koreans' failure to observe the "moving of residence" (qianju)

As the funeral bier leaves the village, a "road rite" (noje) is held to help the deceased bid farewell to his or her home.

step and their inclusion of a ritual meal for the messengers of death. According to the *Family Rites*, qianju meant moving the corpse to a special room in the principal quarters of the bereaved household. In Korea, the deceased was left in the room in which he or she passed away. In fact, when people are gravely ill, they are often moved to the main room before passing if they are not there already.

This distinction is directly linked to the family's pattern of living and habitual use of space. A family's use of space is closely associated to the distribution of labor and status within that family. Death signals the transfer of one person's role to another member of the family. The special room for the passing of family members mentioned in Zhu Xi's classic work was con-

meal offered to the messengers because the living want to be sure that the spirit of the deceased makes contact with the messengers and follows them directly to the underworld. Their greatest fear is that the spirit might get lost and wander between this world and the underworld. The *Family Rites*, on the other hand, describes the "calling of the spirit" as an act aimed at reviving the dead by calling the name of the recently departed spirit. This is a truly filial interpretation. Thus, Korean families who follow strict Confucian principles do not provide food for the death messengers.

The "arranging of the corpse," or sushi, signifies the mourners' recognition of the deceased family member's new status, and yŏkbok, the dressing in mourning clothes, signifies the descendants' acceptance of the death. At this point, the living assume the role of mourners. To facilitate this process, the *Family Rites* calls for the designation of a chief mourner, a main female mourner, a funeral director, a custodian and a treasurer to handle condolence money. In practice, however, only the chief mourner (*sangju*) and funeral director (*hosang*) play prominent roles in Korea. The role of the funeral director is given to an experienced neighbor or a friend of the deceased. His familiarity with the deceased's acquaintances helps in the smooth running of the funeral.

According to the *Family Rites*, these roles are restricted to family members, but in practice they are extended to neighbors and friends. This Korean distinction is evident in local mutual aid societies that specialize in funerals (*sangp'ogye*). The ostensible purpose of these societies seems to be economic, but in fact the amount of money they contribute is minimal. Their real purpose is elsewhere. Members of these groups oversee the smooth operation of funeral proceedings. When one member's parent passes away, all members of the society become mourners.

Thus, while a funeral is essentially a family affair, it becomes a community event affecting the entire sphere of the deceased's life. It is only natural that a whole village will stop work to help the bereaved family or participate in funeral procedures. If they do not, they risk societal criticism and may make enemies. In fact, when people are not on good terms, funerals provide a good opportunity to mend fences by paying respects to the bereaved family.

The handling of the deceased is the core of the funeral. However, the procedures laid out in the *Family Rites* and the reality of Korean funerals are quite different. In the *Family Rites*, the transport of the body to the burial site is central, while in Korean practice, the washing and shrouding of the dead body are the most important procedures. These differing emphases reveal themselves in the offering of food. The *Family Rites* calls for a simple offering of wine and fruits (*chŏn*) before burial. A full-fledged *chesa* is performed after returning home from the burial. On the other hand, in Korean practice, a chesa is performed after washing and shrouding the body, while the formal wearing of mourning clothes begins on the third or fifth day after death. According to the *Family Rites*, the simple offering before burial is hosted by the "Reader of the Announcement for the Spirit" (*ch'ukgwan*), and a chesa is held by the chief mourner. In Korean practice, chesa is hosted by the chief mourner after he formally dresses in mourning.

sidered a communal space. However, Korean homes did not have such a space. Even when there was a communal space, it was not used for this purpose. From this perspective, the "moving of residence" was not practiced because of preexisting Korean customs.

The meal for the messengers of death appears to be related to a shamanic concept of an underworld. According to popular Korean belief, food is prepared for the messengers as an incentive to guide the dead on a comfortable journey to the underworld. There are three messengers. Three bowls of rice, three pairs of straw shoes, and three packets of "travel money" are offered.

In Korean practice, the "calling of the spirit" is linked to the

The differences seem to originate from differing understandings of death and the role of ancestors. The *Family Rites* assumes that only after burial does the deceased become an ancestor god. In Korean practice, on the other hand, the deceased is recognized as an ancestor god from the moment of death.

The funeral's significance is also quite different. Funeral practices stipulated in the *Family Rites* emphasize treating the deceased with the respect due an ancestor god, while in Korean practice, the funeral is a mechanism for handling or facilitating death. In Confucianism, death is one of several life processes, but in Korean culture, death is viewed as the end of life. This distinction is clearly a reflection of the shamanic view of death that has been the foundation of the Korean people's approach to death since ancient times.

The *Family Rites* stipulates 108 different kinds of mourning clothes for the main family, relatives and maternal relatives. Relatives are expected to wear mourning every day. In Korean practice, however, only patrilineal relatives—siblings and patrilineal descendants—and spouses are expected to wear mourning attire. In this respect, a wife's family and maternal relatives are only important during a person's lifetime, not in death. This seems to have derived from the Korean emphasis on patriarchal consanguinity. In Korean practice, close relations with one wife's family, maternal relatives and other relatives are thought to be less than complete for they only operate during one's lifetime.

In traditional Korean society, ordinary people's social relationships appear to have been relatively narrow. They rarely extended beyond the scope of two families or villages brought together by marriage, and this only during the couple's lifetimes. On the other hand, the *yangban* elite appears to have operated in a much larger social milieu. Intermarriage across longer distances and between a broader range of renowned families must have produced a larger circle of acquaintances. Yangban relationships were more durable and stable because of the necessities of social activity.

Consequently, Confucian funeral and mourning rites for parents were, generally speaking, closely observed for three years, but for ordinary people, the rites were simplified for practicality's sake. In most cases, mourning rites extending to the second anniversary of death (*taesang*) were considered important. Consanguineous relations were also only important when relatives lived in close proximity. Otherwise, regional ties, which were more important in the formation of practical human relationships, took precedence. Hence the Korean proverb, "A good neighbor is better than a brother faraway."

During the Chosŏn Dynasty, villages dominated by one surname came into being as Koreans attempted to harmonize blood and regional ties. When a village expanded to the point that it could no longer accommodate collateral relatives, a new village was formed. The consanguineous ties of the two villages were reconfirmed through various rites of passage, including funeral and ancestral memorial ceremonies and ancestor worship. For this reason, we must consider Korean lifestyle not only within the context of a single village but also in the context of neighboring villages, with a distinction made between villages sharing consanguineous ties and those based

on other connections. By considering everyday life together with ritual life we may better grasp the nucleus of Korean life.

Koreans accept the three-year mourning period as an ideal and thus make every effort to observe ritual procedures through the second anniversary of a death. The three-year mourning period is a time for the bereaved to demonstrate their self-control. Mourning is a process by which the bereaved gradually return to normal life. During the initial mourning period, they use straw bedding and do not eat. From the "end of keening" (*cholgok*), they exhibit self-control in eating and drinking, and sleep on reed mats with wooden "pillows" to show penitence. After the first anniversary (*sosang*), they start eating vegetables and fruits. After a rite performed two months after the second anniversary (*tamje*), they may drink wine and eat meat. One month later, after *kilche*, the "good" rite, they return to their own beds and normal life.

In Korean practice, keening does not accompany all procedures despite the rules of Confucian etiquette. The *Family Rites* indicates that the "end of keening" and the first anniversary of

The funeral bier is carried to the grave by family and community members (left). The grave is covered with a sod-covered dome (above). Dramatic keening is part of all Korean funerals, rural and urban (below).

the death are important procedures. They provide an opportunity for the bereaved to return to normal life. This is more evident at the "end of keening" than at the first anniversary. In Korea, mourning sometimes ends after 100 days or on the first anniversary. These procedures indicate a return to normal life.

According to the *Family Rites*, the "end of keening" should be conducted two days after *samuje*, the third rite after death. For scholar-officials (*taebu*), cholgok is conducted three months after death. For a gentleman-scholar (*sa*), it is conducted after one month. In general practice, cholgok occurs about 100 days after death or three months after burial. According to the *Family Rites*, the funeral itself takes place three months after death, then comes the "end of keening." In Korean practice, the funeral takes place first and the "end of keening" three months later. This reflects differing views of life and death. As mentioned earlier, Confucianism views death as part of life while in Korean practice death is not recognized as part of the framework of life.

A casket could remain in the home for three months as a

demonstration of filial piety. The process of "calling of the spirit" can be interpreted as an expression of the longing for the departed spirit to reenter its body and remain as a living entity for three months. The significance of the three-month or 100-day interval appears to be closely related to the 100-day mourning period observed at the end of the Koryŏ Dynasty when the *Family Rites* was first introduced to Korea.

The preparation of a grave has the specific purpose of informing descendants of the deceased's contributions to his or her family and, more broadly, to society. The deceased's spirit should be remembered forever by generation after generation. This gives social significance to the spirit and reflects a humane and cultured way of life. In other words, the creation of a tomb or grave site is a cultural act aimed at encouraging descendants and future generations to make their own remarkable contribution to family and society. It also symbolizes the existence of the ancestors. In this way we recognize that the present is based on the past and the future is based on the present. ◆

Ancestral Rites

Kim Yong-duk

In traditional society Koreans were taught to respect their dead ancestors as they would their living elders. Respect for living elders was an act of filial piety, and *chesa*, or ancestral rites, was an extension of filial piety. Filial piety is the most fundamental human act because it constitutes a repayment of the debt we owe our parents for giving birth to us. Chesa, a means of paying respect to ancestors, originated as a way of thanking ancestors and asking them to watch over their descendants.

According to the *Book of Rites* (*Lishu*), a Chinese Confucian classic, the emperor performed rites to Heaven, feudal lords to Nature and the literati to their ancestors. From early times, chesa fell into two categories: collective community rites appealing to heaven and earth for communal well-being, and ancestral rites performed by individuals or extended families to memorialize ancestors and confirm familial ties.

The concept of "ancestral god" (*chosangshin*) is implicit in the word "ancestor" or *chosang*. Synonyms include "founder" (*shijo*), "progenitor" (*sŏnjo*) and "forebear" or "previous generation" (*sŏndae*). All these words refer to the deceased members of several generations of one family. However, not every dead person becomes an ancestor god. Ancestor gods must fulfill certain essential requirements, and their deaths must be solemnized by proper rites. Someone who dies young without a son does not become an ancestor god, and ancestors for whom proper funeral rites were not performed because, for example, they died on the battlefield or were traitorous also do not qualify. In these cases, specific funeral rites must be performed before the dead are recognized as ancestor gods.

Ancestors represented with a spirit tablet (*shinwi*) in Confucian ancestral rites are gods of goodwill who exist in a state of contentment in the "other world" (*chŏsŭng*) thanks to the respect and obedience of their descendants. They meet their descendants on chesa days and protect them out of goodwill. These ancestors become the objects of religious belief, and in some cases, when the concept of "god" expands spatially and historically, they are embraced as familial founding gods or regional guardian deities. Tan-gun, the legendary founder of Korea, is Korea's most exalted deity. Kim Al-ji is the founding god of the Kyŏngju Kim clan, and Kolmaegi is the guardian deity of the Kyŏngsang region. Founding gods and regional guardian deities have evolved into the deities honored at village rites and other rites deriving from folk religion.

Ancestor veneration and chesa are related to religion. According to the English philosopher and evolutionist Herbert Spencer (1820-1903), the worship of the dead developed into the worship of ancestor gods, and later into a religious faith. He believed that religion originated from a belief that living descendants must revere the dead with affection and respect and in turn the dead will protect their descendants. Thus, ancestral rites must have originated in a belief in the immortality of the soul.

Korean chesa are religious rites in which gratitude founded on filial piety is the basis for the veneration of ancestor gods. This has been especially true since the founding of the Confucian Chosŏn Dynasty. Chesa also link ancestors to descendants and strengthen ties of solidarity among living relatives.

Chesa can be categorized by purpose and

Clan elders preside over an ancestral rite.
Ancestral rites and funerals express filial piety, link family members to
clan history, and strengthen ties among living relatives.
Shije (right) are rites at which more than four
generations of ancestors are honored in concert.

form. There are rites for individuals and rites for communities. Rites for individuals are family rituals in which descendants pray for the well-being of the deceased and ask the deceased to watch over the living.

The word "chesa" normally refers to these familial rites. According to traditional etiquette, nine types of chesa are performed for three years after a death. These are directly related to an individual's death, beginning with the funeral and ending with the discarding of mourning clothes. *Kije* is the term for rites performed on the anniversary of the ancestor's death after three years have passed. *Ch'arye*, performed at the home of the eldest son, and *myoje*, performed at the family grave site, are held on major festival days such as Hanshik (the 105th day after the winter solstice) and Ch'usŏk (the Harvest Moon Festival on the 15th day of the eighth lunar month). *Shije* are rites at which more than four generations of ancestors are honored in concert.

Community rites involving entire villages may honor common ancestors or forces of nature. These rites begin with a shamanic ceremony (*kut*) or a Confucian-style chesa, followed by the sharing of food and wine used as ritual offerings and a festival with dancing and singing. The shamanic ceremony and Confucian ritual coexist because the latter is a relative newcomer that was incorporated into an indigenous folk religion. Typical regional or community festivals are Kangnŭng's Tano festival and the *Ch'ilmŏridang kut* of Chejudo Island.

Historical records indicate that rites venerating the heavens have been performed in Korea for more than 2,000 years. During the Koguryŏ Kingdom, state rites (*tongmaeng*) honored the kingdom's founder, Chumong. The *yŏnggo* "spirit-invoking" rites of the Puyŏ Kingdom were also communal rites honoring the heavens and ancestors. The Koryŏ Dynasty, a Buddhist state, observed several state Buddhist festivals. The *yŏndŭnghoe* and *p'algwanhoe* incorporated elements of indigenous folk practices in Buddhist rites. In Chosŏn society, with its Confucian-centered ideology, Confucian rituals were performed at Chongmyo, the Royal Ancestral Shrine where the spirit tablets of deceased monarchs were housed, as well as at Munmyo, the National Shrine to Confucius, and at Confucian schools scattered around the country where the spirit tablets of Confucian sages were enshrined.

The Chongmyo royal ancestral rites were once conducted five times a year, but since the fall of the Chosŏn Dynasty, only one

Confucian ancestral memorial rites are performed at the family grave site on Ch'usŏk, the Harvest Moon Festival (right). Villagers often join together to perform community rites which may begin with shamanic ceremonies (above) or Confucian-style rites. Folk and Confucian ritual practices often overlap.

annual ceremony is held as a familial ritual for the Chŏnju Yi clan, the ruling house of the Chosŏn Dynasty. Ceremonial procedures, music and dance are strictly observed. In fact, the shrine and the rites associated with it were recognized as a unique world cultural heritage and included on UNESCO's World Heritage list in 1995.

Confucian scholars performed similar rites honoring revered Confucian dignitaries at Munmyo. The National Confucian Shrine, located at Sŏnggyun-gwan, the National Confucian Academy in Seoul, houses spirit tablets of Confucius and several Chinese and Korean Confucian worthies. The highly stylized rites are still performed twice a year, in spring and autumn. Traditionally, local Confucian schools (*hyanggyo*), which housed similar shrines, held rites on the same day as

Confucian rituals are still performed at Chongmyo, the Royal Ancestral Shrine where spirit tablets of deceased monarchs are housed. The rites were once conducted five times a year, but since the fall of the Chosŏn Dynasty, only one annual ceremony is held as a familial ritual for the Chŏnju Yi clan, the ruling house of the Chosŏn Dynasty.

the National Confucian Shrine.

Early Koreans did not make a clear distinction between village rites and ancestral rites. With the increase in population and expansion of populated areas, however, village rites and individual rites began to differentiate. In accordance with state ideology, Buddhist rituals were performed during the Koryŏ Dynasty and Confucian rituals during the Chosŏn Dynasty. As Confucianism became more important, filial piety was emphasized, and as a result, individual rites were deemed more important than village rites. Individual rites are still widely performed with little modification. Today the word "chesa" is generally understood to mean a family rite, specifically the memorial services performed on death anniversaries (*kije*). These rites are performed at the family shrine where ancestors' portraits

KIM SOO-NAM

KIM SOO-NAM

Memorial services performed on death anniversaries (kijesa) are performed in the home of the eldest son. The spirit tablet is taken from the family shrine and placed behind an altar (top), and offerings of wine and food are made (above).

or spirit tablets are kept. When there is no shrine, rites are held in the main room or open hall (*taech'ŏng maru*) of the principal family.

Family shrines originated in Confucianism and were first introduced to Korea during the Koryŏ Dynasty. They house the portraits or spirit tablets of ancestors. Spirit tablets are made of chestnut wood. The ancestor's name is carved or written on the tablet. On the day of a ceremony, the portraits or tablets are removed from their protective cases and family members bow before them.

Chesa begin with the careful preparation of ritual offerings. Special containers and plates, usually made of brass, porcelain or wood, are reserved for ancestral rites. Today, wood is most popular. Wooden *chegi* (ritual vessels) from Namwon, in the heavily wooded Chirisan Mountain region, are prized by modern Koreans.

Kije, the rites held on the anniversary of a death, are performed at the first hour of that day, in the wee hours of the morning after the

participants have cleansed their minds and bodies during the evening. On this special day, no one sings or drinks. They concentrate on revering the deceased ancestor. After bathing, the participants unfold a wall screen on the north side of the main room or hall, polish the ritual vessels, fill them with offerings of food and arrange them on a table in front of the screen. Two candles are lit on either side of the ceremonial table, and objects representing the deceased ancestor, such as the spirit tablet, a portrait and ceremonial documents, are arranged on the table.

When preparations are complete, the ceremony is performed. It follows a predetermined order, which may differ somewhat from family to family. Each procedure has its own meaning.

1. Lighting Incense (*punhyang*): Sticks of incense are lit and placed in a censor. The incense cleanses the ritual site. The principal participant prostrates himself before the ceremonial table and bows twice.

2. The descent of the spirit (*kangshin*): The ancestor is invited to descend from heaven. The principal participant pours wine in a cup and bows twice.

3. Participation by the spirit (*ch'amshin*): The ancestor is welcomed. All participants bow twice.

4. Offering food (*chinch'an*): Food is offered to the ancestor. Noodles, rice (called *me* to be differentiated from the ordinary word for rice, *pap*) and soup are placed on the table, which is already laden with other foods. A spoon and chopsticks are laid on the table.

5. Making the first offering and reading the invocation (*ch'ohŏn tokch'uk*): Wine is offered and an invocation is read. The invocation states that the humble dishes have been prepared for the ancestor's death anniversary by descendants who cannot endure their sorrow. The descendants entreat the ancestor to enjoy the offerings.

6. Making the second offering (*ahyŏn*): Wine is offered again. In the past, women were not permitted to attend these ceremonies, but now they are allowed to participate. The principal woman participant offers wine and bows four times. Women always bow twice as many times as men, because in accordance with traditional cosmology, women represent *yin*, and it takes two yin to make one *yang*, the male element.

7. Making the final offering (*chonghŏn*): Wine is offered once again, prompting the ancestor to eat to his or her fill.

8. Waiting for the ancestor to eat (*yushik*):

The ancestor is encouraged to have more food. The spoon and chopsticks are stuck vertically in the rice bowl.

9. Leaving the room: The light is then turned out and everyone leaves the room. The idea is to allow the ancestor to eat at leisure if he or she is shy.

10. Opening the door (*kyemun*): The participants open the door and reenter. They make sure to cough a few times before opening the door to avoid surprising the ancestor.

11. Putting rice in soup (*chinda*): In order to prompt the ancestor to eat more, three spoonfuls of rice from the ritual offerings are placed in the ancestor's bowl of soup.

12. Bidding farewell to the ancestor god (*sashin*): Wine is offered and all participants bow in farewell to the ancestor god.

13. Burning prayer paper (*punch'uk*): Now that the ancestor has departed, the spirit tablet is moved to its original place and the prayer paper and wishing paper are immolated in an act of cleansing.

14. Taking away the food (*ch'ŏlch'an*): All food is cleared from the ceremonial table.

15. Eating the ceremonial food (*ŭmbok*): The food from the ceremonial table is thought to hold the ancestor's spiritual touch. Sharing this food brings the ancestor's grace to living relatives.

After the ceremony, the participants gather to share the wine and food from the ceremonial table, reminisce about the ancestor and take pride in their family's illustrious past. In this way, chesa reflect a strong filial consciousness among the descendants who at the same time wish for the ancestor's benevolence. The elaborate procedure is a means of demonstrating filial piety and praying for good fortune.

This mentality is tangible in the careful preparation of food and the attention paid to the arrangement of offerings on the ceremonial table. Food is prepared with special care, using only the freshest ingredients. The kinds of food and their arrangement on the table reflect Confucian logic. For example, fruits are placed in a certain order. Plates of fruit are arranged from left to right. Jujubes are placed first because they have only one firm red seed, which symbolizes one consistent heart or loyalty to the sovereign. Chestnuts come next, symbolizing the three fundamental Confucian bonds (*samgang*). A chestnut burr usually holds three nuts. The three fundamental bonds refer to the relationships between the people and the king, between a father and his sons, and between husband and wife. Pears have five seeds, which symbolize the five

moral disciplines (*oryun*): the obligations inherent in the relationship between a king and his subjects, between parents and their offspring, between adults and children, between husband and wife, and between friends. Persimmons have six seeds, symbolizing a desire for descendants to advance in the world as one of the king's six ministers.

The color of foods also follows a code. Red fruits are placed to the east, while pale-colored fruit are placed to the west, in accordance with the Confucian principle of the east corresponding to red and the west to white. Other rules stipulate that fish be placed to the east and meat to the west. The fish's head must point east and its tail west.

These elaborate rules are thought to reflect the depth of descendants' filial piety and their heartfelt hope for good fortune, which their ancestors may bestow on them. Filial piety is one of the most prized virtues in Confucianism. Ultimately, the spirit of chesa is realized in the veneration of ancestors, the purest of human emotions, and in the spirit of Confucianism. ◆

After offerings are made, the food is cleared from the ceremonial table (below), and the spirit tablet is returned to the family shrine (bottom).

KIM SOO-NAM

49

Chokpo: Clan Genealogies

Chung Seung-mo

In traditional Korean society, succession of the family line was essential. The perpetuation of the bloodline was the ultimate act of filial piety and the prime means of ensuring prosperity for descendants. The keen awareness of family was extended to kin of the same lineage, thus nurturing a strong sense of cohesion among clan members. The clan genealogy, or *chokpo,* underpinned this cohesion.

Genealogies identify the clan's progenitor and subsequent generations of clan members. They are systematic records of the line of descent beginning with the clan's progenitor, and include historic documentation about the founding of the clan and the names, sobriquets and major contributions of all clan members from the progenitor to those living at the time of its compilation. Through this record, we see the vertical genealogy of a clan from the founder to the present members and the ties of kinship linking clan members of each generation.

Chokpo are not records of one individual's or family's line of succession but a combined record of an entire clan or lineage within a clan. These combined genealogical tables are made possible by private records kept by individual families. Private family records include family genealogies, patri- and matri-lateral genealogies, and "eight-ancestor" tables (*p'algojodo*), which document the parentage of an individual's paternal and maternal grandparents. It was only after the mid-Chosŏn Dynasty that clans began to compile genealogical tables on the basis of information provided in these family records.

Although these genealogies originated in China, their compilation was much more ardently undertaken in Chosŏn Korea because social status was inherited through blood relations. For *yangban,* the ruling elite at that time, chokpo were irrefutable evidence of social privilege bequeathed by ancestors.

Chokpo identify individuals by surname and *pon-gwan,* the clan seat where the lineage originated. The surname is the name of a kin group of unilineal descent, that is, either patrilineal or matrilineal descent. Because the surname and pon-gwan identify both the clan and place of origin, the two are often used together as identification.

Koreans traditionally feel a strong sense of consanguineous belonging through their surnames. This is apparent in several customs. Koreans always specify patrilineal bloodline by indicating the pon-gwan in their family registers. Marriage between persons of the same surname and pon-gwan is strictly prohibited, and generational "markers" are often used in the names of members of the same generation of a clan, even if they are distant relatives. This sense of belonging also explains the continued compilation of genealogies.

Most Korean surnames consist of Chinese characters imitating the Chinese system. The history of these surnames can be traced to the end of the Three Kingdoms period, when Korean royalty adopted Chinese surnames and awarded surnames originating from China to privileged aristocrats. Surnames were popularized among public officials and commoners during the Koryŏ Dynasty, and even the low-born came to have surnames during the Chosŏn Dynasty.

In an effort to undermine the Shilla hereditary "bone-rank" (*kolp'um*) system of aristocratic privilege after establishing a new unified dynasty, Koryŏ rulers awarded powerful provincial clans who actively participated in the unification campaign surnames of native origin and established clan seats, which later came to be subdivided into various pon-gwan. However, over the centuries many of the locations for which the pon-gwan were named were superseded in reorganizations of the local administrative system. From the end of the 15th century, many pon-gwan with obso-

Carefully maintained clan genealogies reflect a family's commitment to filial piety and perpetuation of the bloodline.

50

敬文

玄見 子礦

配瑞寧柳后

目及翰院題 名錄韓山李瑞山柳文化柳首陽吳譜皆作礦故正之

天順己卯文科與弟曁高榜官止翰林○按舊譜作勵而國朝榜

進義校尉

配瑞寧柳
氏考方敬祖瑞寧君沂曾祖三司右尹厚思菴淑○玄孫女外祖開國功臣復

○永同金光輔女金勵翰林无后豈前后室耶今姑並錄

縣令晉卿从
氏考咸從鄭
祖生員生員
韻忌十月
忌十月二
十六日
二十九日

墓海州西

配文化柳
氏祔

高山有碣

子玩

墓海州北

子李文馨
城府院君后室无后

女閔汝慶參判汝慶子閔
林兵使死節孫女張晩玉

女李寶
子李文郁
縣監

子李文華
別坐

子李文髻
文吏判

文李公遂
縣監全義人父判決事
○全義李為全義李之壻殊涉可疑

全義人父都事義錫
城君禮長

此派子孫

---

lete geographic names were consolidated with those named after towns that still existed. With the development of elite yangban society during the Chosŏn Dynasty, the pon-gwan of distinguished families were so highly regarded that some yangban of less powerful stature adopted the more prestigious pon-gwan. As a result of these two developments, the number of pon-gwan decreased.

Following the Reforms of 1894, which brought sweeping changes to government administration, the economy and Korea's social structure, even the lowest of the lowborn were given the opportunity to have their own surnames, and with the enforcement of the census registration law in 1909, all citizens were granted a surname and a pon-gwan.

The oldest systematic royal genealogy is the *Chronicle of Emperors and Kings* (*Chewang yŏndaeryŏk*), compiled by Ch'oe Ch'i-won (857-?), the renowned Shilla scholar, statesman and poet. The surname system was institutionalized in the early years of the Koryŏ Dynasty. From the mid-Koryŏ period, royal annals (*Wangdae shillok*) and royal genealogical records (*sŏnwollok*) were compiled. The use of terms such as *kabo* ("family treasure") and *kach'ŏp* ("family album") by royalty and aristocrats dates to the reign of Koryŏ's King Munjong (1046-1083), suggesting that the elite was keeping systematic records of their lineage under those titles. However, there appear to have been no special organizations devoted to the recording and recharting of lineage tables generation after generation.

The royal house of Chosŏn compiled royal genealogical records and an official record of royal relatives (*chongch'innok*) in 1412. At the same time, a number of documents were compiled in an effort to distinguish primary descendants from secondary descendants in the royal family. These documents included the *Royal Genealogy* (*Kukcho poch'ŏp*), the *Current Royal Genealogical Record* (*Tangdae sŏnwollok*), the *King's Eight-Ancestor Chart* (*Yŏlsŏng p'algojodo*), and the *Genealogy of Royal Relatives* (*Tonnyŏng poch'ŏp*), a record of royal sons-in-law and the royal family's maternal lineage.

In 1679, upon the recommendation of Prince Nangwon-gun, a grandson of King Sŏnjo (r. 1567-1608), King Sukchong (r. 1674-1720) ordered the compilation of a simplified royal genealogical record entitled the *Genealogical Table of the Royal Clan of the Chosŏn Dynasty* (*Sŏnwon kyebo kiryak*) for distribution to government officials. Until 1931, the record was intermittently reedited and

51

supplemented by subsequent kings. In 1680, the court published a 50-volume royal genealogical record. A temporary office was established for each update of the record until 1757, when the Office of Royal Genealogy (Chongbushi) was established. It was absorbed by the Bureau of Royal Relatives (Chongch'inbu) in 1864.

In the meantime, the Chŏnju Yi clan, to which the kings of Chosŏn belonged, authorized the descendants of each sub-clan headed by a brother or son of the king to compile their own "augmented royal genealogy" (sŏnwon sokpo) to maintain links with the royal bloodline recorded in the royal genealogy.

After the Chŏnju Yi clan lost the kingship with the fall of the Chosŏn Dynasty in 1910, clans descending from kings of previous eras, such as the Pak, Sŏk and Kim clans of the Shilla Kingdom and the Wang clan of the Koryŏ Dynasty, began to include the terms sŏnwon or wanggye, meaning "royal," to their genealogies.

In East Asia, clan genealogies first appeared in China in the form of imperial genealogical records. Common people began to compile genealogical tables from the Han Dynasty (202 B.C.-A.D. 221). During the Six Dynasties (221-589), when family pedigree was of prime social consideration, the compilation of genealogies was undertaken most actively because the court institutionalized a screening system to review genealogies to ensure that only members of illustrious clans were promoted to high public office.

In Korea, genealogies are believed to have originated in records of royal lineage compiled during the Koryŏ Dynasty. Commoners began to compile joint genealogical records by combining records kept by individual families of the same ancestry. The first such record was the *Genealogical Table of the Munhwa Yu Clan* (*Munhwa Yussi yŏngnakpo*) published in 1423, but it has since been lost. Some of the earliest extant records are the *Genealogical Table of the Andong Kwon Clan* (*Andong Kwonssi sŏnghwabo*) dated 1476, the *Revised Genealogical Table of the Munhwa Yu Clan*

This genealogical table is recorded in mixed Korean-Chinese script.

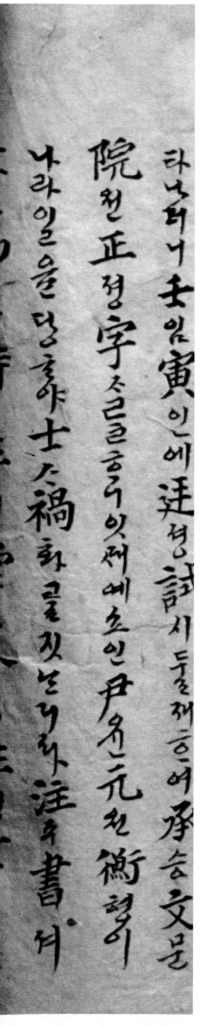

(*Munhwa Yussi kajŏngbo*) dated 1565, and the *Genealogical Table of the Ch'ŏngsong Shim Clan* (*Ch'ŏngsong Shimssi chokpo*) dated 1649. These early records comprised relatively few generations and duplicated all information kept in family records. Therefore, even descendants by daughters were entered. They also included the total number of clan members at the time of compilation.

Joint genealogical records as we know them today were first compiled in the late 17th century and became most prevalent in the late 18th century. By that time clans were organizing into sub-clans centered around localities. Each sub-clan compiled its own genealogy dating to its founder. However, from the beginning of the 19th century, integrated clan genealogies were compiled as various sub-clans attempted to chart their descent from a common progenitor.

A family genealogy usually includes:

1. A preface and postscript describing the genealogy's significance, the history of the clan, and sometimes the preface and postscript of a previous edition.

2. An introduction of the clan progenitor, sub-clan progenitor and eminent ancestors with their biographies, epitaphs, and inscriptions from the memorial steles marking their graves, as well as chronicles and written addresses to their spirits.

3. A map indicating the location of the graves of the clan progenitor, sub-clan progenitors and eminent ancestors.

4. Introductory remarks explaining the circumstances of the genealogy's compilation and the recording system used.

5. The table and chart of lineage, which comprise the main part of the record. The page number is indicated by Chinese characters in their order of appearance in the *Thousand-Character Text* (*Ch'ŏnjamun*), a primer of Chinese characters.

6. The publisher, the place where the record was printed, and a list of those who participated in the compilation.

During the early Chosŏn Dynasty, genealogies were printed at temples, which were often equipped with printing tools and paper. In the latter part of the dynasty, when genealogies were compiled by lineage, they were published at private Confucian academies (*sŏwon*) or sometimes by provincial offices.

In multivolume genealogies, the volumes are numbered by Chinese characters, which normally appear in compound words or phrases. For example, two-volume genealogies are marked *kŏn* ("heaven") and *kon* ("earth"), or *sang* ("up") and *ha* ("down"). Three-volume genealogies are marked *ch'ŏn* ("heaven"), *chi* ("earth"), and *in* ("human"); or *sang* ("up"), *chung* ("middle"), and *ha* ("down"). Ten-volume genealogies are indicated by the characters for the ten celestial stems or calendar signs.

Sometimes sub-clans collaborate to publish a joint genealogy. The first volume includes the biography and lineage of the clan progenitor. Subsequent volumes are then compiled independently by individual sub-clans and combined with the first volume for distribution.

Chokpo is a generic term for lineage records of all kinds. There are many other names for these records. All refer to chokpo but are slightly different in nature. *Taedongbo* is the most comprehensive genealogy, a corporate effort, which includes the genealogies of all constituent lineages of a clan sharing the same pon-gwan. A *p'abo*, on the other hand, deals with only one of the numerous sub-clans. P'abo thus has the advantage of including every member of the particular sub-clan and also detailed biographies of the sub-clan's eminent ancestors. *Sebo*, like p'abo, is a sub-clan genealogy, but it is generally more detailed, often including information on ancestry preceding the relevant sub-clan's branching out from the main line, such as the circumstances of its separation, its relationship with other sub-clans, and the history of the progenitors of all sub-clans. *Kasŭngbo* generally records the immediate relations only or at most the genealogy originating with the great-great-grandfather. Each family or lineage compiles their kasŭngbo on the basis of the clan genealogy, which is usually kept in the house of the clan head. The kasŭngbo is used to remember ancestral birthdays, the anniversaries of deaths and other important dates. The kasŭngbo of various families are sometimes combined to form a family album, or kach'ŏp. *Kyebo* is a record of sub-clans or posthumous titles that the government conferred on deceased ancestors.

Genealogies of towns and villages are also compiled. The *hyangbo* documents the clan distribution of a town, and the *tongbo* of a smaller village. *Sŏnwonbo* is the genealogy of the royal family. *Oebo* is a limited matrilineal genealogy. *Naeshibo* were genealogies of court eunuchs, *naeshi*. *Nobi chongch'inbo* chronicled the lineage of slaves, and *p'alsebo* were official genealogies of yangban officials.

Genealogies are revised every 30 years, that is, every generation, in order to include new clan members and the accomplishments of older ones. The decision to revise a genealogy is made at a meeting of clan elders, which takes place after ancestral memorial rites held in the tenth lunar month each year. The revision usually starts in the 11th month. Clan officers first send letters to each family of all subclans requesting updated information. Sometimes they visit each household to expedite the census process. The information is meticulously crosschecked against historical records before it is included in the genealogy. A draft is often made in brush calligraphy and bound in bookform before it is printed.

During the Chosŏn Dynasty, genealogies were printed with wood blocks or movable wood type, the latter prevailing in Chosŏn's waning years. Metal type was used from the Japanese colonial period.

Publication expenses are generally shared equally by all living clan members, although some clans prorate contributions according to the financial status of each member. Toward the end of the Chosŏn Dynasty, adult members paid 1 *ryang*. Unmarried members were assessed half that amount. Sometimes well-to-do members make special donations, or the clan makes a donation from its treasury.

Compilation and publication generally take two or three years but there can be delays depending on clan circumstances. The printed genealogy is dispatched to each family. A charge is made for additional copies. In the past, families who could not afford a printed chokpo borrowed one and copied it by hand.

Early genealogies included not only patrilineal but also matrilineal descendants. However, after the clan organization was reinforced in the late Chosŏn Dynasty, entries were limited to patrilineal descendants, except for sons-in-law, their fathers and the wife's father. At first, offspring were entered by order of birth, regardless of sex, but in late Chosŏn chokpo, sons were entered before daughters and their husbands, reflecting a strengthening of Confucian patriarchal thinking.

Adopted sons were commonly entered under their birth name and the name they were given by their adoptive family. Illegitimate sons and sons born of concubines were not supposed to be included in clan genealogies, and if they were entered, their illegitimate status was noted. In more recent times, this principle has not been strictly followed.

A perusal of genealogies from the late Chosŏn period reveals the frequent use of *hangnyŏlcha*, or generation characters. The prevalence of generation characters is believed to be an outgrowth of the development of large lineage organizations. Generation characters were used to confirm relationships among the ever-increasing constituents of the clan.

Individual entries vary according to ranking within a generation. For example, the entry of a lineage heir is more detailed than those of other lineage members. It includes not only his name but also his sobriquet, pen name, birth and death dates, examinations passed, public offices held, posthumous title, and the exact location of his grave. His wife's entry includes her birth and death dates; her pon-gwan; the name of her father and grandfather and their public titles; the name, pon-gwan and public title of her maternal grandfather; and the location of her grave if she is not buried next to her husband.

Side notes are added when needed to show the accomplishments of the persons entered. Most refer to "honorable achievements" (*hunŏp*), "virtuous deeds" (*tŏkhaeng*), loyalty and filial piety, and writings. If a person has no heir, it is so noted. For adopted sons, the circumstances of adoption are specified in the genealogies of both the adoptive and birth families.

During the latter part of the late Chosŏn Dynasty, the credibility of clan genealogies came into question. One of the most frequent abuses was the false entry of young men to avoid corvée labor service. The false or exaggerated recording of public office, rank and civil service examination results was also common. If a family claimed descent from a person who had no heir in the previous genealogy and there was no historical evidence to countercheck their claim, the family's lineage was entered in a supplement or a separate volume, not in the main genealogy.

Korean genealogies are presented in two formats: vertically or horizontally. The vertical format is seldom used today because it is confusing and difficult to find lineages or identify horizontal relationships. The horizontal bar format describes each generation in a bar with its ancestor at the top, making it easy to determine the degree of kinship.

Some scholars discredit the historic value of clan genealogies on the grounds that most entries on ancestors predating the Koryŏ period cannot be historically verified and that many entries made in the late Chosŏn Dynasty were intentionally fabricated. Nevertheless, clan genealogies are a priceless source of information on the population and social relationships of the Chosŏn Dynasty.

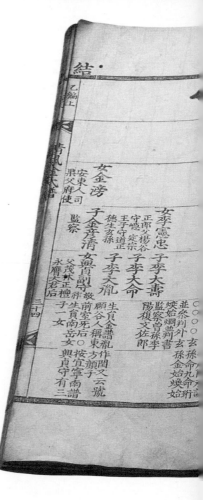

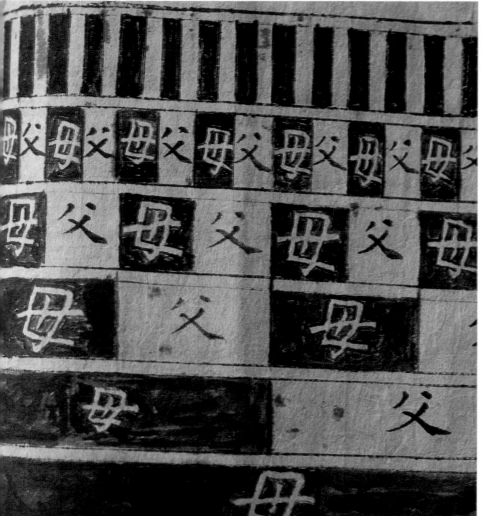

Clan genealogies are invaluable historical documents and tools in the study of traditional society. Clockwise from below: a genealogical schedule of ancestral rituals; the genealogical record of a Chosŏn yangban clan; and a genealogical diagram showing the immediate male and female forebears of a particiular individual.

The traditional clan genealogy is now undergoing a modernization for the sake of the younger generation, which is not familiar with Chinese characters. Some clans translate difficult Chinese terms into the Korean alphabet, *han-gŭl*, or include photographs for the benefit of relatives who seldom see each other. The most recent development are videotaped genealogies with a formal introduction of the life and achievements of ancestors.

Tradition should neither be blindly praised nor condemned. Clan genealogies are a product of the past. They were developed to meet the needs of the people living in another time. But just as history is related to the present, clan genealogies, maps of past lives and achievements, are linked to our lives today. Today's feminist protests against the male-dominated inheritance system and laws prohibiting clan intermarriage are modern developments. Such protests would have been unthinkable in traditional society. By the same token, clan intermarriage was and remains completely abhorrent to traditional Confucians. That is the reality of Korean society. ◆

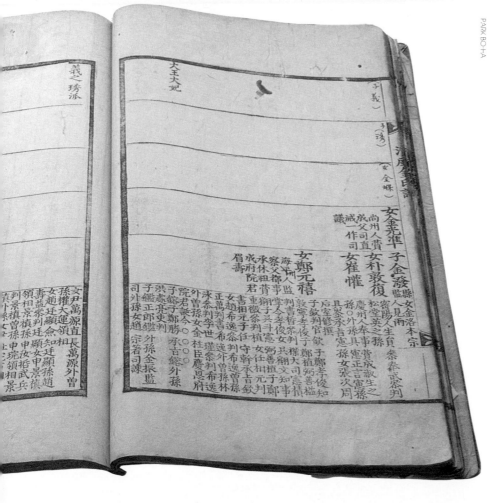

HOUSING AND THE NATURAL ENVIRONMENT

Architecture and land use are mirrors on traditional culture. In Korea, residential housing and landscaping reflect traditional beliefs and social structure.

The history of habitation on the Korean peninsula, provided here by Kim Bong-ryol, describes changing social structure and Korean attitudes toward nature, natural forces and the land. Professor Kim looks at the development of Korean dwellings from the Paleolithic era through the Chosŏn Dynasty, considering how housing mirrored social class divisions and regional differences.

Folk belief and Confucian teachings have both had a profound influence on Korean habitation. Kim Kwang-on examines Confucianism's influence on structure and function in the strict segregation of the sexes and veneration of ancestors. The folk belief in a broad pantheon of household gods was also a crucial influence on living patterns.

Geomancy, the divination of natural forces, which influences human habitation and the location of graves, houses, and even cities, has been an important factor in Korean life since ancient times. Choi Chang-jo, a professional geomancy practitioner, compares Chinese geomancy with indigenous Korean beliefs and practice, describing Korean geomancy as a philosophy-science that perceives nature as a loving, yet sometimes imperfect, mother who requires our understanding, acceptance and accommodation.

Architect and educator Joo Nam-chull considers architecture's role as a mirror of social status in the Chosŏn Dynasty's strict Confucian society and, like Choi, notes the importance of the Korean people's reverence for nature and their surrounding environment in their homes.

Furnishings and tools also reflect traditional Korean values. Lim Young-ju describes the furnishings and function of the men's and women's quarters, communal open spaces and work areas.

In the early 19th century, Chosŏn's King Sunjo ordered the construction of an ideal noble home in the back garden of one of Seoul's royal palaces so that he could experience life outside the court. While Sunjo never actually lived there, this structure, Yŏn-gyŏngdang, still stands today, a valuable representation of an ideal Confucian lifestyle where the sexes were strictly segregated and people lived in meditative harmony with nature. Kim Kwang-hyun focuses on the layout and architectural features of the outstanding structure.

Traditional rural villages and houses were literally born of nature. Lee Sang-hae's contribution discusses the development of rural villages and the relationship between rural dwellings and the surrounding environment.

Korean homes are unique in part because of the *ondol* under-floor heating system that has evolved since prehistoric Koreans began erecting stone fire pits thousands of years ago. Choi Young-taik provides the historical background of the ondol heating system as well as an explanation of its benefits and influence on Korean lifestyles.

Since ancient times, Koreans have incorporated nature into their lives in the form of water. Professor Yoo Byung-rim discusses the use of water in landscape architecture in East Asia, emphasizing its "mind-cleansing" qualities and unique ability to link humanity to nature and supernatural forces.

A History of Korean Housing

Kim Bong-ryol

The oldest evidence of human habitation on the Korean peninsula is Paleolithic relics dating back some 500,000 years. Paleolithic people lived among rocks, under trees or in caves. Their homes bear little resemblance to what we call "houses" today. It was not until the end of the Paleolithic period that man-made dwellings appeared on the peninsula.

In the Neolithic era, hunting and fishing were the primary lifestyles, but primitive forms of tilling had begun in some regions. Agrarian life necessitated permanent dwellings. It was around this time that pit dwellings, Korea's first man-made dwellings, were introduced. They consisted of circular or square pits, about 20 meters wide and 0.6 to 1.2 meters deep, covered with a straw or reed thatch roof that was supported by rafters. Pits were used because they conserved heat in winter. Lacking the technology to erect vertical walls, Neolithic Koreans used the cut faces of the pits as walls. The pit's interior was open. At the center was an open hearth for heating and cooking. Completing the meager household facilities were storage holes designed to store food.

It was not until the Bronze Age that a settled agrarian lifestyle dominated the peninsula. Pit dwellings underwent important changes during this period. They were larger now, up to 70 meters square, and many had two hearths, suggesting that the function of the inner space was beginning to change.

As pits grew larger, their shape also changed, from square or circular to rectangular. A separate building was constructed to take the place of the old storage holes. This differentiation of function gave rise to the tradition of separate quarters and functional buildings in the Korean house.

Structural technology also changed dramatically. As pits grew shallower, vertical walls appeared. Woodworking technology developed enabling the construction of larger buildings with vertical walls. In the northern and central parts of the peninsula, *ondol*, a hypocaust, or under-floor heating, system, was coming into use. Ondol and the pattern of separate functional quarters gradually came to distinguish Korea's traditional housing.

As iron culture was transmitted to Korea in the fourth century B.C., a new ruling class developed and society became increasingly stratified. With this stratification came more diversification in dwellings. Power and wealth were concentrated in the hands of a new elite, and the qualitative gap in lifestyles widened.

Common people still lived in pit dwellings, but the ruling classes now constructed dwellings above ground with vertical walls, and often with several different wings or buildings. Not only were their houses comprised of several buildings, but the elite lived in different types of dwellings depending on the season. In winter, they stayed in luxurious pit dwellings or buildings in which ondol was installed. In summer, they lived in cottages constructed on wooden platforms well above the ground. This dual lifestyle was a forerunner of the housing tradition in which ondol rooms coexisted side by side with *maru*, wooden-floored rooms that were often open to the outside.

While ondol was an invention of the colder north, maru and *tarakbang*, a small loft over the kitchen, originated in the warm southern region. Open wooden floors and lofts were probably quite common in the Paekche and Kaya territories, and over time the custom slowly spread northward. Conversely, the ondol custom of the Koguryŏ Kingdom, which was located in the northern part of the peninsula, began to spread southward. Eventually, ondol and maru came to coexist in dwellings throughout the peninsula.

A pumpkin vine finds a sunny home on a thatch roof in Chŏllanam-do province.

The advancement of iron culture resulted in more sophisticated building tools, which in turn brought more advanced construction techniques that enabled craftsmen to process building materials and assemble parts in a more precise manner. Dwellings grew in size as a result, walls were higher and structures stronger and more sophisticated.

As the three kingdoms of Koguryŏ, Paekche and Shilla established themselves, class differences in housing became even more evident. The development of advanced structural technologies meant large multistory buildings could be built. Elaborate multiroom houses were built not only within the walls of the royal palaces but also by members of the aristocratic elite. Wooden construction techniques newly imported from China had a revolutionary influence on building construction. Larger interiors were constructed and heavy roof tiles could now be used.

With the development of a centralized monarchy, urban culture flourished, giving rise to a new genre of city dwellings. However, the common people and farmers in rural areas still lived in pit dwellings or huts.

Lifestyles in Koguryŏ, the most culturally advanced of the three kingdoms, can be inferred from historical records and murals found in royal tombs. A typical aristocratic mansion consisted of ten or more structures. The owner's main building was surrounded by subordinate structures such as servants' quarters, rice mill, well, kitchen, stables, barn, and cart shed. The buildings were connected by corridors or separated by walls where needed, and the main building was built in the magnificent style of a two-story pavilion.

The popularization of ondol and the development of multistory structures were two prominent features of Koguryŏ dwellings. Because of the cold climate, the common people used ondol as their main heating system. In aristocrats' dwellings, however, it was customary to install ondol in only part of the room. The nobles slept in wooden beds and sat in chairs. Koguryŏ houses were also distinguished by their private storehouses, or *pugyŏng*. These storehouses were probably loft-like structures made of stacked logs.

During the Koguryŏ Kingdom, improved technology led to the construction of two-story buildings among the common people as well as at royal palaces and aristocratic homes. Timbers were the main building material, but in some cases bricks were used, evidence of Chinese influence.

Paekche dwellings were generally smaller

These straw-covered pit dwellings (above and left) reconstructed near Seoul stand on the site of similar Paekche dwellings.

A field of red peppers surrounds thatch cottages in this typical Korean landscape.

than those of Koguryŏ but similar in style. Many remains of pit dwellings dating to early Paekche have been discovered. These dwellings are characterized by separate kitchens equipped with fireholes and ondol heating systems. No remains of two-story structures have been discovered but earthenware shaped like two-story houses has been excavated in the southern part of the peninsula. From this we can assume that private houses in the southern part of Korea had wooden-floored living areas on the second floor, which were reached by ladder.

According to a reliable historical record, Kyŏngju, the capital of the Shilla Kingdom, had 178,936 houses within its walls. They were all tile-roofed. The record also says that no smoke came from their chimneys because charcoal was used for cooking and heating instead of firewood. Inside the city walls, 35 palatial mansions formed the nuclei of various neighborhoods. The eaves and walls of these structures connected in a complex web of

urban housing. The houses themselves were formalized with walls and gates and lavishly decorated with colorful trim and ornaments.

From historical records scholars assume that Shilla's more luxurious homes were "one-room buildings" (t'onggan), where the entire building consisted of one room. These houses had no fixed interior walls. Instead, the large interior space was divided by blinds or screens. The floor was covered with fired bricks, and a maru-like wooden platform was built over part of the floor to serve as a seating and sleeping area. Records indicate that charcoal was used for heating in Kyŏngju. From this it appears freestanding braziers were used during the winter months.

The Koryŏ Dynasty was marked by greater local autonomy than the Shilla period. As a result, noble families constructed large mansions, even in the rural areas, and surrounding commoner homes improved in style and quality.

Because of the many hills, valleys and com-

plex river systems that mark Korean topography, the selection of a building site was one of the most important elements of the construction process. Aristocrats were especially keen on interpreting natural environment and gradually developed various theoretical methodologies for selecting a "good" site. The twin concepts of *yin* and *yang*, elements of ancient Chinese cosmology, were basic to one methodology. According to this theory, Korea's complex, mountainous topography corresponded to yang, the masculine, active element. In order to balance this element, houses should be low and flat, corresponding to the negative, absorbing and receptive nature of yin. This is one reason why there are so few multistory structures in rural areas.

On the other hand, the larger homes in urban areas were equipped with two- or three-story pavilions, which symbolized authority and at the same time offered views of the surrounding area. According to the yin-yang theory, urban areas, crowded with the low-lying houses of the common people, were yin by nature. Therefore, lofty yang houses were needed. The urban dwellings of Koryŏ nobility were further embellished with glazed blue tile, lavishly decorated walls and colorful trim.

Chinese geomancy, or *feng shui*, was introduced to Korea around the tenth century. It provided a theoretical basis for the interpretation of the natural environment. According to feng shui theory, all matter in nature, including heaven and earth, consists of a universal energy called *qi* (Korean, *ki*). One can draw nature's qi into a house by locating the house in such a manner as to be in harmony with natural qi. This good qi will eventually be transmitted to the people living in that house. They in turn will enjoy prosperity and longevity. Feng-shui theory had an immense influence on Korean lifestyles, for Koreans had always sought to harmonize with nature. Ultimately, feng shui came to be the dominant tradition in Korean architecture.

During the Koryŏ Dynasty, the main building of a private house was typically made of three rooms with the main hall flanked by two side rooms. The division of one building into several rooms was already popular in the Koryŏ Dynasty. However, ondol and maru did not coexist in one building yet. The main building had only ondol, while open-air pavilions, set away from the main structure, were unheated maru. The differentiation of functional buildings that had started during the Bronze Age divided the private home's many functions among several buildings. The differentiation of functional buildings and the subsequent differentiation of functional rooms became

one of the main distinguishing features of Korean housing.

These Koryŏ traditions—the simultaneous use of differentiated functional buildings and rooms, the use of feng shui to select housing sites, and the coexistence of ondol and wooden flooring in one house—continued into the Chosŏn Dynasty. In fact, one could say that the major structural characteristics of the "Korean house" had been solidified by the Koryŏ Dynasty.

Confucianism, the state ideology of the Chosŏn Dynasty, had a powerful influence on housing patterns and lifestyles. The state regulated house styles, strictly distinguishing between the homes of the *yangban* elite; the *chungin* "middle people," a social class that served as technical officials and local government clerks; the *sangmin*, freeborn commoners; and *ch'ŏnmin*, the lowborn, which included public and private slaves. The homes of the Neo-Confucian yangban were inward-oriented and closed to the outside. The houses of the common people and lowborn, on the other hand, had insubstantial walls and gates and were relatively open to passersby.

Under the exacting Confucian Chosŏn regime, men and women were strictly segregated. In upper-class households this segregation was reflected in the maintenance of separate quarters for men and women. Men were forbidden from entering the *anch'ae*, where women lived and worked, and women only went to the *sarangch'ae*, the master's quarters, to serve men. Household servants worked in a separate building near the main gate, the *haengnangch'ae*. Male servants were strictly prohibited from entering the anch'ae.

Confucian etiquette demanded absolute respect for elders. The Chosŏn home reflected the generational hierarchy. In the sarangch'ae, there was a large *sarangbang*, where the senior male lived, and smaller sarangbang for his sons. Similarly, in the anch'ae, the lady of the house lived in the main *anbang*, while her daughters-in-law lived in *kŏnnŏnbang*, across from the main room. In other words, there was a systematic division of rooms within the larger context of the division of buildings.

During the Chosŏn Dynasty, families began building separate private ancestral shrines, or *sadang*. The establishment of special buildings for these shrines had important symbolic value as each family held at least ten rites a year.

Confucian scholars, who despised bravado and materialism, rejected any decorative elements in their houses. Instead, they attempted to express abstract concepts. Blank white walls, geometric latticed windows and unadorned courtyards are just a few examples of the metaphysical elements expressed in the traditional Korean house.

During the 18th and 19th centuries, however, the value system of the yangban elite had changed dramatically. The yangban concern for political and scholarly achievement gradually gave way to more pragmatic values concerned with economic gain. The yangban who embraced this new value system are sometimes referred to as *punong*, or "wealthy farmers." The homes of these pragmatic yangban complied with traditional Confucian formalities, but functional convenience and economical rationality were also taken into consideration. There was also an ostentatious trend toward larger and taller homes.

Ondol was the main heating method for commoner and yangban homes. It was during this period that the floor-sitting lifestyle was finally universalized, and the combined use of ondol rooms and maru in one home was accepted throughout Korea. Many families had attempted to install both ondol and maru from the Koryŏ period, but various material and technical obstacles prevented the successful application until the middle of the Chosŏn period. Thus it was not until the middle of the Chosŏn Dynasty that Korean homes took on the form familiar to us today.

Agricultural productivity improved dramatically during the Chosŏn Dynasty, bringing a similar improvement in rural lifestyles. As a result, housing in the provinces improved and differentiated to reflect differing regional cultures and climates. Construction technology itself saw great improvement. Among the innovations of this period were changes in the placement and combination of rooms in a single building, new roof-framing techniques, new construction materials and new styles of buildings. Generally speaking, housing during the Chosŏn Dynasty became more varied in function and style in accordance with social class divisions and regional differences, creating a diverse housing culture in striking contrast to contemporary Korean society, where high-rise apartment complexes have become the norm. ◆

In large homes, heated ondol rooms are flanked by wooden-floored maru which offer relief from summer's heat.

Spiritual Traditions in the Korean House

Kim Kwang-on

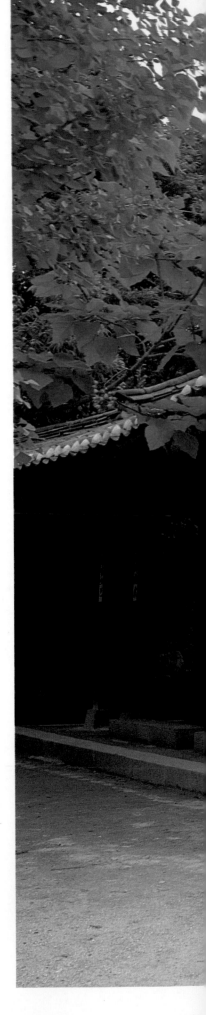

Built with clay and wood, Korean houses seldom last more than 200 or 300 years. Most traditional houses standing today date from the mid- to late Chosŏn Dynasty.

Confucian teachings prevailed in every aspect of Chosŏn life. The gentry who embraced the cultivation and practice of Confucian virtues as a lifelong mission naturally strived to build their houses within the framework of Confucian norms. Gentry homes were not living spaces so much as venues for the inculcation and practice of Confucian precepts. They also served to demonstrate the righteousness of their owners to others.

Confucian teachings had a profound influence on Chosŏn lifestyles. Strict segregation of men and women, a basic Confucian principle, led to a life of virtual separation. Separate quarters for men and women were required. Faithful reverence of ancestors, another paramount Confucian virtue, meant that parents and long-deceased forebears were accorded the utmost respect and care. The younger generation was bound to yield to their elders in all matters, and housing arrangements reflected the elder generation's absolute power.

The homes of the Chosŏn gentry were divided into two distinct areas: one centered around the *sarangch'ae*, the men's quarters, and the other around the *anch'ae*, the women's quarters. A wall made the division complete. No one from the sarangch'ae could enter the anch'ae when the inner gate between the two areas was locked from inside. Food was cooked in the anch'ae and carried, meal by meal, to the sarangch'ae by servants for the household's male members. Clothes too were brought from the anch'ae. It was rare for a husband and wife to be seen together, even by their family. When the husband entered the anch'ae, he was no better than a visitor. He was expected to dress formally and make the warning coughs that Koreans have long used instead of knocking before stepping through the inner gate.

Ideally a wife would have little reason to go out beyond the inner gate at any time during her life. The few times she did leave the anch'ae was when she visited her parents with her husband shortly after their wedding, when her parents died, and finally, in a coffin, when she died.

This segregated life was perpetuated in her children's lives from early on. When boys reached age five or six, they were sent to the sarangch'ae to grow under the tutelage of their grandfather while girls remained in the anch'ae to be trained by their grandmother.

Men from outside the immediate family were not allowed to look at the anch'ae, much less enter it. Outside contact stopped at the freestanding wall that was built in front of the inner gate to ensure even greater privacy. It was the convention of the time not to inspect the anch'ae even when buying the house.

Conjugal relations were a problem in this segregated environment, a problem doubly troublesome in an era when a woman's most important mission was to produce a male heir; otherwise, she risked expulsion from her husband's family. But how was a woman supposed to get pregnant? The solution to this problem lay in secret passages that ran through most homes. For example, the Kim family home in Sanoe-myŏn, Chŏngŭp, Chŏllabuk-do province has a small opening in the wall of the anch'ae. Barely wide enough for a man to squeeze through, it is normally hidden with sorghum stalks and other objects. In the Ch'oe family home in Kyŏngju, a tiny

The men's quarters (sarangch'ae) of a noble household was a place for quiet study and socializing.

A gate connects the men's and women's quarters.

door inside a walk-in closet in the sarangch'ae opens to a passage leading to the wife's quarters.

The segregation tradition lives on in some parts of the country. For example in the Son household in Yangdong-ri, Kyŏngju, the elderly husband and wife and their only son, a middle school student, lead separate lives in their sarangch'ae and anch'ae. In the Kim house in Chŏngŭp, on the other hand, the wife lives in the main room of the anch'ae while her husband occupies the room right next to it. In the conservative Kyŏngsang region, a man who frequents his wife's quarters is still the brunt of merciless teasing.

In houses facing south, the sarangch'ae, the men's quarters, was built in the east and the women's anch'ae in the west. The ancestral shrine stood behind the sarangch'ae. The sarangch'ae and the shrine stood in the east because that was the direction of the masculine force *yang*, the rising sun and light from which auspiciousness derived. The notion that the main gate should stand in the east also originates from this belief. The west, on the other hand, was the direction of the setting sun and thus the feminine *yin*, representing darkness and inauspi-

ciousness.

Filial piety was the paramount virtue in Confucianism. Children were admonished to perform their filial duties while their parents were alive and after their death. Household shrines reflected the ideal of ancestral veneration. The construction of these shrines was vigorously promoted by the Chosŏn rulers from the beginning of the dynasty. Aristocrats without ancestral shrines were punished, and Buddhist monks, who had already renounced secular concerns, were urged to follow Confucian funeral and memorial protocol.

The importance of the ancestral shrine system grew over time. The location of the family shrine was the first decision made when a house was built. The shrine had to be taller, or on higher terrain, than the rest of the house. Once built it was never to be moved. From the point of view of traditional geomancy, the shrine had to sit at the most auspicious spot in the residential compound. This explains why shrines were always behind the sarangch'ae, in the direction of the nearest protective mountain, thus basking in the positive energy of nature.

Most shrines were three-*kan* structures separated from the rest of the house by a wall and gate. (A kan is a traditional unit of measure referring to the space between two columns). The building was often painted with the multicolored *tanch'ŏng* and surrounded by plantings. The shrine in the Son clan house in Kyŏngju is six kan across and protected by a gate three and a half kan wide. It also has its own well-tended garden. In this case, the shrine takes up more than half the residential compound. The Chosŏn people's tendency toward ostentatious family shrines has produced the popular expression, "like adorning one's shrine" (*sadangch'ire hadŭt*), which is still used to describe impractical, ostentatious displays.

However, the Chosŏn people believed that their ancestors lived in the shrine. Some visited the shrine every morning to bid morning greetings to their ancestors. Some even made daily food offerings. In addition to the regular memorial rites held on death anniversaries and seasonal holidays, families paid tribute on the first and fifteenth day of each month and made offerings of freshly harvested grain and fruit at the turn of the seasons. Coming-of-age ceremonies and other important family rites were held in front of the shrine. The master of the house reported to the shrine before and after any outings. He also went there to report on family affairs such as marriages, births, new jobs, military service and other major undertakings involving family members. The Ŭisŏng Kim clan of Andong in Kyŏngsangbuk-do province still meet in front of their ancestral shrine when they have important matters to discuss. In this way they include their ancestors in each family undertaking and prevent future discord on items decided at the meeting. The Kim clan is famous for standing by their commitments.

The memorial tablets of up to four generations of ancestors, back to the great-great-grandfather of the current master of the household, and their wives are ensconced in the shrine. The oldest generation is enshrined at the left (when viewed from the entrance). When a new generation of ancestors enters the shrine after death, the tablet of the senior ancestor is removed and buried in front of his or her grave. Ancestors beyond the fourth generation are accorded memorial rites at graveside in the tenth lunar month.

In some cases, the memorial tablets of especially illustrious ancestors, who made outstanding contributions to their country while alive, are enshrined at the family shrine indefinitely. These tablets were referred to as *pulch'ŏnwi*, "never removed," or *kuksŏn*, "state designated," tablets.

Families who could not afford a separate shrine building kept their ancestral tablets in small niches in the back wall of their *maru*, the unheated wooden-floor hall usually found at the center of the house. Commoners kept small earthen rice jars, called *chosang tangsegi* in the Kyŏngsang region and *mom-ogari* in the Chŏlla region, on a shelf in the main room. The rice jars symbolized ancestral

The family shrine (top) houses ancestral tablets. Elders often discuss important clan affairs when they gather for ancestral rites (above).

spirits, much like the memorial tablets, and were usually found in the house of the direct-line descendant of the clan. Like memorial tablets, there could be a jar for each ancestor honored or one for each generation. The enshrining of memorial tablets in a detached shrine was a Confucian custom that began to spread during the Chosŏn Dynasty. Prior to the Chosŏn Dynasty, Koreans may have venerated their ancestors through the symbolic rice jars as part of their indigenous folk beliefs.

The Confucian principle that the elder shall preside had a considerable influence on the spatial arrangement of upper-class residences. Even the names of the different rooms and

69

The senior daughter-in-law rules the women's quarters (above). She is in charge of running the household. One of her most important duties is caring for the many sauces stored in jars on the changdoktae (below).

buildings reflected the Confucian deference to seniority. The father's room in the sarangch'ae was called the "big" *sarang* and the son's room the "small" sarang. In the anch'ae, the mother's room was the *anbang* (or "big room" in the Kyŏngsang region) and her daughter-in-law's room was the *kŏnnŏnbang*, the "room across."

The nature, importance and size of a room was evident from its name. The big sarang was generally two kan wide, while the small sarang was only one kan across in most houses. The big room was sunny and airy because it opened to both the garden and the maru. It also had a closet that often led to an attic and a small inner room. Sometimes, there was a side room which housed a young servant who attended the master of the house. In short, the best parts of the sarangch'ae belonged to the master, and only a meager space was given to his son. The big room was also furnished with expensive furniture while the son's room was quite bare.

The distinction between young and old was apparent in the anch'ae as well. The anbang was larger and had a closet, an attic and sometimes a pantry. The kitchen was more or less the domain of the mother. So were the storehouse and the maru next to the anbang. The daughter-in-law's kŏnnŏnbang, on the other hand, was small, barren and had only a narrow veranda attached in front.

In the Kyŏngsang region, the kŏnnŏnbang, which is also called *mŏribang*, was even smaller. More often than not, its floor was covered with rush mats instead of expensive varnished paper, and its ceiling was bare with the framework of the roof exposed. The room was reached through a small, single-panel door from the maru, not a two-panel door like that leading to the mother-in-law's room. On the other hand, it was also a custom of this region that the mother-in-law confer all responsibility for household management to the daughter-in-law when she had acquired the necessary knowledge and skills (about ten years after marriage). At that time, the mother-in-law traded her large room for that of the daughter-in-law and often relinquished the all-important pantry and storehouse keys.

A similar transference of power occurred in the men's quarters as well. When the senior male relinquished decision-making powers to his son, the older man moved from the big room to smaller quarters. Thus differences in room size did not necessarily mean discrimination against younger family members. The size of someone's quarters represented their rights and responsibilities in the family.

Traditional Korean homes house a pantheon of gods. Koreans have long believed that gods inhabit all parts of the house—the ground, the front gate, the kitchen, the cow shed, even the outhouse. In addition, they venerated the ŏpwang, the god of family fortune, and sŏngju, the house god.

Sŏngju oversees household affairs and is the highest in the hierarchy of household gods. When a family builds or moves into a new house, they hire a shaman to perform a kut, a shamanic rite of cleansing, to welcome this god into the house. Sŏngju is offered food on major holidays and during ancestral memorial rites. As the representative of all house gods, sŏngju was revered by every household.

Sŏngju varies from region to region. On the islands off Kyŏnggi-do province, the house god is represented by a bundle of mulberry paper strips hung over a beam or mulberry paper folded in a square and glued on a pillar. In the Kimp'o and Koyang areas of mainland Kyŏnggi-do, the house god takes the form of a hemp cloth hung on a beam. In the Ch'ungch'ŏng-do province, mulberry paper, folded in a square or mashed into a papier-mâché ball, is stuck on a pillar. People in the Kyŏngsang region, on the other hand, venerate sŏngju in the form of earthen rice jars, reverently replacing the old rice with new at harvest season. When family fortunes improve, the amount of rice is said to expand. Conversely, the rice offering will shrink or become discolored when disaster is imminent.

Ŏpwang, the god of family fortune, takes many forms, as a human, a snake, a weasel, even as soy sauce. For example, a child whose birth brings good fortune to the family is called ŏptong-i, "ŏp child," and is naturally cherished by the entire family.

Animal ŏp, believed to dwell somewhere in the house, are revered because the family may slip into poverty if they leave the house. Snakes are especially popular ŏp on Chejudo Island. The soy sauce ŏp is venerated in the Ch'ungju area in Ch'ungch'ŏngbuk-do province. This homemade soy sauce is only used at seasonal festivals or birthdays of family members and is replenished each time with equal amounts of fresh soy sauce, lest family fortunes should shrink.

T'ŏju shin, the house site god who is responsible for day-to-day household affairs, is embodied in an earthenware jar of uncooked rice on the stone terrace at the back of the house where soy sauce and other preserved condiments are kept.

The gate god is represented by a branch from a kalopanax tree hung over the gate. The tree's thorns are believed to expel evil spirits. Chinese ideograms for "tiger" or "dragon" are written on paper glued to the gate, and sometimes a horse bone is also hung there because the horse is considered a sacred animal.

The kitchen god, chowang, is manifested in a bowl of water placed behind the firehole or stove in the kitchen. Every morning the housewife fills the bowl with fresh water from the well and prays for another day of safety and prosperity for her family.

Since oxen are one of the farmer's most valuable possessions, many rural families venerate so-samshin, the birth goddess of oxen, to pray for the health and fertility of their animals.

The outhouse god is the only household god believed harmful by the Korean people. The outhouse god takes the form of a young woman. To avoid startling her, people take care to cough once or twice on their way to the outhouse. ◆

Household gods manifest themselves differently in each household and region, and offerings vary from region to region. Here an offering of rice is made to the house god (sŏngju).

Korea's Indigenous Geomancy

Choi Chang-jo

Korean geomancy derives from the concept of "Mother Earth." All problems related to geomancy are solved within the context of the Mother Earth concept. In Korea, all sites, for buildings or tombs, originate from a mountain. That mountain is the "main mountain" (*chusan*), or mother. The selection of an auspicious site begins with an assessment of the element of truth and falsehood, agreement and disagreement, safety and danger, and life and death inherent in the land leading toward the mother mountain. This assessment is called "examining the dragon" (*kallyongpŏp*). It is tantamount to reviewing one's mother's lineage. The ideal site is characterized by softness and stability but also exudes vitality and the ability to change.

A mother opens her arms to embrace her children. The next step is determining whether her embrace really is warm, soft and full of vitality. Chinese *feng shui* (geomancy) practitioners judge a site by examining its alignment in relation to the directions of the compass, which coincide with four "celestial" animals: the Green Dragon for east, the Red Bird for south, the White Tiger for west and the Black Tortoise for north.

Of course, just because a site is within a mother's embrace does not mean it is a good site. Even mothers are sometimes tired or irritated. The embrace of an irritated or enraged mother is thought inauspicious. When a mountain, the mother, is upset, it may radiate deadly energy. Such sites must be avoided.

Interestingly, in Korean geomancy a ritual method has been developed to augment or compensate for a mother's shortcomings. The important thing is the heart, not simply external appearances. Once in the mother's embrace, the geomancy practitioner searches for her breasts because they are the source of her energy. This process is called "finding the right spot" (*chŏnghyŏlbŏp*). Geomancy practitioners distinguish between the "location" (*hyŏlchang*) and the "site" (*hyŏlch'ŏ*). The former corresponds to the whole breast, the latter to the nipple. Finding the breast is not particularly difficult, but it is not easy finding the nipple. This is the goal of geomancy.

The next step is surveying the flow of water and the wind direction within the mother's embrace. Korean geomancy pays little attention to this, but in Chinese geomancy, identifying the flow of water and wind is important. In fact, it is one of the more complicated elements of Chinese geomancy. Because of the relative scarcity of water in China, some method of attracting water or reaping its benefits, even if only as a means of demonstrating one's wealth, is necessary. Similarly, directional differences play an important practical role in Chinese geomancy because of the country's rough terrain and harsh climate. It is quite natural, therefore, that the Chinese pay more attention to directional orientation. Korea's topographical conditions are quite different. In Korea, no site, not even one facing north, is dismissed out of hand.

The final step in site selection is determining what it resembles. A mother's embrace is unchanging, but just as each mother resembles something, so too does a site have a unique appearance. Identifying a site, giving it a name, also helps the owner and future generations feel a certain psychological satisfaction about it. It makes a huge difference knowing that one's residence, or tomb, is in a good place. Traditional geomancy's theory of shapes can be understood as an application of this psychology.

I recently had an opportunity to review the land ownership status of several leading figures in Korean society. I was astonished to find how many "mothers" they had. They do not cherish their mothers so much as own

Korean geomancy seeks to complement the forces of nature, compensating for topographical shortcomings and achieving a harmony between earth and humanity.

them. Many of them had one mother in the city, another in the countryside, one in a remote mountain area and some even in poor villages. But which is their true mother?

We all depend on our Mother Earth. Children like to play with earth because it is their mother's skin. And we are buried in the earth when we die. We store some food in the earth because by doing so, the smell of our mother's milk penetrates the food. When we walk down a country road on a spring day, we smell the earth's distinctive odor, our mother's breath. That is the core of life: energy, or *saenggi*. All living things begin to stretch awake after a long winter's sleep. According to the philosophy of the "five elements" (*ohaeng*), spring's wood element drives out winter's water element to create new buds. This is the beginning of new life, made possible by Mother Earth.

Let us now examine the details of Korean geomancy, as distinct from Chinese geomancy. What is the basic attitude of Korean geomancy? All Korean geomancy originates in the belief that the earth is a living thing. In other words, Koreans regard the earth as our mother. No one discusses geomancy unless they are capable of viewing the earth as a living dragon or a mother's warm embrace. This stage in a geomancy practitioner's development, often called *toan*, an "eye for truth," is only achieved through a genuine love for the earth and humanity. Once you have arrived at this stage, the mountain that had appeared like a pile of stones or clay before is transformed into a body alive with terrestrial energy. With an eye for truth, geomancy theory is unnecessary. The awareness of truth is the road to the art of geomancy.

The mountainous region from Mt. Sŏraksan's Hangyeryŏng Pass to Chŏmbong-san and Kach'ilbong is famous for having the greatest variety of trees and wild plants in Korea. However, the region's topography is incomparably unfavorable with uneven terrain, large rocks and a poor climate. So why this abundance of plant life?

In geomancy, the answer lies in the secret harmony between earth and plant life. Replace the trees in this equation with human life and we have the definition of Korean geomancy. In effect, no site is inherently good. If

anything, it is a question of harmony between earth and humans. The wisdom of Korean geomancy lies not in distinguishing a good site from a bad one, but in determining whether the site agrees or disagrees with our lifestyle.

Sometimes a site that is not auspicious from an objective point of view is appropriate for certain people. It is geomancer's job to identify such sites. The search for places where land and human life harmonize developed over time and experience into geomancy. The selfish practice of finding auspicious grave sites is a vulgar form of geomancy developed by recent generations.

How did geomancy begin? It originated in the human desire for a safe, stable life, free of anxiety and troubles. Finding an ideal site means discovering a place where there is an exchange of energy (*ki*) between the earth and living creatures. Living beings rooted in a good location radiate harmony and stability. The peace of mind one feels in such a place is what all humans strive for.

Those of us living in the cold world of our modern cities long for that peace of mind all the more. To find such a place, where mountains, trees, streams, houses, fields and people are all in the right spot performing their natural function, is what geomancy is all about. That place, that land, is again our mother's embrace. There we forget our anxieties and troubles and discover peace of mind.

People who see the mountains and earth through their mind's eye can find an ideal site resembling a mother's embrace. There is no reason why they must study the theories of geomancy. The basic methodological principles of Korean geomancy are instinct, intuition and love.

The geomancy practitioner observes the land with pure human instinct. This instinct naturally, inevitably, embodies our innate longing for our mother's warm embrace. We simply follow that instinct. Sexual instinct is not excluded from Korean geomancy. After all, sexual desire is a pure instinct pursuing the preservation of the species. Wantonness and the desire for domination through the sexual act are unnatural developments. In Korean geomancy, some fine sites go by seemingly crude names, such as "Cock Peak" or "Penis Valley."

Instinct, intuition and love for the land and humanity are at the heart of Korean geomancy.

Intuition is the pursuit of purity. Reasoning, knowledge, logic and calculations cloud purity. Unfortunately, in modern life we are more interested in these impure elements. We tend to think purity is something found only in literary imagination or poetic images. Geomancy is different, however. A geomancy practitioner must not depend on reason. The geomancy practitioner must follow instinct and intuition. However, there is one condition here: Intuition should be free from all prejudice.

Love should encompass not only the earth but all the people who rely on the earth. The great Korean geomancy theorist, Tosŏn, a Buddhist master who lived in the ninth century, focused on "diseased land." Filial devotion to a mother who is ill reflects a nobler and truer love. Similarly, the geomancy practitioner must not limit his or her search to "good" sites. A mother is a mother no matter what. Korean geomancy does not discriminate against a mother who is now old and sick. We do not long for our mothers when we are sick and lonely because she can do something for us. It is simply because she is our mother. She does not ask for anything. Her love is absolute and sacrificing. That is why a mother's love is true love.

This does not mean, however, that we should simply ignore our mother's infirmities. As mentioned earlier, Korean geomancy attempts to augment or compensate for a mother's shortcomings. Throughout Korea, people carefully pile small stones in man-made hills (chosan) or towers (chot'ap). These structures are thought to balance the forces of nature. They work on diseased earth as acupuncture works on the sick.

Geomancy is to the earth what the medical doctor is to a patient. A geomancy practitioner surveys land conditions. If the land is sick, he or she finds the cause and develops a healing method. In Korean this is called "saving the land" (kujibŏp) or "healing the land" (ŭijibŏp). There are numerous examples of this practice around the country. For example, at Noch'e Village in Chian County, Chŏllabuk-do province, the left "branch" of the "mother mountain" appears to pierce the left side of the mountain. Villagers have erected a stone tower at the top of this branch to compensate for the topographical flaw.

Years ago there was a tower on this site, but it was removed 15 years ago during the "New Village" (Saemaŭl) Movement's campaign to eradicate superstition. The tower was reconstructed after village elders noticed that several village youths had died or suffered injuries since the removal of the tower.

How does Noch'e's tower work? In geomancy terms, it is a compensatory measure, a way of overcoming negative forces (*yŏmsŭng, apsŭng*). But environmental psychology is also at work here. The left branch of the mother mountain may have been a psychological burden to the villagers' daily lives. By erecting a tower there, villagers obtained psychological comfort. They believed that everything would be fine. It was a symbol of comfort and confidence.

Unfortunately, while hard geomancy practitioners insist that geomancy is a traditional philosophy of love for the land, modern Koreans see its primary purpose in selecting auspicious family grave sites. This is a reality that cannot be ignored. I once engaged in that mundane form of geomancy but realized the dangers of its abuses and stopped it altogether, at least officially. However, when there is a death in the family, relatives cannot help but rely on that form of geomancy. Hence, I offer a few specific suggestions on what to do when one loses a parent or other loved ones.

In Korean geomancy, a spot cannot be selected without knowing the person who will be managing it. The relationship between the site and the person who will manage it is essential. Any geomancy practitioner who says a certain spot is auspicious without knowing the person who will be responsible for it is a fraud.

The person who has lost a parent or loved one must make the final decision on the site. If the deceased had a geomancy practitioner as a personal friend, he may be consulted, but such cases are rare. I would like to recommend, therefore, that you sit on the earth where you intend to bury your parent and think hard about him or her. In an hour's time, you will know whether the spot agrees with your parent or not. You will sense whether the deceased will find this place comfortable or not through instinct, intuition and love. In other words, the earth will respond to your piety and let you know whether it will accept your parent or not.

The grave's directional orientation should be determined in the same manner. Simply choose the direction that the deceased would like. That is the best lesson that Korea's traditional geomancy has to offer.

Still, three kinds of sites should be avoided at all costs. The first is any site under which water flows. The second is any site where land energy comes together in a vortex. The third is any site where movement under the earth is apparent. In modern geomorphology, this phenomenon is called "mass wasting" or more precisely, "soil creep." The term "soil creep" refers to gradual earth or rock slides caused by gravity. The sliding movement is imperceptibly slow, but the result is obvious. A cross-sectional view of the weathered layer shows that the movement of soil or rock is more rapid on the surface and slows underneath. This phenomenon is common and most obvious in the way utility poles or trees lean down slopes.

When soil thaws after a hard freeze or becomes wet after a long drought, it goes through a process of repeated expansion and contraction. When the soil expands, particles are lifted at right angles to the slope. When they contract again, they fall vertically because of gravity, instead of returning to their original position. Naturally, the soil tends to move down the slope during this repeated expansion and contraction.

The degree of slope at this stage plays an important role. Soil creep will not take place at a degree of slope less than 5 degrees. The steeper the slope, the less stable the soil layer. Trees and plants slow down soil creep. In fact, soil creep is a more serious problem in arid locations with little vegetation than in wet areas where trees and plants flourish. Thus the Korean people's anxiety when grass does not grow well over family tombs is not entirely groundless.

If a body is buried in an area where soil creep is a problem, strange things can happen. The body may disappear altogether, or it may

When a site is found inauspicious or lacking, geomancy practitioners often recommend "treatment" such as the erection of stone towers (below) which compensate for topographical shortcomings.

turn over or shift in direction. Some unscrupulous geomancy practitioners claim that this is a bad omen and offer to perform costly rituals to correct it, but that is a deception. With a little understanding of the properties of the soil, this can be avoided. If people recognize that the shifting and disappearance of bodies are caused by nature, many unscrupulous practices can be prevented.

How do Chinese geomancy and Korean geomancy differ? The difference, as I mentioned above, lies in the Koreans' love for the earth. Love does not exist in isolation. It requires an object. The earth's object is humanity. Only in the relationship between the earth and human beings can love be born. That is why human beings are as important as the earth in Korean geomancy. That is also why the earth cannot be evaluated without understanding the people who may be using it.

Love is truly glorious because it does not simply deal with the good. Anyone can love something good and noble. True love means loving imperfect things, troublesome things, things that are not so good. Korean geomancy is based on this philosophy. Ideal spots, good spots or lucky spots are foreign to the true meaning of Korean geomancy.

Love for imperfect soil is the direction that Korean geomancy has been taking, reflecting the compensatory nature of the geomancy school promoted by the monk Tosŏn centuries ago. In Tosŏn's geomancy the land and mother are one. Mother Earth's embrace is our home. If Mother Earth was always perfect, warm and without care, everyone could easily love her. However, that love would not be filial piety so much as simple reciprocity.

A good mother is in herself an ideal yearning for perfection. But there is no such thing as perfection or an ideal mother in the real world. All mothers are somehow imperfect. They may be tired, sick or angry. But they are still our mother. Korean geomancy professes love for an imperfect Mother Earth, a love for our own land.

True love for our mother is expressed by seeking to relieve her fatigue, heal her illnesses and make her happy. Anyone can be kind to a good mother, but attempting to heal and comfort an imperfect mother is Korean geomancy's way of complementing natural forces.

As I toured the Buddhist temples that Tosŏn helped to build centuries ago, I realized once more how much the monk loved his native land. He never took advantage of auspicious spots, even if they were within easy

access. He chose problematic sites for temples. No geomancy specialist with an "eye" like Tosŏn could have selected these sites without understanding their inherent defects. He acted out of love for his motherland. It was obvious from the temple sites he chose that he intended to heal the ills of this land. The temple sites are not particularly auspicious. In fact, almost all of them have been abandoned because they do not suit the needs of the egotistical geomancy of a later age.

Today's geomancy is not geomancy at all. How can a greedy mind hoping to gain something from the skeletons of dead parents be called love? As wise men of the Shirhak school of Practical Learning said centuries ago, self-aggrandizing geomancy is nothing more than fortune-telling, bound to destroy the country and the Korean people. The true nature of Tosŏn geomancy lies in love for humanity and the earth and the search for ways of healing the objects of our love. ◆

Pŏpchusa Temple (top) and a village shrine (above). Although geomancy is a traditional philosophy of love for the land, modern Koreans see its primary function in selecting auspicious grave sites for parents.

Gates, Posts and Beams: Signs of Class and Changing Times

Joo Nam-chull

In the tenth lunar month of 1394, King T'aejo, founder of the Chosǒn Dynasty, moved his capital from Kaesǒng to what is now Seoul. This, of course, entailed the construction of many houses, which was actively undertaken in styles complying with the master plan of the new capital.

It is quite probable that Seoul had considerable housing before .it was designated the Chosǒn capital, because it was already a city, known as Namgyǒng, during the Koryǒ Dynasty. In fact, the city's history can be traced back to the Paekche Kingdom, which was founded in its environs. Today, however, only a few traditional houses remain. Most were built in the 1880s during the latter years of Chosǒn.

The rigid social system, which dictated every aspect of Chosǒn life, had a great influence on residential construction. Houses were generally divided into three grades: upper-class houses for the *yangban* elite who were qualified by birth to apply for government service; middle-class houses for lower echelon officials, such as medical doctors, astronomers, translators and minor government employees; and houses for the general populace. In addition, there were huts for servants who lived outside their yangban masters' residences, though most servants lived within the walls of the master's compound.

At the time of the capital's relocation to Seoul, the government distributed housing plots according to social rank. A 1396 entry in the *Annals of King T'aejo (T'aejo shillok)* notes that housing plots of 4,504 square meters were given to Grade 1 officials; 3,861 to Grade 2; 3,217 to Grade 3; 2,574 to Grade 4; 1,930 to Grade 5; 1,287 to Grade 6; 1,030 to Grade 7; 772 to Grade 8; 515 to Grade 9; and 257 to commoners.

In 1431 King Sejong designated house size by rank. A prince was allowed 60 *kan*; a prince by a royal concubine, or a princess, 50 kan; a princess by a royal concubine, other royal family members and Grade 2 officials and above, 40 kan; offi-

The front gate of a Korean home reflects the status and values of its residents.

cials of Grade 3 or less, 30 kan; and commoners, 10 kan. A kan is a traditional measure of length, approximately 1.8 meters. However, because the kan referred to both the length between two columns and the square space within four columns, Sejong's size limits had little meaning. A kan could easily be enlarged by spacing columns further apart. The size specification was thus amended in 1440 to include the length of columns, girders and beams.

With time, however, powerful yangban families built larger houses, going far beyond the 60-kan limit and stimulating a general escalation in house size. The government eventually upped the permitted size for private houses to 99 kan, allowing only palaces and public buildings to be larger. The 99-kan limit was so popular that Koreans came to describe a very large private house as a 99-kan house even when it wasn't.

Other architectural restrictions were enjoined at the time these size limits were imposed. For example, the use of decorative eaves bracketing, *tanch'ǒng* coloring, and dressed stones, except for post stones, were prohibited for houses of princes down to the lowest commoner. Bracketing on private homes, though less ornate than on public structures, was not uncommon in the countryside where government supervision was less vigilant, but all traditional houses found in Seoul today are of a square-beam style with no bracket clusters. The restriction on the use of tanch'ǒng was also rigidly observed.

Chosǒn was a strict Confucian society. Families held memorial rites honoring four generations of ancestors as prescribed in the *Family Rites of Chu Xi (Chuja karye)*. This necessitated an ancestral shrine within the residential compound of each clan head.

During the Chosǒn Dynasty, geomantic theories that prevailed in the Koryǒ Dynasty and ancient Chinese cosmological

The "lofty gate" (sosŭl taemun) of a noble residence was a status symbol in Chosŏn society. The gate at Sŏngyojang, a yang-ban home in Kangnŭng has been carefully maintained (above).

theories greatly influenced the selection of housing sites, design and building layout. Housing sites were chosen carefully to fit the geomantic prescription for an auspicious location, and the layout of the house—from the main living room to the kitchen, gates and even the lavatory—was planned in a way to best guarantee harmony with the "five elements," which were represented by the cardinal points.

The layout of buildings was often in the shape of auspicious Chinese characters: for example, the characters 口 ("entrance"), 日 ("sun"), 月 ("moon"), and 用 ("use"). Characters such as 尸 ("corpse") or 工 ("to fabricate") were never adopted, the former for obvious reasons and the latter because it might involve the need to break down the structure and build again.

One of the finest and best preserved Chosŏn-period houses is Yŏn-gyŏngdang in the back garden of Ch'angdŏkkung Palace. It is representative of elite houses of the 1800s, having been built in 1828 at the request of the crown prince who hoped to become better acquainted with the yangban lifestyle.

Yŏn-gyŏngdang stands on a hill behind the palace gardens. The *haengnangch'ae*, or servants quarters, which forms its front wall, is the first part of the house to come into view. A stream, spanned by a small stone bridge, flows past the gate, and a square pond lies at the side of the house. In upper-class houses a pond for growing lotus often stood near an auxiliary building or in a spacious yard outside the haengnangch'ae. A pond and some unusual rocks mounted in stone boxes were essential to a well-planned garden. The stone boxes in Yŏn-gyŏngdang's garden are ornately carved. One is decorated with carved frogs,

The men's quarters (above) was a sitting room, bedroom and study for the master of the house. The floor of the taech'ŏng maru (opposite), an unheated hall generally used in summer and for large family gatherings, was usually made of rough boards.

two crawling into the box and two crawling out. This motif gives the impression of mobility to the heavy object.

The stream flowing in front of the haengnangch'ae originates west of Yŏn-gyŏngdang and curves south of the haengnangch'ae, weaving its way between buildings. Yŏn-gyŏngdang's architects used the stream to link separate space much as modern architects employ the interpenetration technique in their designs. The curves of the stream provide a certain flexibility to the garden harshly divided by the straight lines of the buildings and are reminiscent of the fluid lines of the uplifting eaves and ridges of traditional houses.

A "lofty gate" (*sosŭl taemun*) is in the middle of the haengnangch'ae. This type of roofed gate is taller than the walls of the haengnangch'ae which flank it. Lofty gates have a groove in their thresholds because they were originally designed to accommodate one-wheeled palanquins used by officials above Grade 2. With time, lofty gates became status symbols among the Chosŏn elite and were built long after the wheeled palanquin fell into disuse. The gate in Yŏn-gyŏngdang does not have a groove, though it is taller than the walls that flank it.

This gate leads to the courtyard associated with the haengnangch'ae, which is actually two build-

ings. The east part of the first building, which opens on the courtyard, consists of a room, a stable and an outhouse for men. The west part is made up of rooms and a shed. Two entrances to the house proper, a lofty gate in the east and a simple, rather nondescript door in the west, are located in the second building which stands opposite the first across the yard. The lofty gate leads to the *sarangch'ae*, or men's quarters, while the simple door leads to the *anch'ae*, the women's quarters. This distinction is a reflection of traditional cosmology as well as the male supremacy that characterized Chosŏn society.

Past the inner lofty gate is the sarangch'ae, which faces south. To its east is the west-facing Sŏnhyangjae, a book depository. The sarangch'ae developed out of the Confucian precepts of strict sexual segregation and male supremacy. Men and women were required by law to keep separate sleeping quarters as early as the reign of King T'aejong (1400-1418). Yŏn-gyŏngdang's sarangch'ae thus comprises a room for sleeping, a *sarangbang*, or master's room, a *taech'ŏng*, or unheated wooden-floored hall, an elevated veranda and an attic. The taech'ŏng and veranda were important living spaces in summer, but at other times the hall served as an antechamber to the sarangbang and veranda.

A sarangbang usually had a built-in cabinet, which led to the attic. A thick, cotton-stuffed mat, or *poryo*, was spread on the warmest part of the *ondol* heated floor in front of the cabinet. A thick, stiff cushion was propped against the wall for the master to lean against when he sat on the mat. It was flanked by two large arm rests. In front of the mat was a reading table, and sometimes a large tray to hold the master's long-stemmed pipes, ash tray and other necessities. Next to these was an inkstone box. Writing brushes were kept in a jar on a low chest, or *mun-gap*. One or two decorative objects, such as an interestingly shaped stone or a potted plant, often sat on the mun-gap.

Cushions for visitors were arranged around the inkstone box and the tobacco tray. A tea cabinet sometimes stood against the north wall, and a letter holder hung on the wall next to it. A pair of shelves called *sabang t'akcha* stood in the far corners to hold books brought from the book storage and perhaps a bowl of quinces or other fragrant fruits. If possible, windows opened to the south, calligraphy or paintings were glued on the window panels, and a tablet hung over the window.

The bed chamber was similar to the sarangbang. Bedding was kept in the loft during the day, a thick mat placed on the warmest part of the floor in its absence. An elevated wooden bed with a latticed bottom was often used in the summer. A safe was kept in this room as well as the man's toiletries, including his head band.

The tacch'ŏng was the coolest spot in summer. Rush mats were spread there and sometimes the latticed bed was brought outside. The elevated veranda was furnished in the same way.

At Yŏn-gyŏngdang, the beams in the sarangch'ae are round, whereas those in the anch'ae are square. This is a thought-provoking contrast considering that round beams were of higher stature than square ones.

At the west end of the sarangch'ae garden is a low wall which separates it from the anch'ae area. Near the wall is a line of interestingly shaped rocks in stone boxes. In the east corner of the garden is a lotus pond. A large tree stands in another corner. This is the "center tree" but it was planted in the corner because when the Chinese character for tree (木) is written inside a square (口), the shape of the garden, it becomes another character meaning predicament (困).

To the east of the sarangch'ae is the book depository and study. Sŏnhyangjae has a spacious taech'ŏng hall at the center. This is flanked by an ondol room. A canopy on the west side blocks the afternoon sun. Canopies were commonly found on sarangch'ae and auxiliary buildings of upper-class houses. This canopy has slatted panels like modern louvered shutters which can be lifted up.

A small hill rises to the east of Sŏnhyangjae; on it is a pavilion called Nongsujŏng. The hill is terraced into flower beds. Because more than 70 percent of Korea is mountainous, Korean houses are often bordered by a hill in the back or on one side. The hills are made into terraced gardens and have pavilions on them. Deciduous trees were planted in the garden because they best reflect the passage of the seasons.

The anch'ae is approached from outside through the door built in the inner haengnangch'ae. The door opens on a courtyard to the south of the anch'ae. The L-shaped building has an *anbang*, or living room, a taech'ŏng, and a room across from it. The southern end of the anbang is a loft, and the area underneath it houses a fireplace to heat the anbang via the underfloor flues. In an ordinary upper-class house, there would be a kitchen here, but this house's kitchen is separated from the anch'ae by a low wall.

The anbang is the wife's living room during the day and bedroom at night. Like the sarangbang, a typical anbang was furnished with a thick poryo mat, cushions for the back, and arm rests. The mat and cushions in the men's quarters were dark blue silk, but in the anbang they were purple. Low mungap chests stand under the window, and a small chest stands against the opposite wall. A mirror box was on top of the chest and a comb holder on the wall over it. Sometimes there was a reading table in front of the poryo mat and, during the winter, a brazier with small mats around it for visitors.

Various devices were used to keep out the winter cold. A folding screen was often placed across the built-in cabinet behind the poryo, a thick curtain hung over the walls, and the shutters outside were closed. Sometimes curtains were draped across the ceiling to block drafts.

The taech'ŏng, or wooden-floored hall, often housed the rice box, on top of which were a neat array of jars containing preserved foods. In the summer, when the hall was used as a parlor, a bamboo blind hung from the ceiling to block the sun and curious eyes.

Though Yŏn-gyŏngdang does not have one, an extra room called the "upper room" was usually attached to the anbang. Chests of various sizes and use lined its walls and on them were small boxes such as sewing kits and thread holders. The two rooms were separated by papered doors, which were usually kept open so that the two rooms seemed one.

The room across the taech'ŏng was for the daughter-in-law. It was furnished similarly to the anbang.

Servants who worked for the mistress of the house such as seamstresses, cooks and nannies were quartered in the haengnangch'ae. An outhouse for women stood in the courtyard behind the west haengnangch'ae.

The oldest residential structure in Seoul may be the Yi Chinsŭng House in Kwanhun-dong, believed to have been built in the 1700s. The residence of Pak Yŏng-hyo (1861-1939), politician and a son-in-law of King Ch'ŏlchong, was built in the 1850s. It has been designated Folklore Material No. 18.

The second oldest house is the Kong Tŏk-kwi House in Anguk-dong, Folklore Material No. 27. It was built toward the end of the 1800s. The sarangch'ae, anch'ae, haengnangch'ae and an auxiliary building remain but the exterior of the anch'ae has been remodeled.

The sarangch'ae of the Kong House comprises a sarangbang, a bed chamber, a wooden-floored taech'ŏng, an elevated veranda and a canopy to the south. The canopy on the sarangch'ae and the one on the auxiliary building were originally built of wood panels but these were replaced with slate tiles, which became available in the 1900s.

The Chŏng Kyu-yŏp House in Seoul's Chegi-dong, Folklore Material No. 24, was built to accommodate Yun Tŏk-yong, a son-in-law of King Sunjong, who came to the area to attend memorial services held at his ancestral shrine. The layout of the buildings was planned so that, together with the shrine, they

The Kong Tŏk-kwi House in Anguk-dong, Folklore Material No. 27, was built toward the end of the 1800s. It is the second oldest residential structure in Seoul.

formed the Chinese character meaning "prime" (元).

When the social ranking system was virtually abolished by the Reforms of 1894, the middle class began to model their gates after the yangban's lofty gates. Scandalized by this transgression, some yangban replaced their lofty gates with low ones. The Shin House in Mugyo-dong is an example of a middle-class house whose original gate was replaced by a lofty gate brought from another house in the early 1900s.

After Korea reluctantly opened its ports to foreign trade at the end of the 19th century and Western diplomats, missionaries and traders built residences in their own style, Western architectural styles began to influence the construction of traditional houses. The most conspicuous change was the introduction of foyers and corridors, which were absent in traditional Korean houses. The houses of the Min brothers in Kyŏng-un-dong, Folklore Materials Nos. 15 and 17, which were designed around 1930 by the Korean architect Pak Kil-yong, exemplify such changes. They have foyers and the anbang, sarangbang, bathroom and toilet are in the same building, connected by corridors.

Seoul continued to expand in the 1930s, and city development continued in earnest. Real estate developers began the mass construction of U-shaped houses to make the best use of the limited size of urban housing plots. By design, the view from a U-shaped house was blocked by the back of the house in front of it. This wall faced the taech'ŏng of the back house and was decorated with floral designs and auspicious ideographs.

Freed from housing restrictions that had limited the use of ceiling beams to three or four for commoners' residences, house sizes were expanded by using five beams as in a Chosŏn yangban house. Because round beams were more prestigious than square ones, round beams, or halved beams with the circular side down to appear round, were used. The roofs were hipped and gabled and the eaves double-rafted, in a fashion reminiscent of upper-class Chosŏn houses. ◆

Furniture in the Traditional House

Lim Young-ju

Much of a traditional Korean house's beauty derives from its simple interiors and arrangement of furniture. The elegance and comfort of a Korean room are created by sunlight filtering through papered lattice windows and the natural sheen of the varnished floor. In the traditional house, few artificial decorations cluttered the rooms. The nobler the occupants, the more austere the decor.

The traditional Korean house was divided into two parts, one for women and children, the *anch'ae;* and one for men, the *sarangch'ae.* For families of higher social status the division was more clearly marked. The furniture used in the two parts of the house was also quite different.

The *anbang,* the innermost room, was the center of family life for women and children. In upper-class houses, the inner room was both cozy and elegant. The mistress's sewing kit, a brazier for the clothes iron and an ironing board of sorts were found in every traditional anbang. A folding screen decorated with painted or embroidered flowers and birds or a

landscape design usually stood by the window or just inside the door to block drafts. Various clothes chests, boxes for jewelry and other small items, and reading tables served the mistress's needs.

Clothes chests were of two kinds. *Nong* was a simple chest used individually or stacked in two or three tiers. *Chang* was a tall chest with an interior space divided by two or three shelves. Originally, nong used by women were made of woven bushclover or willow twigs. Many nong were made with wooden boards, but some consisted of wood-framed paper panels, made entirely of multiple layers of paper pasted together. Others were made of rush.

Upper-class women sometimes had lustrous lacquered nong inlaid with mother-of-pearl, *hwagak nong* paneled with painted ox horn, or embroidered nong. Chang were of various sizes and shapes and served a variety of needs. Some were used to store clothes, others smaller items such as cotton-padded socks, bedding, thread, books and medicine.

The wooden furniture found in women's

The women's quarters, or anch'ae (above), was the center of family life for women and children. The men's quarters (right) served the social and scholarly needs of the aristo-
cratic man.

quarters was elaborate with distinct compartments and openings and diverse combinations of wood and decorations. *Pandaji* and *kwye*, wooden boxes of various shapes and sizes, also served women's storage needs. Usually the upper half of the pandaji's front panel opened as a flap door, although some had doors in the lower half. "Dog-hole" pandaji had tiny doors or lids. Some boxes were actually combination box-wardrobes.

In the Chosŏn Dynasty, the *yangban* elite, who often held civil or military posts in the bureaucracy, returned to their ancestral home-towns after retirement to read, meditate, enjoy nature and indulge in hobbies such as poetry, painting and music. The center of a man's life in the home was the study-*cum*-drawing room called *sarang*. In principle, the sarangch'ae, or men's quarters, was a detached building, separate from the anch'ae, but in smaller houses the room nearest the gate served as the *sarangbang*.

Wealthy nobility sometimes had three sarang: the main sarang for the master of the

house, a smaller sarang for his sons, and an inner sarang for his parents, who turned household management over to the younger generation and lived in retirement. The inner sarang was usually connected to the inner quarters. The wealthy man's main sarang often had a library in a detached building, sometimes outside the wall surrounding the house. The size and furnishing of sarang quarters reflected the master's position and prestige.

The main sarang consisted of the master's bedroom, the sarangbang itself where the master spent most of his daytime hours and received guests, the wooden-floored veranda or antechamber, and the *numaru*, or raised terrace. The sarangbang and raised terrace were connected to form the master's study.

The sarang furniture was carefully selected because it spoke so vividly of the master's financial situation and intellectual sophistication. A reading table was essential as was a calligraphy table. A special tobacco table held smoking accessories and the *paduk*, or *go*, board. The master usually sat on a padded silk

mat and leaned on thick-cushioned armrests. A stationery chest, book chest and hanging wardrobe were also necessary.

Anything gaudy or overly decorative was taboo. Simple elegance was the first consideration in the selection of furniture. The walls were hung with white paper, and the ceilings were papered with a somber blue or pastel green paper. The paper covering the *ondol* hypocaust floor was repeatedly varnished with boiled bean extract until it was translucent. Only one calligraphic work or painting was hung on the wall at a time, and folding screens were relegated to the bedroom or women's quarters.

Because the rooms were small, some stationery articles, such as brush racks and letter holders, hung on the wall to minimize clutter on the floor and tables. Light was provided by cast iron candleholders and wooden lamp hangers. Braziers, incense holders and incense tables were also part of the basic furnishings for the sarang. According to the master's taste, interesting stones, orchids, zithers and flutes

The sarangch'ae (above) was often a detached building dedicated to the needs of the cultured male. The furnishings (opposite) reflected the status and intellectual sophistication of the master.

87

The traditional Korean home was functional, yet elegant. The kitchen (above), taech'ŏng attached to the master's quarters (top right) and the women's taech'ŏng (bottom right) were furnished for function and efficiency.

were used for decoration. Most important of all were the "four friends of the scholar"—paper, brush, ink stone and ink stick.

From as early as the Koryŏ Kingdom, when the room was called *sŏjae* or *munbang*, literati men gathered in the sarang to discuss life, politics and art. A sarangbang culture developed, and furniture and accessories for the sarang became more sophisticated and elegant.

The numaru, or raised terrace, was an elevated space, somewhat like a loft. The master of the house went there to relax and meditate, enjoying the view of his garden afforded by the numaru's elevation. In summer it was a pleasant spot for a nap. The master also invited his friends there to share drinks and enjoy poetry composition and calligraphy writing.

The terrace thus required its own reading and calligraphy table, book chest, tea table, lamp, brazier and smoking accessories. A wooden bedstead was usually placed in the middle of the numaru for napping, along with a wooden pillow and a long woven bamboo cylinder called a "bamboo wife," which provided ventilation when held to the body while sleeping on hot summer nights.

Taech'ŏng, the "large hall," was the wooden-floored hall between the two main ondol rooms of the inner quarters. It served as the family's living room. Its wooden floor was made of rows of long and short boards laid at right angles to each other.

The taech'ŏng was usually furnished with a cupboard and rice chest. Seasoning jars were arranged on top of the rice chest, and the fulling stone for pounding fabrics smooth was stored in one corner. The cupboard was made of solid wood, such as cedar, chinaberry or Korean pine. The furniture was quite simple, decorated with cast iron fittings and miter or finger joints to enhance their solid look.

Since women spent almost all their daylight hours in the kitchen, the room's furniture and utensils tended to be designed not only for practical use but also to be aesthetically pleasing. Cupboards, china and brassware chests, food boxes, trays and ceremonial vessels were well-crafted. Buffet chests had shelves and one or two doors and were usually made of pine boards. Design varied from region to region. Most cabinets had hinged or sliding doors.

The *soban* meal tray is a uniquely Korean piece of furniture tailored to the lifestyle of traditional Koreans who sat and ate meals on the ondol floor. The trays were used to carry food and be eaten from. They varied in size, shape and design according to region and use. ◆

The Courtyards of Yŏn-gyŏngdang

Kim Kwang-hyun

The courtyard of a traditional Korean house is the perfect place to enjoy a fresh breeze and the strident chant of cicadas in summer, to gaze at the deep blue sky in autumn, or to feel the pulse of nature in spring. The courtyard is an architectural link between humanity, earth and seasonal changes.

Courtyards and houses—these are the essence of the traditional Korean home. Surrounded by walls and buildings, a courtyard is an open space, which embodies Korean life in its fundamental form. It is an empty space, unrestricted by specific purposes, a place that permits activities not tolerated in other living spaces. It is also supplies air and light to rooms.

Madang, the generic name for courtyard and any vacant area between buildings in Korean houses, is in some ways similar to a Western patio or atrium but is starker, a simple open space with bare ground and few trees. Here, Koreans commune with nature, thrash grain, hang laundry, and hold weddings and other ceremonies. A courtyard is a vacant "space" and a work "place" at the same time. Korean houses are not just buildings in which people dwell; they are inseparable from the courtyards that lie between them.

The courtyard is the point of origin for

Yŏn-gyŏngdang's main gate (lower left) opens onto a courtyard flanked by the servant quarters (above). This was a busy work area.

Korean dwellings. A house without a courtyard might as well be without light, air, without even a sense of life, for it is through the courtyard that Koreans sense seasonal changes and the separate structures serve their true function. A courtyard separates rooms and at the same time links them. To restore courtyards to modern Korean houses would thus rekindle the sense of habitation that now lies dormant in the Korean subconsciousness.

Yŏn-gyŏngdang in the back garden of Ch'angdŏkkung Palace is by far the most beautiful extant residential structure from the Chosŏn Dynasty. It was built in the residential style of the Chosŏn nobility for King Sunjo (r. 1800-1834). Sunjo did not live there, of course. He simply wanted to experience noble life and resided there a few days each year.

Two buildings, the *sarangch'ae* and the *anch'ae*, stand side by side at the center of Yŏn-gyŏngdang. The sarangch'ae is the living quarters of the master of the house; his wife resides in the anch'ae. Sŏnhyangjae, a separate structure, stands to the east of the sarangch'ae.

It served as the master's study. Behind it spreads a back garden landscaped with an eye for harmony with the existing terrain. A picturesque pavilion, Nongsujŏng, sits in the garden. Yŏn-gyŏngdang is surrounded by a stone wall behind the garden and the pavilion, but its southern boundary consists of two rows of *haengnangch'ae*, servant quarters. True to the upper-class norms that demanded strict obedience to the Confucian ethical code, which required separation of sexes, a wall stands between the sarangch'ae and anch'ae. To the north of the anch'ae is an auxiliary building, which housed a kitchen and pantry.

Yŏn-gyŏngdang's ground plan is very simple, but it is spatially diverse and emanates a sense of spaciousness and the ambience of the upper-class literati, thanks to its many and varied outdoor spaces including seven courtyards, in front of the southern haengnangch'ae, the sarangch'ae, the anch'ae, and at the corners of buildings.

From the outside, Yŏn-gyŏngdang's facade is simple, with the long expanse of the haengnangch'ae interrupted by only Changnakmun, the main gate. A small stream flows past the gate from the west into a lotus pond in the east. This movement of water past the front of a dwelling and into an unseen receptacle is extremely auspicious in terms of *feng-shui*, traditional Chinese geomancy.

Past Changnakmun gate stands another haengnangch'ae. The courtyard between this and the outer haengnangch'ae was naturally a work area where servants tended to household chores. It was also designed as a screen against outsiders. The inner haengnangch'ae effectively blocked all approaches to the main buildings, except through the two gates that were located at the middle of the long building: Changyangmun gate at the right, opening in to the sarangch'ae courtyard, and Suinmun gate at the left, opening to the anch'ae courtyard. Changyangmun, serving the men's quarters, has a lofty roof, while Suinmun, which was used by women only, is the same height as the rest of the haengnangch'ae. The conspicuous difference between the two gates tells what kind of buildings stand beyond them.

Changyangmun leads to an enclosed area that centers around the sarangch'ae and the

The anch'ae, the women's quarters, was a closed, private area, sheltering women from the outside world.

auxiliary Sŏnhyangjae, a study. The name Yŏn-gyŏngdang, by which the entire house came to be known, is in fact the name of the sarangch'ae. Typical of this kind of building, the sarangch'ae has a wooden-floor hall (*taech'ŏng*) at its center. It is flanked by an *ondol* (heated floor) room and a pavilion-like hall with a wooden floor elevated on pilotis. The taech'ŏng (or *maru*) and ondol rooms remain basic elements of traditional Korean interiors to this day. They distinguish Korean houses from those of Japan and China, although the houses of all three countries are built with wood. The ondol room is a closed structure originating in the colder regions of the north, and the wooden-floor taech'ŏng or maru is an open area devised to offer summer relief in the southern region where high temperatures and humidity are more common. The ondol room is a space for winter living; the taech'ŏng or maru is for summer. The dual structure of Korean houses developed out of necessity in a country where there are four distinct seasons.

Taech'ŏng, the wooden-floor hall, can be transformed into a private area by closing its partitioned doors. In summer, however, the doors are lifted up and out and hooked under the eaves to welcome breezes. The elevated paper doors block the sun and at the same time reflect light from the courtyard into the room. With light and shadow dappling the floor and a fresh breeze cooling it, the taech'ŏng felt like part of nature and the courtyard.

The elevated pavilion-style hall, or *numaru*, was a spatial representation of the master's authority. The master of an upper-class house was generally a public official or the senior figure in a clan-oriented village. All his social and political activities were conducted here in his sarangch'ae. The sarangch'ae, and especially the numaru, were off-limits to women; they were hallowed places that bespoke the stature of the master in the public world unknown to women.

The anch'ae beyond Suinmun gate also has a numaru but, unlike the one in the sarangch'ae, it was built around the corner at the end of the building. The anch'ae was a closed, private area while the sarangch'ae was open to visitors, educators and public life.

The basic unit of measurement in Korean architecture is the square area within four columns, *kan*, a unit that is also used to refer to the distance between two columns when measuring the width or depth of a house. The interior of any building is thus based on a structural unit formed by four columns and the lintels that link them. It is a major characteristic of a Korean house that such structural units are repeated side by side in a row. This floor plan makes it easy to conform with the lay of the land and also ensures sufficient light and ventilation for every room because all structural units face in one direction.

Numaru, the elevated wooden-floor hall, is, in a sense, an "internalized pavilion." In his book *The Diminution-Oriented Japanese*, Professor Yi Ŏ-ryŏng compares the Japanese garden culture, which tends to bring nature inside and views the universe through artificial rearrangements of nature, and the Korean pavilion culture, which reflects the Korean tendency to plunge into nature and experience it first-hand in its essential form. Koreans built pavilions not to bring nature to them but to go to nature. In his "Essay on the Pavilion with Four Wheels" (*Saryunjŏng ki*), the Koryŏ poet Yi Kyu-bo (1168-1241) toyed with the idea of building a moving pavilion in which he could travel to nearby hills and mountains. He thought it would eliminate the drudgery of packing and unpacking his *kayagŭm* zither, books and wine bottles every time he traveled. Yi's essay exemplifies the Korean outlook on nature. He wanted to embrace nature in a scenic yet sequestered environment.

Architects often use the term "scale." The concept of scale refers to proportions used to determine the dimensional relationship of one object to another. It is indispensable in a field like architecture, which deals with large objects in a limited space. Its most important manifestation is "human scale," which refers to human perceptions of objects and the relationship between objects and the humans that use or inhabit them.

Strolling through Yŏn-gyŏngdang, one ponders the relationship between oneself and the structure, between the viewer and the viewed. The various spaces within Yŏn-gyŏngdang were created on a human scale. They have a calming effect and sometimes produce the uncanny feeling that one is not simply looking at the structure but being embraced by it.

The layout of the buildings reflects human scale. At first glance the ground plan appears informal and spontaneous, with buildings placed casually according to their function, but more careful consideration reveals that Yŏn-gyŏngdang's seven courtyards unfold like a windmill, following the turns of stone walls and buildings. This effect is quite common in traditional Korean architecture, but Yŏn-gyŏngdang has by far the most pronounced use of this deceptive naturalness born of meticulous calculation.

All traditional Korean houses of any size meet the outside world with a closed facade. Hidden behind a tightly closed gate and tall walls, the house is a mystery to outsiders. However, once inside the gate, the outdoor spaces open up gradually until they reach a

back garden with a pavilion or a hill behind the house. In this respect, Korean houses, of which Yŏn-gyŏngdang is a good example, stand in stark contrast to Japanese houses which become darker and more closed as one moves inside.

Yŏn-gyŏngdang typifies the Korean house in this respect. Beyond the main gate and haengnangch'ae, visitors enter a courtyard, a space visually enclosed by the sarangch'ae, Sŏnhyangjae, the haengnangch'ae and the side wall. The anch'ae is adroitly hidden by Chŏngch'umun gate and a wall, so the visitor's eyes naturally turn to the sarangch'ae, and past it, to Nongsujŏng Pavilion in the back garden.

Stepping past Sŏnhyangjae to the right, the visitor's vision, once blocked, opens to the tranquil back garden. Thus, as the visitor walks through the compound, the house opens and closes, opens and closes. Most noble houses would have an ancestral shrine in the back garden, but Yŏn-gyŏngdang does not because it is located within a royal palace. Instead, a pavilion in the back garden serves to expand the living space.

The sense of tranquil comfort exuding from Yŏn-gyŏngdang takes the visitor back to a different age when Confucian ethics and the traditional Korean love of nature ruled. I recommend a leisurely tour of this house to experience first-hand the eclectic unfolding of space and human scale in traditional Korean architecture. ♦

The men's quarters (opposite), Chŏngch'umun gate leading to the women's quarters (above) and Nongsujŏng, a pavilion in the master's back garden (below)

In Tune with Nature: Rural Villages and Houses

Lee Sang-hae

Korea is a nation of mountains, which cover almost 70 percent of its land area. Mountains have had a profound influence on the Korean people's view of nature and on their lifestyle. Many villages have developed naturally around the base of mountains, adapting to the local topography. The spatial composition of the traditional village and its rhythms of life originate in the harmony between communi-

Nak-an Ŭpsŏng, a traditional village in Chŏllanam-do province

ties and the mountains around them. Koreans empathize with nature, and nature responds by molding their villages, their houses and their spirits.

Rising behind many villages is a mountain, *chinsan*, which serves as the villagers' spiritual mainstay. Chinsan functions as a village symbol and guardian. Ideally a small brook flows in front of the village, and beyond it lies a flat expanse of arable land. On the other side of

the fields is another mountain, *ansan*, which faces the village. The villagers see this mountain every day, so its form has an important influence on the villagers' mental attitude. The majority of Korean villages are situated in this manner.

From ancient times, Koreans developed a variety of ways of determining auspicious village sites. In his *Ecological Guide to Korea* (*T'aengniji*), Yi Chung-hwan (1690-1752), the *Shirhak* scholar, listed the criteria for the selection of a village site.

Geographical conditions are the utmost consideration in choosing a place to live. Physiological conditions are the second most important, followed by the mentality of the local villagers, then mountains and rivers. A site lacking in any of these four conditions cannot be considered a good place to live. People cannot enjoy longevity on land that is geographically good but lacks physiologically, or in a place with good physiological but poor geographical features. What's more, regrettable things happen in a place with fine geographical and physiological aspects, but where the villagers are wicked in mind. And one cannot build character in a place without mountains and rivers nearby.

For Yi Chung-hwan, the natural environment was of premier importance when selecting a village site; then came the social environment and finally topography. Traditional Koreans established the layout and shape of their villages in response to the given social and natural environment. Villages were not created by a single individual in a set period.

Rural villages and houses embrace nature in search of peace and harmony. The wooden-floored **maru** *(above) was always ready for cool summer breezes. Spirit posts and auspicious stones mark the entrance to a village (below). Thatch, earth and stone meet in a farmhouse (opposite).*

They were developed over years by many people aware of the surrounding natural and human social environment. Physical layout was not important for its own sake. Rather, it was important in its contribution to the harmonization of human habitats with nature. For Koreans, one's attitude in selecting a site was crucial.

In *Ecological Guide to Korea*, Yi Chung-hwan listed the auspicious characteristics of renowned dwelling sites around the country. In *Sixteen Treatises on the Development of Nature and the Comforting of the People* (*Imwon kyŏngje shimnyuk-chi*), a mid-Chosŏn period agricultural tract, the scholar-official Sŏ Yu-gu (1764-1845) spoke of the traditional village, which stood with its back to a mountain and faced a river or stream. Such villages provided a place of comfort and serenity, safeguarding against negative natural forces. These ideal villages corresponded to the rules of traditional geomancy: the Green Dragon to the east (*chwach'ŏngnyong*), the White Tiger to the west (*upaekho*), the Black Tortoise in the rear (*huhyŏnmu*), and the Red Bird in front (*chŏnjujak*). According to Sŏ, these elements, named for figures in Chinese astronomy, did not have to be naturally formed. The Green Dragon, for example, normally a hill or mountain to the left of a village, could sometimes be flowing water, and the White Tiger, a mountain to right side of a village, a road.

Yi Chung-hwan asks, "How should we evaluate geographical features? First, we must look at the water outlet (*sugu*), the configuration of fields and mountains, and the color of the soil. Then we must consider the water

supply, mountains and rivers." Yi's suggestion is important to an understanding of the conditions affecting the location of a village and its configuration. The water outlet was the point at which a river or stream flows from a village. Yi said that the outlet had to be covered, and fields should stretch along its inner side. In other words, a village should be located at the foot of a mountain with arable land in front and a river flowing into the distance. The configuration of fields and mountains and the soil's color should be conducive to farming and a proper mentality among villagers. If a village is nestled at the foot of a protective mountain and faces another mountain and a stream or river in the distance, it is considered to be in an auspicious site.

A site with these geographical conditions is economically advantageous because it possesses fertile land and a good water supply. If the water outlet is in the distance and surrounded by mountains, the village will feel cozy and have an unobstructed frontal view. Korean villages are invariably located in sunny spots that are cozy and warm like a mother's embrace.

The road that connects a village to the outside world usually wraps around the skirt of the surrounding mountains and follows the river that flows past the village. The road often cuts across farmland to reach the village entrance. In many instances, spirit posts (*changsŭng*) stand in pairs at the foot of the nearby mountain to ward off evil spirits. They mark the preliminary boundary to the outside, and a tree or a pavilion at the village entrance marks a secondary boundary. While the changsŭng, a reflection of indigenous religion, suggests the boundary separating the village from the outside world, the village entrance is the actual boundary in the villagers' lives. The tree or pavilion at the village entrance provides a place to gather and discuss important village matters as well as to relax. The stream or river that passes nearby is the laundry center and public meeting place for local women. In fact, everyone entering the village has to pass the wash place, so it is the place for news from neighboring villages as well as local gossip.

The spatial dynamic of a village thus created corresponds to human movement. The village is hidden from the outside by a mountain, but appears suddenly as one draws closer. The twisting road reaches deep into the heart of the village, naturally following the fences and stone walls that separate each house. The road, which extends like branches

on trees, is not precise or geometrical, and side alleys zigzag between the houses. The twisted paths allow changes in the spatial flow and create unexpected spaces. In this way space is endowed with a sense of time. In his *Farm Management* (*Sallim kyŏngje*), the Shirhak scholar Hong Man-sŏn (1643-1715) said that straight roads were undesirable. For him, the ideal road to a village was twisted and circuitous.

According to Hong, no more than two houses should be built side by side, and the gates should never face each other. This custom was born of experience. The lay of a house was determined by the topographical features of nearby mountains. In *Farm Management,* Hong suggests that a compass be used to establish a dwelling's layout in relation to the neighboring mountain because the layout directly influences the mentality of the people who live inside. Neighboring houses should not be built parallel to the dwelling, and the side street should curve naturally between the various lots. Thus Koreans chose to reflect the surrounding topography over geometrical order in the construction of individual homes and communities.

The relationship with other houses in terms of the natural environment and the social environment was an important consideration. The lay of the house and the direction it faced were decided in relation to the surrounding environment and other houses. The layout and exposures were traditionally associated with how the house "leans" into the earth. A well-situated house offered comfort and stability. A gradually inclined backyard was considered a positive feature. Ansan, the mountain in front of the village, also played an important role in the mentality of the people living in a house. An unobstructed frontal view was thus a valuable asset. The distant mountain served as a front garden, a gift of nature.

The hill that reached into the backyard was connected to the main mountain (*chusan*) behind the village. Although villagers did not face the mountain in their daily lives, the mountain was a symbol of the village to the outside world and at the same time marked the position of the village to people coming to the village from outside. As the mountain villagers faced it each day,

Paper-covered lattice windows and doors (above, opposite) provide relaxing diffused light and ventilation.

ansan plays a significant role in determining their state of mind. In short, the principal mountain behind a village, chinsan, is important as a symbol seen from the outside, and ansan is important as the spiritual foundation of the village.

Generally, Korean houses are similar in composition although they may differ in size. The houses of commoners were generally composed of a women's quarters (*anch'ae*) and a storeroom with an open front. A new wing was usually added when family fortunes improved. A house composed of only the anch'ae formed a straight line. If a second wing was added it was another straight line, parallel to the first. A new wing could also be added at right angles to the first, and if another wing was added, the house resembled an open-ended square. Larger homes were enclosed in a square with a central courtyard. One or more additional wings, such as a separate men's quarters or servants' quarters, were sometimes built across the courtyard. Houses on sites that required protection from intruders were built facing a tiny inner courtyard over which only a patch of sky was visible.

In all houses, regardless of design, the women's anch'ae is located at the innermost part of the house. The master's sarangch'ae is always near the main gate. This design is in keeping with the norms of Confucianism, the state ideology of the Chosŏn Dynasty, and also derived from the necessities of everyday life.

Korean houses composed of several wings naturally include external space, which is created by the wings. The front courtyard of the sarangch'ae was the outer courtyard, the yard in front of the servant's haengnangch'ae was the "front" courtyard, and the yard in front of the anch'ae was the inner yard, or *anmadang.* Each courtyard was distinguished by the surrounding buildings and walls, and was accessible through a door. Generally, a series of gates leads through the buildings from the outer courtyard to the inner courtyard. One usually has to pass through several courtyards to reach the innermost courtyard from the main gate. The path is never straight. It zigzags to create the perception of layer after layer of buildings and walls. These houses were built in the traditional belief that the essence of living space was layers. Even small thatched houses with only three rooms were built inside a courtyard created by stone walls, adding to the depth of living space.

The distinct sense of domain or territory in each wing or room of the house is extremely important. Separate wings come together to form a single house, and rooms are placed in accordance with their function and purpose. Korean houses, therefore, are designed in separate wings on the basis of practicality. In a small house with a single wing, the rooms are designed to accommodate all necessary functions. These functions are dispersed to different wings when the house expands.

A wing generally consists of a series of rooms—for example, a kitchen, the *anbang* (the main room for women), a wooden-floored *maru*, and an extra bedroom—all built in a single row. Sometimes additional rooms, another wooden-floored maru and storerooms are added in the various configurations mentioned earlier.

The method of choosing a village site, the spatial composition of a village and the layout of houses are important elements that made Korean villages and houses unique. Together with these elements, *ondol* and maru are features found only in Korean houses. Ondol is a system of under-floor flues used for heating. The maru is an unheated wooden-floored hall, generally used in summer. The ondol and maru are two distinct ways of using space seasonally.

Rooms are named according to their inhabitants. The anbang, the main room in the women's quarters, is used by the mistress of the house and by young children. The *kŏnnŏnbang* is used by grown children or by a married son and his wife. *Sarangbang*, the main room of the men's quarters, is where the master of the house stays.

Depending on the season and circumstances, the anbang, maru, sarangbang and the inner courtyard functioned alternatively as the place for family gatherings and discussions. Each person slept in the room that he or she used during the day. As for meals, the head of the household ate in the sarangch'ae and other members of the family in the anbang or maru. Today these customs are changing, but Koreans' fundamental use of space reflects the traditional hierarchy based on seniority and the strict distinction between sexes.

A house is a vessel that protects against the rain and wind and surrounds the space that contains human life. The traditional architectural ideal derives from this concept. The planning psychology, spatial aesthetic and traditional values of the Korean people are also evident in the structure of their houses. Through the maru and ondol, Koreans experience the rhythms of the four seasons. The layout of the Korean house also brings outdoor scenery into the house itself. As such, Koreans did not build their houses as objects to be viewed from the outside. The foundation of the Korean house is in the internal space around which the external space is developed.

In traditional society, houses were built from materials readily available. In mountainous areas, wood or stone were generally used. In flatter terrain, wood was used for the framework and clay for the walls. Construction materials determined the structure of the house. Generally, there was only one way to build a tiled-roof house. Wood had to be used to build the framework. There were several different types of thatched houses, however. Some had stone or earthen walls, whereas others were made of stacked logs, much like a log cabin.

Above all else, traditional Korean houses were environmentally friendly. Each building was carefully planned to take into account the surrounding environment. The angle of the eaves reflected an awareness of the sun's altitude in winter and summer. Sunlight penetrated deep into the house during cold weather and never shone inside the stone threshold during the summer months.

Traditional homes also took advantage of summer breezes. Houses were situated to take best advantage of breezes from the front and back. The maru was built at the center of the house to catch any breezes blowing through the courtyards. A door was installed in the maru to be closed in winter and lifted for ventilation in summer.

Korean houses also adjusted to the environment through the careful use of construction materials. A thatch roof is particularly effective for blocking solar heat but also serves as excellent insulation in winter. Thatch is ideal in the Korean climate where temperature differences are so great. Earthen walls also block out the sun's rays in summer and hold in heat in winter. The mulberry paper used to cover latticed windows diffuses sunlight to provide a pleasant natural light. At the same time, it allows ventilation and absorbs sound.

As such, Korean houses were built to naturally adapt to the local environment. They were a kind of climate filter, offering protection and order, while at the same time embracing the natural surroundings. ◆

Ondol:
A Uniquely Korean Lifestyle

Choi Young-taik

The discovery and use of fire formed the basis of human life and culture. The importance of fire is still evident in many human rituals, from the Olympic flame to the eternal flames at the Arc de Triomphe in Paris and Arlington National Cemetery in Washington, D.C.

Until the 1950s, it was the Korean custom for every housewife to nurture a live coal, believed to have originated in the mountains during prehistoric times, and hand it down to the next generation. The creative acquisition and use of fire—in other words, the wisdom of preserving fire—was thought to be the secret behind the Korean people's survival. Housewives buried a lump of charcoal under a 15-20 centimeter layer of leaves or wood, then sealed the pile with a 10-15 centimeter layer of earth. Thus insulated, the coal would stay alive for two to three days.

In prehistoric society vast amounts of wood were needed to keep a fire burning day and night through the long cold winters. To conserve firewood, early Koreans tried to maintain the heat from their bonfires as long as possible. They protected their fires from rain and snow by erecting stones around the fire pit and placing a wide, flat stone over the top. The stones surrounding the bonfire heated up and remained warm even when exposed to out-

side air. Sometimes people sat or lay on top of the horizontal stone. It was only a matter of time before Koreans cemented the top stone to the verticals with mud to create a fire chamber that sustained energy and heat. This in turn led to the development of the *ondol* hypocaust, an under-floor heating system.

Ondol is unique to Korea. It consists of a fire-hole that vents to the outside. The fire-hole is connected to ridged flues, the equivalents of the pillar stones mentioned above, made of mud and stone. On top of these flues are flat stones. At the back of the flues, opposite the fire-hole, is a chimney. A large kettle could be placed in the round hole over the fire-hole. This was used for cooking and heating water, and at the same time raised the room temperature by forcing heat through the flues. The entire floor and the air inside the room remained warm for some time after the fire was out because the flat stones retained heat. Only the smoke was let out through the chimney. In summer, colder air from beneath would pass through the flues, cooling the flat stones.

The ondol system gave rise to a uniquely comfortable lifestyle. Koreans always take off their shoes before entering a room because the warm floor is conducive to a floor-sitting lifestyle. Koreans have traditionally slept on

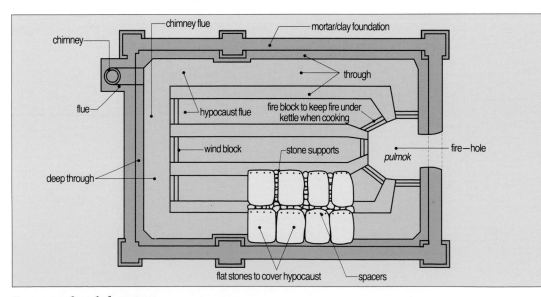

Diagram labels: chimney flue, mortar/clay foundation, chimney, through, flue, hypocaust flue, fire block to keep fire under kettle when cooking, wind block, stone supports, *pulmok*, fire—hole, deep through, flat stones to cover hypocaust, spacers

Layout of ondol system

Unheated wooden-floored rooms (above) were used together with ondol rooms such as this woman's room (left).

mattresses stuffed with cotton covered with cotton quilts. The heat released from the ondol system is absorbed in the mattress. The warm mattress enhances blood circulation. If the blanket is larger than the mattress, the released heat concentrates in the blanket, warming the whole body. When the body comes in direct contact with the ondol floor, gamma rays stimulate body cells, accelerating blood circulation and cellular regeneration during sleep.

There were other benefits as well. Thanks to the ondol system and floor-sitting custom, a "bedroom" could be transformed into a living room simply by folding up the mattress and blanket. While the rooms in traditional Korean houses were quite small, they were versatile in their lack of furniture.

The most important room was the *anbang*, the "inner room" at the center of the house. It was connected to the kitchen. In smaller homes, where there was no separate men's quarters, family members gathered there to eat, to perform rites and to hold holiday ceremonies.

103

The warmest part of the anbang, closest to the fire-hole, is called the *araenmok*, or "lower part." It was a place of honor for the elderly and sick and for guests. During the daylight hours a blanket was spread over the araenmok to keep it warm. Family members often warmed their hands and feet there when they returned home. Mothers also placed the portable dining table there at meal times. The "upper" part of the room, or *winmok*, opposite the araenmok, was not as warm. This area was often covered with a large chest to store clothes or blankets, or it was used for chores.

Traditionally, Koreans were born and raised on the anbang araenmok. As they grew up, boys lived in the *kŏnnŏnbang*, "the room across," and girls in the *twibang*, the "back room," for they were expected to get married and leave home. When Koreans grew old and infirm, they returned to the araenmok to die. After death they were honored there by their descendants on important holidays and the anniversaries of their passing.

On winter days in farming villages, farmers sat on the winmok reading, making straw rope or wooden or straw shoes, or culling seeds for spring farming. Their wives sat on the araenmok spinning hemp, sewing, ironing or preparing side dishes. The children studied in the middle of the room. And in the evening the family sat in the anbang sharing sweet potatoes, corn, potatoes and chestnuts cooked in the coals of the fire.

The traditional Korean house consisted of ondol floors made of mud, walls plastered with mud and a mud ceiling and roof. It was like living in a mud cave. Yet mud provided effective insulation, maintaining an almost constant temperature. Before refrigerators were invented, Koreans followed this principle by digging a deep tunnel close to a river and allowing it to fill with water, which froze during the coldest months of the season. They then cut the ice into manageable blocks and stored the blocks inside the tunnel, covered with rice straw and a thick layer of earth to protect them from the heat. This method of refrigeration was used until the 1950s and 1960s, when modern refrigerators were introduced to Korea. According to ancient Chinese documents, this technique dates to the Shilla Kingdom. One example of a Shilla icehouse (*sŏkbinggo*) remains in Kyŏngju today. It consists of a pile of granite stones covered by a mud mound and turf. Similar icehouses believed to date from the Shilla Kingdom are found in five other areas. Seoul's Tongbinggo-dong ("East Ice-Storage District") and Sŏbinggo-dong ("West Ice-Storage District") are named for underground tunnels where ice was stored.

The ondol system also contributed to the development of Korea's unique culinary tradition based on fermentation. In the mud underneath the ondol flues were countless microorganisms beneficial to the human body. The flow of summer air into the flues facilitated reproduction of these microorganisms and discharged them into the room. *Meju*, a staple of the Korean diet used to make soy sauce and soybean paste, was made by kneading boiled soybeans into large lumps, which were then laid on rice straw on the ondol floor for several days. The heat and enzymes emitted from the rice straw and ondol floor helped the meju ferment. When the blocks of meju had hardened, they were piled on the heated floor for further fermentation, then hung from the ceiling by rice straw ropes. The leaven from the mud walls, ceiling and floor aided the fermentation process, producing tasty meju, which was the foundation of Korea's unique diet of fermented foods.

In addition to aiding fermentation, the ondol system also helped adjust humidity in the home, dried laundry and food, and produced ashes used to make lye.

Despite Korea's urbanization and the boom in high-rise apartments, the majority of Koreans still live in homes heated with a modified ondol system. In apartments a boiler heats water that passes through copper pipes laid in the cement floor. In recent years, the quest for health and longevity has led many people to install modified mud ondol systems. Traditional ondol flues are nearly extinct, but a modified system, called *kyŏpkudŭl*, or "double ondol," offers the benefits of mud construction without the danger of carbon monoxide leaks. ◆

Firewood was carried in A-frame backracks (opposite). A large iron kettle was always kept over the fire-hole (lower left). Soybean cakes (meju) were dried over ondol heat (above).

Water in the Traditional Garden

Yoo Byung-rim

Koreans used water wisely in traditional society. Literati sought spiritual tranquility in the still water of a small pond and enjoyed gazing at portable flower trays placed in their gardens. They lingered wherever they could hear the sound of water, near waterfalls or mountain streams. Traces of this tradition live on in the gardens of virtuous scholars who led reclusive lives away from the secular world.

At times, the scholars' obsession with water was extreme, but generally they used water as a means of cleansing their minds and soothing ruffled emotions. Some scholars meditated while gazing upon their reflections in still water. Others enjoyed a playful atmosphere, watching fish frolic in a pond. Water was indispensable to the traditional gentleman-scholar's personal space. It was an essential part of their lives. No wonder the word *seshim*, "mind-cleansing," was so often part of the names used for ponds and outdoor pavilions in traditional society. It signified the purification of the mind through water.

A painting of Okhojŏng, a summer house owned by Kim Cho-sun (1765-1831), the father-in-law of the Chosŏn Dynasty's King Sunjo, shows the many aesthetic uses of water. Near the men's quarters in the front courtyard are a small flower tray, an herb garden, some strangely shaped rocks, small pine trees and a beehive. On the slope leading to the upper part of the garden are a small tile-roofed pavilion and a thatched pavilion. In front of the pavilions are flowering trees, stone figures, a stone-lined stream and a small pine grove. The stream empties directly into the pond through a bamboo pipe. Locating two ponds at different levels doubled the observer's pleasure. The sound of a mountain stream gushing by the house must have heightened the flavor of summer.

It was not difficult drawing water into the garden because during the Chosŏn era houses were purposely built near rivers or mountain streams. Homeowners drew water directly from rivers and streams to feed artificial ponds. The water supply from streams varied through the year, however, so a small wooden or bamboo conduit was developed to ensure a constant flow. Soswaewon in Tamyang, Chŏllanam-do province, offers an outstanding example of this technique. The water flowing into the pond from the bamboo conduit creates a different sound in autumn when water was often in short supply.

People living on flat terrain stored surface water during the rainy season or drew water from distant rivers and mountain streams for their gardens. Because of the general lack of water, most ponds in the gardens of ordinary homes were small and shallow. To compensate for the ponds' limited size and depth, garden owners emphasized the sound of water. Traditional gardens usually included either a pond or water flowing down an incline, or both. When one pond was located in the upper part of the garden and another below, water was allowed to flow beneath the surface, out of sight. Every garden in Woe-am-ri in Asan, Ch'ungch'ŏngnam-do province, used water in this manner. In the Songhwa-taek garden at Woe-am-ri, water flows through a narrow waterway instead of along the mountain stream. The sound of the water in the waterway can be heard from the men's quarters.

One way to understand traditional Korean ideas about space is to examine the attitudes of gentlemen-scholars and gentry who were concerned about creating a suitable personal environment. Their gardens and the use of water in creating those gardens are the best examples of their spatial understanding. Gardens were the man's traditional domain. They were usually located in a quiet and isolated spot. Rocks, pine trees, ponds and lotus flowers—in short, nature itself—were typically included in the gardens. The peacefulness of the garden allowed a person to forget the outside world, if only for a brief moment, and to indulge in idealistic

Soswaewon in Chŏllanam-do province

The pond at Anapchi, the royal garden in Kyŏngju (above), is fed by a stream which passes through a stone channel (right) regulated by a wooden sluice gate.

thoughts. The garden allowed the resident to enter a state of utopia.

Water often took the form of a pond in traditional gardens. A small island called *chungdo*, or "island in the center," was placed in the middle of rectangular ponds. Koreans believed the island may be inhabited by supernatural beings. This belief was based on *shinsŏn* ideology, a Taoist belief in immortals who live in mountains.

Ponds vary stylistically in each of the three East Asian countries, although all three cultures embraced Confucianism. In Chinese gardens, ponds are usually wide enough to be crossed by boat and, in many cases, are molded artificially. Chinese gardens are generally built for strolling around these ponds. The Chinese try to transplant the natural scenery of large mountains and streams in their gardens.

Japanese gardens, on the other hand, usually do not loop around ponds. In the famous Japanese garden Hiraniwa Karesansui, which is

believed to have been modeled after Korea's Anapchi, the royal garden in Kyŏngju, the ancient capital of the Shilla Kingdom, the sea and rivers are represented by carefully raked sand and pebbles, instead of water.

In Korean gardens, mountain streams are incorporated in their natural form, while ponds are usually rectangular with an island in the center, featuring abstract rather than natural forms.

One particular quality of Korea's traditional gardens were ponds that could not be crossed. The central island was viewed from the pond's edge or from within a structure beside the pond. Pine trees, Chinese arborvitae, bamboo trees and other landscaping were recreated in abstract, idealistic forms. Thus, the observer confronted each natural object from a certain distance and perceived it as an abstract and ideal object. Ponds were small because Koreans could not afford large gardens, and most were located near valleys, rocky areas or hills.

An island sits at the center of the pond at Anapchi, the royal garden in Kyŏngju. The pond is not rectangular, however, because that was not a practical shape for such a large pond. The pond's size also made it logical for the designers to utilize existing natural forms. An interesting feature of Anapchi is its perspective. The pond cannot be seen in its entirety from any point around it. This makes it seem larger than it is. In fact, Anapchi is quite small compared to ponds in Chinese and Japanese palaces, but it gives the impression of space and depth. The magnificent panorama created by the ponds at Versailles is a function of the garden's vast size, but the smaller ponds in Korean gardens relied on illusion and imagination for their special ambience.

Koreans' use of water in traditional gardens is fundamentally different from the way the Chinese or Japanese use water. This difference is most evident in the relationship between a pond's shape and the island at its center.

Chinese gardens usually had a pavilion on the central island, and it was possible to cross over to the opposite side of the garden. The central island was a practical space. On the island, people admired the view around them. It was thus only natural that ponds needed to be quite large, large enough for people to paddle about in small boats.

The Chinese also liked to build buildings or corridors around the pond, turning the island into an element of the scenery. For this reason, a bridge was built to the island itself, enabling people to walk to it and lean against the railings of the pavilion, admiring the surrounding scenery. Poets often alluded to such scenes. The Chinese carefully arranged objects to create an idealized overall effect. They also built structures in a way that would emphasize the framing effect, capturing the beauty of a tree or flower through a gate or window.

Japan's traditional gardens, on the other hand, were constructed so as to bring people back to the original point of departure, instead of allowing them to cross over to the other side. Ponds tended to be natural shapes. Japanese gardens were similar to Chinese gardens in their use of water as a given element of nature. The raked sand and natural rocks of Karesansui Garden symbolize the vast sea and mountains.

In Piwon, the Forbidden Garden or back garden of Ch'angdŏkkung Palace in Seoul, Aeryŏnji Pond, is filled with lotus flowers in summer. From ancient times, Korea's gentlemen-scholars revered lotus flowers because they blossom in muddy water. In observing nature, gentlemen-scholars paid close attention to an object's ultimate form in its natural surroundings and

tried to perceive all things from an ethical standard. In Confucian thought and Buddhism, the lotus flower symbolized purity and forthrightness in a secular world.

In their gardens, gentlemen-scholars planted trees and shrubs that represented the values of Confucianism. The "Four Gracious Objects"—water, rock, pine and bamboo—are found in all Chosŏn-era gardens. Gentlemen-scholars often planted plum trees because plum blossoms sprouted through the snow in early spring and were valued for their symbolism. Natural elements were chosen for their symbolic significance, not necessarily for their innate beauty. To classical scholars the beauty of a pure plum blossom was not as important as its embodiment of the moral values which they revered.

Puyongjŏng in Piwon is a picturesque pavilion. Its shape resembles a person dipping his or her feet in a stream. Half of the pavilion is on land; the other half is in the water. The same is true of Hwallaejŏng in Kangnŭng, Kangwon-do province, and Namganjŏngsa in Hoedŏk, Ch'ungch'ŏngnam-do. How did this unique configuration come about? The answer lies in the concept of nature held by traditional scholars.

From early times, classical gentlemen-scholars believed that the scholar's path meant executing the king's wishes in the administration of government, then returning to a life of rural isolation once his bureaucratic career ended. A life in seclusion was the life of a scholar. Much of Korea's classical literature depicts this isolated lifestyle. The terms t'aksa and t'akchok, which refer to dipping one's feet in a stream in summer and spending one's time idly, came to represent the life of gentlemen-scholars who lived in the country, away from worldly avarice and greed. As these concepts represented the gentlemen-scholars' basic attitude toward the viewing of objects, it was natural that they should be present in the gardens and pavilions where the scholars spent most of their time.

A pavilion with two columns in the water resembles a gentleman-scholar with his feet in a stream. Accordingly, a pavilion reflected in a garden pond symbolized the scholar and his life. This is why the names of many pavilions in Korea include the term "t'aksa." Korea's classical scholars tried to realize their philosophical ideal of moderation by building their pavilions in this manner. They sought to take one step closer to utopia. The traditional Korean concept of human surroundings can only be understood when one looks beyond the simple visual beauty of an object or structure and attempts to understand the spiritual world of the traditional gentleman-scholar. ◆

Pond-side pavilions are part of most traditional gardens such as Aeyŏnjŏng (previous page) and Puyŏngjŏng (above) at Ch'angdŏkkung Palace and Hwallaejŏng at Sŏngyojang, a yangban residence in Kangnŭng (right). The pavilions were welcome retreats to members of the royal family and gentlemen-scholars.

CLOTHING

In all cultures, national costume is an indicator of national character and values. The clothes that Koreans have worn over the millennia—everyday clothing, ceremonial garments, official uniforms and shrouds worn in death—vividly reflect the values and social structure of the people who made and wore them.

In this section, Cho Woo-hyun considers the development of Korean clothing over time, focusing on structure, function and symbolism. Cho Hyo-soon looks more closely at ceremonial garments and accessories used in rites of passage and at the use and care of traditional fabrics.

Professor Kum Ki-sook contributes two essays: one on changes in the traditional *hanbok* over time and the other on modern interpretations of the hanbok. Cheon Wan-kil looks at the historical development of women's accessories, hairstyles and cosmetics from the founding of Korea, recorded in the myth of Tan-gun, through the Chosŏn Dynasty.

Embroidery expert Huh Dong-hwa focuses on the hopes and desires of women in his study of Korean embroidery over the centuries. Needlework and weaving skills were essential skills for women in traditional society. Huh examines the development of these crafts and the use of embroidery as a reflection of social status and personal desires.

Journalist Kim Yoo-kyung interviews artisans devoted to the re-creation of traditional garments and accessories and considers several traditional items such as embroidered baby carriers and shoes, which are still in use today.

Korean Costumes: Design and Development

Cho Woo-hyun

National costume is the most accessible guide to any culture. A nation's clothing offers insights into national consciousness and character.

The Korean word for garment, *ot*, 옷, was designed to resemble a person with arms and legs extended. The word, coined by the Chosŏn Dynasty's King Sejong (r. 1418-1450), inventor of the Korean alphabet *han-gŭl*, embodies the idea that clothes reveal the character of the person wearing them. This article examines the basic principles and philosophy underlying the traditional Korean costume *hanbok* and how the costume evolved from ancient times.

The hanbok currently worn by Koreans fall into three categories: daily wear, ritual wear, and costumes worn for special purposes. Today the older generation is most likely to wear hanbok as daily apparel. Women wear *chŏgori*, a bolero-like blouse, *ch'ima*, a skirt, a *sok ch'ima*, or full slip, and thick padded socks called *pŏsŏn*. In winter, a long overcoat, *turumagi*, is worn outdoors. Turumagi are also worn on formal occasions.

Men wear chŏgori, *chokki*, a vest, *magoja*, a jacket or short coat, and *paji*, baggy trousers. For undergarments, they wear variations of the chŏgori and paji. Men also wear pŏsŏn and sometimes a turumagi when they go out.

Ritual garments are worn at rites of passage. On their first birthday, boys wear *k'waeja*, a knee-length vest, a five-colored top coat called *kkach'i turumagi*, and on their head *hogŏn* or *pokkŏn*, peaked or plain hoods. Girls wear *tang-ŭi*, a ceremonial jacket with hanging front lapels, over ch'ima and chŏgori, a small bejeweled toque called *chokturi* on their head, and *tarae pŏsŏn*, quilted pŏsŏn decorated with embroidery and pompoms, on their feet.

For weddings, the groom wears a gossamer hat called *samo* and *tallyŏng*, a kind of topcoat with a rounded neckline and a belt. The bride wears *wonsam* or *hwarot*, a long decorative jacket, on top of *sŭran ch'ima*, a long skirt decorated with embossed gold at the hem.

For Chosŏn-era burials, the corpse of an upper-class man was dressed in the official attire of the highest office he held during his lifetime. Upper-class women were dressed in attire corresponding to the rank of her husband's last official post. Lower-class men were dressed in tallyŏng, and common women in hemp robes patterned after the wedding attire.

There were also special garments for rituals held at Chongmyo, the royal ancestral shrine of the Chosŏn Dynasty, and for shamans, folk dancers and other performers.

Structurally, the hanbok resembles the caftan, another front-opening, right-fastened garment. Anthropologists A.L. Kroeber and Yasuro Ogawa have noted that men's and women's clothing fastened on different sides in the West, but in the East, the determining factor was the wearer's way of life—whether he or she was from an agrarian or hunting-nomadic culture.

In traditional Korean garments, color is used symbolically. White was the basic color most widely used by the common people. It symbolized a modest and pure spirit. Red signified good fortune and wealth and thus was used in women's wedding garments. Indigo, the color of constancy, was used for the skirts of court ladies and the official coats of court officials. Black, symbolizing infinity and the fountainhead of all creation, was used for men's hats. Yellow, which represented the center of the universe, was used for royal garments. Common people were forbidden from wearing yellow.

The color, decorations and accessories of the garments worn at the royal ancestral rites of the Chosŏn Dynasty (right) are rich in symbolism.

These five colors were firmly established as symbols of the four directions and the center of the universe, and as governing the cycle and order of the universe.

Neutral colors symbolized the *yin* or implicit virtues. They were used for embroidery on garments worn below the waist. The five cardinal colors, symbolizing the *yang*, or overt virtues, were used in patterns on garments worn above the waist. The five-colored garments worn by children, five-colored purses and five-colored dancing costumes are good examples of this symbolism. Colors symbolizing heaven and earth were used for wedding clothes.

Koreans used tie-strings and belts or bands to keep their garments in place. Sometimes knots were used to fasten unlined chŏgori, military wear, or tallyŏng, the official topcoat, but regular garments, such as chŏgori, ch'ima, turumagi and paji, were fastened with tie-strings or held up with tied waistbands. Many garments opened at the sides or bottom for greater comfort and ease of movement. Chŏgori for casual wear opened at the side, and the casual garments of civil and military officials also opened on the side or the back. Even ritual garments were open on the sides to make it easier to put on and take off many layers of garments quickly.

Headgear was of great importance to Koreans, so much so that the coming-of-age ceremony for males was called *kwallye*, the "hat ceremony." Males were regarded as adults only after they went through this ceremony and were officially allowed to wear hats. The head was regarded as sacred; men always carried an oiled paper rain hat (*kalmo*) to shield their heads and hats from the rain. Officials were excused from answering the king's summons if their garments and hats were soaked by precipitation, which made them unpresentable.

Perhaps the most important and characteristically Korean garment is the chŏgori. In ancient Korea, the chŏgori was a unisex garment which reached the hips, had borders on collars and sleeves, and was fastened by a band at the waist. The sleeves were originally quite narrow, as suited the hunting and nomadic life of Koreans at that time and the cold climate of the region. Over time, they gradually grew wider.

Chŏgori were fastened on the left in the early Koguryŏ period, but the fastening changed to the right in later years. Collar and sleeve borders began to disappear during the Koryŏ Dynasty, and the use of tie-strings

Color is a powerful symbol in Korean costumes. The yellow found in this chŏgori blouse was once reserved for royal garments because it symbolized the center of the universe.

became widespread. Sometime during the late Koryŏ to the early Chosŏn dynasties, chŏgori with colorful trim and open sides appeared.

Chŏgori were worn to the waist in the early years of the Chosŏn Dynasty, but from the mid-Chosŏn period they were shorter. In a genre painting by Shin Yun-bok (1758-?), women are depicted in chŏgori that stop above the waist. By the late Chosŏn Dynasty, the chŏgori reached only to the armpits and had rounded front panels to cover the breasts. In the mid-20th century, longer chŏgori became the norm.

The chŏgori collar also underwent many changes, from straight to rounded and from stiff to soft. Together with the detachable collar strip called tongjŏng, the collar served as an eye-catching focal point. The length of the sash fasteners of the chŏgori, korŭm, varied in inverse ratio to changes in the garment's length.

While the woman's chŏgori changed repeatedly over time, the man's version has remained more or less the same in form and length since the Shilla period. The long unisex chŏgori with open sides became exclusively women's wear from the mid-Chosŏn period, and developed into the tang-ŭi ceremonial jacket with hanging lapels. The tongsang, a variation worn by Buddhist monks today, is almost identical to the chŏgori which appears in Koguryŏ murals, except for the tie-string and shape of the collar.

Paji, or trousers, also reflected changes in lifestyle. The narrow legs suited to hunting and nomadic life became wider. Men's paji continued to be worn as an outer garment with divided legs, or cut on the diagonal. Paji for women evolved into undergarments, after undergoing many variations. Women wore sŏn-gun and malgun, hybrid paji-ch'ima, for many years. After the Japanese invasions of the late 16th century, numerous variations of the paji, such as soksokkot, tansokkot and nŏrŭn paji were worn under the skirt. The Japanese hakama, the voluminous, pleated trousers worn by Japanese men on ceremonial occasions today, derives from Korean women's tansokkot with front and back openings.

Salwar trousers, of which Korean paji are a variation, are typical of the baggy lower garments worn by settled agricultural peoples. They were worn across a vast area, from Southeast Asia to India, Iran, Turkey, Greece and all the way to North Africa and Spain. From this one can surmise that the boundaries of East Asian culture stretched much farther than is presently demarcated, a contention reinforced by the widespread distribution of straight-sleeved caftans.

The ch'ima was imported from China in ancient times. Pleated skirts and colorfully striped skirts are found in Koguryŏ murals. During the Koryŏ Kingdom, women wore ch'ima as casual and ritual clothing. The man's skirt, called *sang*, which was part of ritual attire, was open on both sides. During the Chosŏn Dynasty, chŏgori grew shorter while ch'ima for formal and ritual occasions became more voluminous and were puffed up by many layers of undergarments which served as petticoats. The length and volume of the ch'ima and the way it was worn were indicators of the wearer's status.

Kisaeng, professional women entertainers, hiked up the left edge of their skirts to reveal a glimpse of their bloomers, an indication of their profession. Sometimes the wives and daughters of members of political factions wore their skirts in a distinct manner as a sign of their affiliation.

The Korean ch'ima is a tubular garment similar to the sarong widely worn in Southeast Asia, Africa and New Guinea. In many cultures, skirts are worn around the waist and fastened with strips of cloth or by tucking a corner of the surplus fabric into the waistband, but in Korea the ch'ima is wrapped around the chest and fastened with straps attached to the ends of the waistband (which is actually a chestband). This variation must have been influenced by the Korean climate and lifestyle. It provides greater freedom of movement, essential to Korea's floor-sitting culture, and better retains body heat.

The turumagi was originally worn over paji and chŏgori for ceremonies and for warmth. Yasuro Ogawa contends that the Korean word for garment, "ot," derives from the Chinese word *ao*, meaning an "outer coat" much like the turumagi. However, in Korea the word "ot" is widely believed to have been coined by King Sejong, as previously mentioned. The turumagi in Koguryŏ murals have borders on the lapels and sleeves, like the chŏgori, and are fastened in the back or on the side to avoid overlapping with the chŏgori fastener. Like the sleeves of the chŏgori, the sleeves of the turumagi grew fuller over time.

A painting of a Chosŏn beauty by painter Shin Yun-bok (1758-?) (left, Kansong Art Museum) and a mural at the Koguryŏ Tomb of the Dancers (below, Jian, China) reveal changing hanbok styles.

Some scholars attribute this change in sleeve width to Chinese influences, but such changes can and do occur spontaneously, as Fluegel's theory of decoration suggests. A change in Korean lifestyles no doubt stimulated the development. It would be wrong to credit Chinese influences alone for changes in the hanbok.

During the Koryŏ period, the turumagi's lines became less distinct, as shown in an *Illustrated Account of Koryŏ*, a painting by Xu Jing of Song China. A white hemp turumagi dating to the mid-14th century, which was discovered among Buddhist relics, provides some important clues to late Koryŏ clothing. This turumagi has a stiff, straight collar, and apparently had tie-strings to fasten it. It is evidently a forerunner of the Chosŏn turumagi pleated at the armpits. During the Chosŏn Dynasty, numerous styles of turumagi, variously called *ui*, *chingnyŏng*, *top'o*, *ch'ŏmni* and *ch'ŏllik*, were worn by the literati, but after the Reforms of 1894, they were unified in the narrower-sleeved turumagi. The waistband that had fastened the turumagi closed was replaced by strings tied at the chest. This indicates that an active and functional lifestyle had given way to an inactive, sedentary one.

In general, aristocrats wore long, full robes. During the reign of King Pŏphŭng (514-540) of Shilla, a four-color official robe system was established. A century later, during the reign of King Munmu (r. 661-681), Shilla adopted the official robe system of Tang China for diplomatic activities. The move was also an attempt to reinforce the dignity of the ruling class.

From the reign of Koryŏ's King Munjong (1046-1083), elaborate dress codes were established for the king, queen and various grades

This wonsam, a long ceremonial robe, is heavily embroidered on front (above) and back (opposite, top). A modern rendition of the wonsam steals the spotlight at a fashion show (opposite, bottom).

of officials. During the Chosŏn Dynasty, the official robe system of Ming China was adopted and codified in the 1394 Administrative Code of Chosŏn (*Chosŏn kyŏngguk-chŏn*). The system persisted as a means of maintaining class distinctions and preserving the dignity of royalty. Women wore official robes corresponding to their husbands' rank.

As daily wear changed, official robes became less varied in design and color, and the utensils for official rituals were simplified. Ironically, however, royal robes became more magnificent after King Kojong (r. 1863-1907) proclaimed himself emperor and renamed the country the Great Han Empire. Shortly thereafter, the country lost its sovereignty. The same thing happened during the Koryŏ Dynasty which was toppled by a coup d'état a few decades after King Kongmin (r.1351-1374) wore imperial robes. The robes had been reserved for Yuan Chinese emperors until that time. The color, patterns and tailoring of royal robes were rich in symbolism.

Other ritual costumes include those worn at weddings, funerals and commemoration ceremonies. Brides wore wonsam, long ceremonial robes, and hwarot, embroidered topcoats. The color and decorations of the wonsam indicated class and rank. Queens wore yellow wonsam with dragons embossed with gold. Princesses and royal concubines of the highest rank wore green wonsam with embossed flowers. Commoners wore simple green.

Hwarot, the bridal topcoat, was made of red cloth lined with indigo. The colors symbolized heaven and earth. Phoenix, peony, butterflies, waves, rocks and longevity symbols were embroidered on its shoulders. On

the back was an embroidered verse: "Marriage is the source of all blessings. Let the couple enjoy longevity like a mountain and riches like the ocean." The primitive shape of the hwarot collar suggests that it has not changed much from ancient times, further evidence that people tend to be conservative when it comes to life's rituals.

For court officials and literati, funeral shrouds were modeled after the official uniform of the deceased's highest office. Mourning clothes worn by the survivors followed strict rules and corresponded to the wearer's relationship to the deceased. Mourning clothes were replaced by everyday garments at set times during the mourning period. When the period of mourning was over, mourners resumed their normal clothes. The wearing of mourning clothes brought sobriety to the survivors' lives and enabled them to overcome their sorrow and consolidate their ties with other relatives. The custom of national mourning for kings, queens and crown princes strengthened national identity and reinforced centralized power.

The development of the hanbok, like any national costume, has been influenced by various factors, external and internal. External factors include the natural and social environment, institutions and customs, government policies and religion. Internal factors are related to personal and community temperaments and dynamics. The natural environment determines the basic character of a nation's costume, but changes in the social environment affect its development.

External factors that have affected the hanbok include climatic changes, political and economic changes, shifts in social classes, the

development of handicrafts and changes in religious practices. Understanding changes in clothing is helpful in evaluating the mores and values of traditional Korean society.

Changes in the hanbok have taken the form of gradual modification and variation. Until the 20th century, few changes were made. In this relative lack of change we recognize the strongly traditional and stable character of Korean society and the Korean people's powerful sense of national identity. Koreans have always worn ch'ima, chŏgori, paji and turumagi. Only length, width and other incidental features have changed. Elements that have changed seem to be modified in an inverse relationship to other elements. For example, when the chŏgori grew shorter, its ties became longer and the ch'ima became longer and fuller. In keeping with changes in ceremonial usage and ornamental value, unnecessary or insignificant elements were minimized or allowed to disappear.

On the other hand, ritual garments have lived on and occupy a significant place in the development of the hanbok. The Confucian ideology that governed the Chosŏn Dynasty for over 500 years placed social order above the individual. Therefore, as individuals derived their identity from the community or group, rituals which consolidated the group or community assumed supreme importance. Thus, ritual garments were considered extremely important.

To study the history of a nation's costume is to understand the culture and character of that nation. It is no surprise that the hanbok, like the traditional costumes of other nations, is increasingly seen as ceremonial or ornamental attire today. ◆

Korean Clothes and Fabrics

Cho Hyo-soon

The earliest physical evidence of Korea's clothing culture dates to 3000 B.C. Neolithic sewing needles, spinning tools and personal accessories such as earrings and bracelets as well as shell necklaces and rings have been excavated from ancient shell mounds in Kimhae. Murals in Koguryŏ tombs show that during the Three Kingdoms period people wore jackets, vests, coats, ornaments such as necklaces, bracelets and rings, and waist belts and shoes.

Weaving is essential to all but the most primitive clothing. We can assume that weaving developed in Korea during the prehistoric era and would have been a major chore for women of that time. According to the Chinese *History of the Three Kingdoms* (*Sanguojhi*), dating to the third century B.C., the people of Pyŏnhan, an ancient Korean kingdom, wove silk to make clothing. The book also includes references to Korean women weaving linen and silk fabrics.

Another written record notes that the Shilla founder King Hyŏkkŏse (r. 57 B.C.-A.D. 4) encouraged the development of sericulture, and King Yuri (r. 24-57) held weaving contests around Ch'usŏk, the Harvest Moon Festival in the eighth lunar month. The Korean *History of the Three Kingdoms* (*Samguksagi*), written in 1146, refers to the Shilla Kingdom's tributary contribution of 30 cartloads of fine ramie fabric to the court of Tang China.

During the Koryŏ Dynasty, King Ch'ungnyŏl (r. 1274-1308) sent embroidered ramie fabric as tribute to the court of Yuan China, and during the reign of King Kongmin (r. 1351-1374), Mun Ik-chŏm, a Koryŏ scholar, brought cotton seeds to Korea from

China. By the Chosŏn Dynasty, the weaving of ramie, silk and cotton fabrics was prevalent throughout the country, contributing greatly to the development of Chosŏn costumes.

In Puyŏ, Ch'ungch'ŏngnam-do, and Yŏngju, Kyŏngsangbuk-do, where the weaving of cotton and hemp, respectively, was communalized, women worked late into the night each summer, making cloth. In some provinces, rewards were given at the Harvest Moon Festival to those who had made the most cloth. Chosŏn women were expected to learn to weave before the age of ten and worked at looms all their lives. Weaving contests were a time for women to temporarily forget the exhaustion of their task and concentrate on camaraderie. While weaving, they sang special weaving songs.

The quality of hemp weaving improved remarkably during the Chosŏn Dynasty. Each region had its own unique cloth. The hemp from Hamgyŏng-do was called *pukp'o*, from the Kyŏngsang region *yŏngp'o*, from Kangwon-do *kangp'o*, from Andong *andong-p'o*, and from Koksŏng *tolshilnai*. Of these regional varieties, pukp'o from Yukjin in Hamgyŏng-do was most highly regarded. Inferior hemp cloth from Andong and Koksŏng was used for summer clothes, while the coarser kangp'o was generally used for farmers' and fishermen's clothing.

The production of hemp fabric is a complicated process involving many steps, beginning with the cultivation and harvest of hemp plants. Hemp is planted in the third lunar month. After harvesting, the plant is steamed and the bark peeled off. For the steaming process, the hemp is placed on a hot stone and

A scene from a Koguryŏ tomb mural in Jian, China (below) shows the variety of fabric patterns produced during that era. Hansan ramie (above) is still one of Korea's most treasured fabrics.

covered with leaves. Water is poured on the stone to produce steam. The hemp yellows, then the bark is peeled off before cooling. The bark is tied in bundles, soaked in water, dried, then torn from the top into three strands. The resulting hemp fibers are bundled together and placed in water to soak again. Next the fibers are spun into strands and placed in a warm room for five to seven days, covered with a straw mat to retain the heat. This prevents the hemp strands from becoming brittle.

The strands are then boiled in water, rinsed and dried in the sun. The weaver prepares threads of varying thickness, depending on use. One *sae* consists of 80 strands. Five sae are usually used for work clothes, seven sae for regular clothes, and three sae for mourning clothes. After the strands are prepared, the hemp is tied together and dried again, this time in front of a bonfire. Then the threads are wound on a reel. After this process is completed, the thread is placed on the loom and woven into fabric.

In early Korea, the most delicately woven ramie fabric was called *hansan sejŏ*. This fabric, from Hansan in Ch'ungch'ŏngnam-do, was sent as a gift to the court of Tang China by Shilla's King Kyŏngmun (r. 861-875). During the Koryŏ Dynasty, embroidered ramie fabric was

introduced. The making of ramie is similar to the manufacture of hemp fabric. Ramie can be harvested three times a year—in spring, summer and autumn.

During the reign of Chosŏn's King T'aejong (1400-1418), the court promoted the production of silk by establishing sericulture facilities (*chamshil*), instituting a law governing sericulture, and introducing silk-weaving contests. During the reign of King Sŏngjong (1469-1494), when even court ladies participated in silk-weaving contests, sericulture flourished to such an extent that domestically-produced silk replaced imported Chinese silk for court apparel.

Silk-making involved not only the weaving of fabric but also the raising of silkworms, preparation of cocoons, and spinning of thread. The best silk was said to be made from cocoons collected in spring because their thread was longer and thicker than that of autumn cocoons.

After cotton was introduced to Korea during the reign of Koryŏ's King Kongmin, the cotton culture flourished, especially in the Ch'ungch'ŏng, Chŏlla and Kyŏngsang regions. Cotton cloth became so popular that it was used in place of money during a 15th century currency crisis. However, the use of cotton as money was abused when cotton was collected for taxes. In some cases taxes were levied on dead family members. The cloth used to pay these taxes was popularly called *paekkolchingp'o*, "skeleton tax cloth." Taxes levied on common people were so excessive that they were forced to remove cotton padding from their clothing and weave it into cloth. *Sŏch'ongdaep'o*, cloth made from used cotton padding, was coarse and had a dark color. This form of taxation greatly hindered the development of quality cotton.

The production of cotton cloth began with the cultivation of cotton bolls, and involved many steps such as carding to remove seeds and spinning cotton fibers into thread. The finest cloth was made of 15- to 21-ply thread, while cloth for commoners was made with 5- to 8-ply thread.

The care of traditional garments was complicated. Careful washing, patching, stain removal, starching, ironing and storage reflect the fastidiousness and wisdom of Koreans in traditional society.

During the Chosŏn Dynasty, in particular, cleanliness was considered a virtue and much emphasis was placed on appearance. A Chosŏn gentleman could not be seen in an outfit that was not spotlessly clean. Women

had to do much washing, starching and ironing and in the process developed many cleaning agents. The most common detergent, lye, was made by boiling scorched hay, wood and bean skins. It was usually used to wash cotton and hemp clothes. Silk fabrics were cleaned with red bean powder, mung bean powder, the milky water left after rinsing rice, and tofu water.

Clothes were starched to keep their shape, give the fabric shine and to make them more stain resistant. Rice, wheat, potato and buckwheat starches were used. After starching, damp clothes were wrapped in a cloth, placed on the floor and trodden on to remove wrinkles. Before ironing with a hot iron, women placed the clothes on a fulling block and beat them with wooden clubs.

To remove stains, the water left from boiling herbal medicine was best. Grease stains were rubbed out with a cut turnip, and the steam produced from boiling cow's feet was recommended for blood stains. To remove tobacco stains, women rubbed the spot with pear leaves and rinsed in cold water. Ginkgo nut, garlic and turnip juice was recommended for removing mildew, and ginger juice was used for rust stains. These old-fashioned laundry methods still work today. ◆

The production of hemp fabric is a complicated process. Clockwise from below: Bundles of hemp fibers are spun into fine threads which are then woven on a loom. The women of Andong specialize in this time-honored craft.

Ceremonial Dress
and Ornaments

Cho Hyo-soon

During the Chosŏn Dynasty, coming-of-age ceremonies, marriage, funeral and ancestral rites were life's most important milestones. The coming-of-age rites were reserved for aristocratic families, but the other ceremonies were performed by the high-born and commoners.

These four ceremonies were introduced to Korea from China in the late Koryŏ period. Chinese influences were particularly evident in ancestral rites, but Korea developed its own distinct ceremonial procedures, as is evident in the *Exposition of Family Rites* (*Karye chimnam*) compiled by the Chosŏn scholar Kim Chang-saeng (1548-1631) and *Procedures for the Four Ceremonies* (*Sarye p'yŏllam*) of the late Chosŏn period. Attempts were made to adopt Chinese rites directly. However, when Chinese procedures proved too complicated, they were modified to conform to Korean customs and lifestyles.

During the Chosŏn Dynasty when Confucianism was the ruling ideology, the four ceremonies were prescribed by law. The rites became an integral part of daily life, serving as the basis for maintaining order in personal lives and households.

Costumes and ornaments were important to each rite. Color, fabrics, symbols and design followed age-old traditions which also served to maintain order and continuity in Korean life.

The coming-of-age ceremony for young men was called *kwallye*, the "hat rite." In the rite, a young man's long hair was tied in a topknot and placed in an ornamental headpiece, or *kwan*, for the first time. The hairstyle was a sign of manhood. Initiates were dressed in a special silk ensemble consisting of a broad-sleeved robe, or *sagyusam*, with a belt and special shoes.

Royal wedding ceremonies (right) require special costumes, rich in symbolism. Pairs of birds and butterflies symbolize marital love and fidelity.
Coming-of-age rites also require special costumes (lower left).

In the rites of wealthy families, initiates changed costumes three times. However, because of the great cost, some initiates simply wore official uniforms.

The coming-of-age ceremony for girls was called *kyerye*. Most girls went through the ceremony on the morning of their wedding. The initiate's hair was twisted in a bun and fastened with a *pinyŏ*, a long hairpin symbolizing womanhood. The initiate wore a long silk gown.

The marriage ceremony was complicated, involving several ritualized stages. First, a proper match had to be found and the families of the bride and the groom had to agree to the marriage. After both families agreed, the groom's family sent the bride's family a paper stating his year, month, day and hour of birth—the "four pillars," or *saju*.

Calculating from the betrothed couple's saju, the bride's family selected a wedding date and sent it to the groom's family. Once the date was set, the groom's family usually sent a box, or *ham*, containing gifts and a letter confirming the marriage to the bride's family.

The letter of confirmation was considered legal proof of marriage. At the same time, it symbolized a woman's vow to remain faithful to her husband until death and was customarily placed in her coffin at death. Traditional gifts to the bride were lengths of red and blue fabric for the bride's wedding costumes. Blue silk was wrapped in blue paper and tied with red silk thread. Red silk was wrapped in red and tied with blue. Small bags containing cotton bolls and red beans were also placed inside the ham to symbolize wishes for fertility. The ham was usually delivered to the bride's house on the eve of the wedding ceremony by a married male friend of the bridegroom.

The actual marriage ceremony was an all-day affair ending with the newlyweds retiring to the bridal chamber. The marriage ceremony ordinarily took place at the bride's house. The newlyweds went to the bridegroom's house two or three days after the wedding. Sometimes the newly-married couple spent months, or a year at the longest, at the bride's family home before moving to the groom's house. However, three days was the customary stay. Upon arrival at the groom's house, the bride greeted her parents-in-law for the first time in a ceremony called *p'yebaek*, in which she presented them with food, such as dried jujubes, chestnuts, wine and dried beef which she brought from her parents' home.

After three to seven days at the groom's house, the newlyweds returned to the bride's house. The couple spent about three days there paying courtesy calls to the bride's family members and relatives. Then the couple returned to the husband's house to live.

After the first autumn harvest, the new couple again visited the wife's house with newly harvested crops. Depending on the region and family tradition, the couple stayed at the bride's house for up to a year or until their first child was born before moving to the husband's house for good.

For the wedding ceremony itself, the groom wore the black silk hat, or *samo*, worn by officials, and a silk robe, or *tallyŏng*, with a loose belt and felt boots. This was the standard male wedding costume from the time of Chosŏn's King Sukchong (r. 1674-1720).

Regulations concerning wedding garments for royalty and commoners were stipulated in the *Procedures for the Four Ceremonies*. The samo and tallyŏng were originally government officials' uniforms during the late Koryŏ period. For much of the Chosŏn period, they were used as burial garments for civil officials, then during Sukchong's reign, regulations were changed to permit their use as wedding clothes for the general public.

In early times, brides wore a simple white gown called *yŏm-ŭi*. However, as tastes grew more extravagant, brides began to adopt the ceremonial clothing of royalty and the *yangban* elite, such as *hwarot* and *wonsam* topcoats and *tang-ŭi*, a ceremonial jacket with hanging lapels. During the mid- to late Chosŏn period, hwarot and wonsam were the most popular wedding dresses. In particular, the hwarot was the most important and luxurious ceremonial dress worn by princesses. The adoption of this attire by common people satisfied their deep aspirations for social advancement.

Commoners were allowed to wear these clothes for weddings. However, because of their great expense, villagers often prepared one set to be used whenever someone in the village married. Families passed down wedding costumes from generation to generation.

Of the four ceremonies, funerals were conducted with the most formality. Since respect for ancestors was one of Confucianism's basic teachings, every step of a funeral was carried out with the utmost solemnity, especially funerals for one's parents. During the Chosŏn period, great care was taken in the preparation of burial clothes as death was considered not the end of life, but the beginning of a new life

The costumes and accessories of a traditional wedding reflected hopes for a long fertile union. A wooden goose (below) symbolized fidelity in marriage.

in the next world. The funeral process involved a number of steps.

First, male mourners loosened their topknots and donned mourning clothes made of coarse, hand-woven hemp. These clothes were worn loosely with only the interior coat string tied and collars folded. Toward the end of the Chosŏn Dynasty, traditional full dress attire was worn instead of mourning clothes. The left sleeve was folded up for a father's funeral, the right sleeve for a mother's funeral. Women in mourning loosened their hair, removed all ornamental accessories, and wore a white mourning dress. All family members of the deceased took off their quilted socks.

Next came the preparation of the corpse. This process, *sŭpyŏm*, involved bathing the body and dressing it in special clothes made of silk or fine hemp cloth. The shroud, called *mŏnŭng-ot* or *chugŭmae-ot*, was often prepared before death. It was made somewhat larger than regular clothes, and its threads were left untied. This was because thread was believed to connect the present world with the next.

Men's burial clothes included inner and outer jackets (*chŏgori*), inner and outer pants (*paji*), a long white topcoat, and a headpiece. Women's shrouds included inner and outer jackets, bloomers, a skirt (*ch'ima*) and a wonsam topcoat. Cloth wrappings for the face, coverings for the hands, a small pouch in which the fingernail and toenail clippings of the deceased were placed, a cloth to cover the abdomen, socks, two quilts, a sleeping mat and a pillow were also essential. Commoners sometimes dressed the corpse in simple pants and a jacket, or in the deceased's wedding clothes.

Once the corpse was dressed, it was placed in the coffin, and the remaining space was filled with old clothes, paper or straw.

Family members then put on proper mourning clothes (*sangbok*). These garments varied according to the mourner's relationship to the deceased. The quality of the fabric, design and needlework also differed. The oldest son of the deceased wore a hemp hood and an outfit made of coarse hemp with a rope belt. He also wore coarse hemp leggings and straw sandals, and carried a mourning staff. Women traditionally wore white cotton two-piece outfits, with belts, headgear, hairpins made of wood, and straw sandals.

On *sosang*, the first anniversary of the death, mourning clothes were worn for rites honoring the deceased. On the second anniversary of the death, *taesang*, mourning

Coarse hemp mourning clothes symbolized the grief of the deceased's family (top). It was the eldest son's responsibility to carry the spirit tablet of the deceased (above).

clothes were discarded and people returned to their former routine.

During the Chosŏn Dynasty, deceased family members were treated with the same care and respect as living elders. Thus ancestral rites, like funerals, were conducted with the utmost propriety. During the harvest season, people reserved the best grains, fruits and meat for ancestral offerings. Loud talking or laughing was prohibited while food for ancestral rites was being prepared because it would disturb the spirits of the ancestors who enjoyed the food's smell.

There were three basic types of ancestral rites: *ch'arye, kije* and *shije.* Ch'arye was usually performed on special days of the lunar calendar, such as New Year's Day, Taeborŭm, the first full moon, Hanshik, the 105th day after the winter solstice, Tano, the fifth day of the fifth lunar month, Ch'ilsŏk, the seventh day of the seventh lunar month, Ch'usŏk, the Harvest Moon Festival in autumn, Chungyang or Chunggu, the ninth day of the ninth lunar month, and Tongji, the winter solstice. Many families chose to simplify, however, and only performed ch'arye on New Year's Day, Hanshik, Tano and Ch'usŏk.

Kije was performed at midnight on the anniversary of the ancestor's death, beginning the year after taesang. According to tradition, kije was performed for four generations of ancestors.

Myoje, also called shije or *shihyangje,* was performed for five generations of ancestors at their graves, which were usually located together at the family grave site. Although the *Procedures for Four Ceremonies* stipulated that myoje was to be held annually early in the third lunar month, most families performed it in the tenth lunar month in appreciation for an abundant harvest.

When performing ancestral rites, men wore *top'o,* long overcoats, over their hanbok, and black headpieces, except during kije when they still wore hemp mourning clothes. Because women did not participate in ancestral rites in most cases, they did not have any specific clothing for such occasions. Nevertheless, upper-class women wore plain white dresses made of thin silk and women of the lower classes wore plain white or light blue dresses. Since Chosŏn-era women usually wore white or light blue dresses, one can assume that they simply washed their everyday clothes and wore them for these occasions. ◆

Modernizing the Korean Costume

Kum Ki-sook

Integrating the beauty of traditional Korean art and culture into modern life and aesthetics is a task faced by all Korean artists. The dual task of preserving and modernizing traditional art and culture seems at first glance to pose a conflict. But both tasks look to the future of an integrated national aesthetic. Toward this goal, Korean fashion designers are actively integrating the lines and colors of the *hanbok*, Korea's national costume, into modern apparel to create garments with a distinctively Korean character.

Clothing fashions change from one generation to the next, often from one year to the next, and aesthetic sensibilities change as well. The beauty of traditional designs and motifs, which had been ignored for much of the period of Korea's rapid modernization, is now being appreciated anew. Although more modern fabrics and colors are used, today's hanbok follows the basic pattern of the traditional costume, with only slight variations to suit modern tastes and lifestyles. Those who have more classical tastes tend to wear hanbok that faithfully adhere to traditional patterns.

The classic hanbok is a variation on the basic combination of a light blue *chŏgori* top and an indigo *ch'ima* skirt. Traditionally, this color combination was worn by married women and was a favorite not only of common women but also of court ladies. The garment consisted of a small blouse-like top and a puffed skirt, creating a fanciful look and a sil-

A ramie hanbok by Lee Young-hee

houette resembling those of Western petticoat dresses. Popular colors were jade blue, blue mauve and gold. The curves of the sleeve and the chŏgori's front panels are more noticeable because of their contrast with the indigo skirt.

One of the most attractive features of the chŏgori is the fastening sashes, or *korŭm*. Judging from their excessive length, these sashes were clearly designed not only for a practical function but also as a means of enhancing the hanbok's beauty.

Stamping gold leaf decorations on the korŭm was one way of drawing attention to them. The sashes often complemented the color of the chŏgori to increase the attractiveness of the garment.

Hanbok fabric is usually plain to emphasize the wearer's figure and the cut of the dress. The uncluttered expanses of fabric also provide space for ornamentation. Gold stamped flowers on the collar, sashes, cuffs and hem provide a sense of unity to the garment.

Summer costumes which use *maedŭp* knots for buttons, are a modern adaptation. Embroidery on the sleeves, lapels and hem create a feeling of elegance and loftiness. The contrasting colors accent the curves of the sleeves and lapels. Replacing sashes with simple maedŭp enhances the simple elegance of the garment.

The feature of the traditional Korean costume most frequently used in modern fashion design is its curves, especially the curves of the chŏgori lapels and sleeves. In the

Lee Shin-woo (Icinoo) experiments with a traditional patchwork motif in this modernized hanbok(opposite).

**A pants and vest ensemble
by Lee Young-hee**

1980s, modern adaptations of the chŏgori and *paji* (trousers) were popular for the freedom of movement the garments' fullness allowed. Ramie and hemp fabrics in black and white and the three primary colors are most common for summer wear.

The peony pattern, often stamped on wedding garments, is also used in designing Western-style ensembles, as are the bow window and roof tile patterns. Traditional Korean clothing accessories, such as *norigae*, knotted sash pendants, and *pinyŏ*, long, stick-like hairpins, have also been adapted for use with Western fashions.

Fine vertical quilting is a traditional feature that many modern designers are fond of using. The quilted cotton jacket by Lee Shin-woo (Icinoo) creates a feeling of neatness and elegance. The jacket illustrates the simple elegance that is the essence of the traditional hanbok. The traditional Korean aesthetic turns the absence of decoration into decoration and the absence of art into art. Lee Shin-woo also deserves praise for her development of printed fabrics, for her creation of pastel tones that reflect the color of the Korean sky, and for her use of motifs from Koguryŏ frescoes to express characteristic Korean sentiments.

Sol Yoon-hyong is another modern designer who uses traditional Korean design elements, such as the color combinations of patchwork wrapping clothes (*pojagi*) and rainbow stripes (*saektong*). One of Sol's one-piece dresses utilizes the patterns and color combinations of traditional paper boxes. The sleeveless blouse and the addition of plastic over the skirt give the outfit an ultramodern look, despite its strong traditional colors and patterns. The rakishly cocked multicolored cap, which imitates the traditional *chokturi*, provides a humorous touch.

The harmonization of primary colors give Chin Tae-ok's designs a gay intensity. The use of red, indigo, green and scarlet on a yellow background is reminiscent of the traditional bridal costume. The triple layering and straight cut produce a feeling of modern sophistication, as do the geometric lines of red piping along the skirt's hem.

Designer Lee Young-hee updates the traditional Korean costume faithfully and creatively. The vest and trousers which she designed for the 94/95 Fall/Winter collection harmonize Eastern and Western aesthetics. The vest is reminiscent of the traditional Korean vest, or *paeja*. It is worn over a Western-style turtleneck sweater. The silk trousers are print-

ed with a phoenix design. These heterogeneous elements combine to create an unusual look that attracted much attention in the fashion circles of Paris.

The task of modernizing Korea's traditional beauty does not fall on fashion designers alone. We must all take an interest in it. Understanding the aesthetic points of the Korean costume and participating in its modernization are important steps in helping the world better understand Korean culture. ◆

A patchwork dress by Sol Yoon-hyong (below) and a filmy ramie hanbok fastened with a traditional maedŭp *knot by Lee Shin-woo (Icinoo)(left)*

A History of Feminine Adornment

Cheon Wan-kil

The women of the Chosŏn Dynasty began their days before dawn, rising early to wash their faces, comb their hair and dress immaculately before paying their respects at the family shrine, or *sadang*, where ancestral tablets were kept, and bowing to their in-laws. It was imperative for them to dress neatly when they visited the shrine and their in-laws' quarters. They powdered their faces, darkened their eyebrows and made sure their hair was held firmly in place with an ornamental hairpin called *pinyŏ*. An unwashed face or messy hair and clothes were a great discourtesy to ancestors and in-laws. Women had to be careful of their appearance in front of ancestors and in-laws, even their own children, not to mention guests. This process of personal adornment was called *tamjang*.

Women dressed quite differently on special occasions such as marriages or sixtieth birthday celebrations and on outings. They used more white powder and eyebrow ink as well as rouge and colored shadows. Their mode of dress and personal ornaments was also different. Pinyŏ for daily wear were usually 13 centimeters long, but these were exchanged for much longer ones extending up to 30 centimeters. Hairpins were also more lavish.

Simple pendants worn at the closure of the *chŏgori* jacket on ordinary days were replaced by more elaborate ones. On outings, women often carried a small dagger (*changdo*) with an ornamental sheath and a pendant in the shape of a tiger's toe. The pendant was worn as protection against wild beasts and the dagger for many uses including warding off unwanted attention from strange men.

The custom of changing clothes for outings began in the Koguryŏ Kingdom and is still observed by most Koreans today. Decking out in beautiful clothes, or *nongjang*, was not limited to outings. Women also dressed up for feasts and celebrations at home.

During the Chosŏn Dynasty, married couples lived in separate rooms: the wife in the

anbang, the main room of the women's quarters, and the husband in the sarangbang, the main room of the men's quarters. Only on auspicious days did they spend the night together. This restraint and the selection of auspicious days were thought to produce bright, gentle and filial children. Traditionally, men were more experienced in lovemaking, because they visited kisaeng, professional female entertainers, and often kept concubines. A wife had to use all means at her disposal to catch her husband's attentions. Women often lit incense, sprayed themselves with musk and applied seductive makeup after bathing. This process of making oneself attractive is called yŏmjang.

The wife usually took off most of her ornaments before retiring, save for ch'ŏm, a needle-sharp hairpin decorated with gems at one end. Ch'ŏm were used like acupuncture needles in medical emergencies such as when a husband suffered a heart attack or stroke during sex.

Weddings are occasions for finery in all cultures. During the Chosŏn Dynasty, brides' long braids were tied in a chignon for the first time and enhanced with a false hairpiece decorated with a large ribbon. For weddings, brides wore larger pinyŏ, usually 30 centimeters in length, which were shaped like a dragon's head. Normally, dragon-head pinyŏ were reserved for members of the royal family, but

Chosŏn women often wore complicated pendants on outings. A small dagger on this three-piece pendant (opposite) was used for personal protection and decoration. The depiction of a woman arranging her hair by Kim Hong-do (1745-?) reflects Chosŏn styles (above, Seoul National University Museum).

137

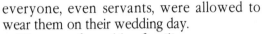

everyone, even servants, were allowed to wear them on their wedding day.

Women of wealthy families wore many different hairpins, including *ttŏlcham*, which were shaped like birds. They also wore magnificent wedding clothes with wide wing-like sleeves. Their makeup was heavy, with white facial powder, dark eyebrow ink and rouge. Virgins traditionally wore a red paper circle on each cheek and on their forehead. Though social status and wealth made some difference, everyone dressed up for their wedding.

The makeup, ornaments, clothes and hairstyle of Chosŏn women varied for each occasion. Dressing appropriately for different occasions was considered basic etiquette. For this reason, a wash basin, a mirror stand and other toiletries such as combs, cosmetics and ornaments were considered essential to every bride.

In traditional Korean society, one's language and behavior also had to match the clothes, personal ornaments and makeup worn on a particular occasion.

How did cosmetics and personal ornaments become a part of Korean culture? Wormwood (*ssuk*) and garlic were the first ingredients Koreans used to enhance their beauty. According to Korea's foundation myth, the mother of Tan-gun, Korea's legendary founder, was originally a female bear who achieved her dream of becoming a human and the wife of the son of the ruler of heaven by eating only wormwood and garlic while remaining in a dark cave for 100 days. Since

Ttŏlcham (above) were used to decorate the hair. They often had moving parts which quivered when the wearer moved. Pinyŏ were long pins used to hold a bun in place. Women from wealthy families often wore pinyŏ decorated with silver cloisonné (below).

ancient times, wormwood and garlic were used to whiten the skin. The legend suggests that the heavenly prince chose a mate who had white skin, enhanced by wormwood, garlic and 100 days out of the sun. Young women of marriageable age have traditionally used wormwood or garlic mixtures on their skin and apply a facial pack of ground garlic mixed with honey to preserve a clear and white complexion.

The Korean people's aesthetic sense is evident in the ancient legend of Pak Hyŏkkŏse, the founder of the Shilla Kingdom, and his wife Aryŏng recorded in the *Memorabilia of the Three Kingdoms* (*Samguk yusa*).

On the first day of the third month in 69 B.C., the heads of the six clans gathered on the banks of the Al River. Sensing the limits of their power, they agreed to unite their six clans and designate a king for the unified country. After this discussion, they climbed a high mountain and looked southward. A strange aura shone over the well called Najŏng at the foot of Mt. Yangsan ... They found a red egg at that spot. From it a handsome boy was born. They bathed him in Tongch'ŏn, the East Spring, and his body shone brilliantly. Birds and beasts danced for joy. The sky and earth trembled and the sun and moon became brighter. Thus the boy was named Hyŏkkŏse, Brightness. People said, "Now that the

Son of Heaven has descended to live among us, we must find him a virtuous queen." That very day a hen-dragon appeared near Aryŏngjŏng, a well in Saryang-ri, and gave birth to a girl from its left rib. The girl had an unusually beautiful body and face, but her lips resembled a chicken's beak. She was taken to Pukch'ŏn, the North Spring in Wŏlsŏng, for a bath whereupon the beak fell off. The spring was then renamed Palch'ŏn, the Eliminating Spring. Pak Hyŏkkŏse became king and made Aryŏng his queen when they both turned 13 in 57 B.C.

What does this legend have to do with the Korean people's concept of beauty and the history of Korean cosmetics and ornaments? Pak Hyŏkkŏse, the first king of a unified nation selected by the heads of six clans, was a man of astonishing good looks, and his bride's body and face were "unusually beautiful." After bathing, Pak's body shone with a brilliant light and Aryŏng become a woman of incomparable beauty. Clearly Koreans believed the ideal leader was both wise and handsome. They also considered fair skin beautiful. That Pak's body shone brilliantly after a bath signifies his skin was extraordinarily white. Both Pak Hyŏkkŏse and Aryŏng became beautiful after bathing. Perhaps this is why Koreans have been devoted to baths for more than 2,000 years. These three beliefs—that beauty signals wise leadership, that fair skin is beautiful and that bathing is a means of personal beautification—are part of the traditional Korean aesthetic.

The importance of physical beauty in the selection of a leader is apparent in the recruitment of hwarang, a troop of handsome young warriors, usually in their mid-teens, organized to supplement the elite units that formed the core of Shilla's military forces. Among the early leaders of the elite force were Nammo and Chunjŏng, two beautiful female recruits who commanded 300 warriors. The two women became jealous of each other, however, and one poisoned the other. After this unfortunate incident, the hwarang became an all-male force. The recruits were handsome young men from the noble class. Records indicate that they wore makeup, dressed in beautiful silk clothing and wore jewelry and elaborate hats. But why did warriors, trained to defend the kingdom, need to be attractive and adorn themselves with ornaments?

As the legend of Pak Hyŏkkŏse and Aryŏng shows, Koreans believed that a beauti-

ful spirit belonged in a beautiful body. The belief that physical beauty, wisdom and courage were interrelated was passed down to the Koryŏ and Chosŏn cultures as well. No matter how old he was, a man of noble character was described as kwan-ok, a term used to refer to a handsome face and a piece of ornamental jade.

Considering the Shilla people's highly developed sense of aesthetics and regular bathing habits, we can assume that their culture encouraged the manufacture and use of cosmetics and ornaments. Shilla women wore wigs decorated with gold, silver, gems, jade and silk in five different colors. Historical records show that the women of Kwanna, one of the independent states that preceded the founding of Koguryŏ, had hair as long as 9 cha, a traditional unit of measure equivalent to 0.33 meters. This sup-ports the theory that long hair was one of the conditions of a beautiful woman during this period. Shilla women's use of wigs reflects their culture's sophisticated aesthetic sense. Shilla wig-making technology was more developed than that of China. Shilla wigs had longer, more beautiful hair than those of Tang China and so became an important export.

In general, Shilla's cosmetics and manufacturing skills were superior to those of China. Shilla wigs were more attractive than those of China for two reasons. First, Koreans traditionally emphasized the importance of clean hair. Hair-washing was an essential part of a woman's basic toilet as well as an important feature of two traditional festivals, Tano, the fifth day of the fifth lunar month when farmers celebrated a lull in the busy farming season, and Yudu, the sixth full moon when Koreans bathed in the clear water of their local stream to drive away evil spirits and impurities. Shilla wigs were also superior because the Shilla people used high-quality hair oil made of camellia seeds, castor beans and rape seed. This hair oil helped maintain black and glossy hair.

The use of white facial powder was also popular during the Shilla period. White powder was widely used until the 1960s to whiten

This celadon rouge case from the 13th century (Pacific Museum) must have been a treasured family heirloom.

This peony-decorated mirrored vanity case dates to 19th century Chosŏn. Such mirrors were considered great luxuries.

the face and camouflage fine wrinkles and small blemishes. One historical record tells of a Buddhist monk from Shilla who in 692 received generous gifts from the Japanese for making facial powder there. From this we can assume that facial powder was widely used in Shilla before 692 but had not yet been developed in Japan.

White facial powder was made from ground rice or other grains such as millet, roasted sea shell powder, white clay or talc. These were mixed with small quantities of ground animal bones. However, these powders did not adhere or spread well on their own. Women had to remove facial hair using a razor, twisted threads that were pulled across the skin, or tweezers. The powder was then mixed with water, spread on the face and left for 20-30 minutes. Women were encouraged to sleep during this time because the production of skin oil and facial movements are limit-

ed during sleep. Despite these complex efforts, however, the powder often did not spread well and the whole process had to be repeated. With the addition of lead, facial powder was much easier to use. The production of lead facial powder was thus a historic event in the development of cosmetics. The discovery of lead's benefits in the manufacture of facial powder appears to have occurred well before Shilla's manufacture techniques were introduced to Japan in 692.

Rouge was also popular in the Shilla Kingdom. The purpose of cosmetics is to enhance good features and camouflage bad features. Koreans traditionally considered young people between the ages of 15 and 16 to be at the height of their beauty and health as girls of that age had cherry-red lips and peach-colored cheeks. Accordingly, rouge was used to color their lips, cheeks and forehead. People who could not afford rouge bit their lips to make them appear redder. People with pale lips were considered weak and sickly, and those with purple lips lecherous. The rouge used to highlight lips and cheeks was made of red flowers.

The Shilla people also used ink to paint their eyebrows. The shape of one's eyebrows has long been important to the Korean people. Thick bushy eyebrows were thought to indicate a violent or lecherous temperament. Thin and soft-looking eyebrows were preferred. For women, half-moon eyebrows were the epitome of beauty. Chosŏn women had ten or more eyebrow models to choose from. *A Composite Guide for the Inner Quarters* (*Kyuhap Ch'ongsŏ*), a Chosŏn-era etiquette guide for women, describes eyebrows resembling mandarin ducks, a small mountain, three mountain peaks, and hooks, among other things, illustrating how important eyebrows were to the traditional view of beauty. Eyebrow ink was so essential to feminine beauty that the Sino-Korean word for it, *pundae*, is synonymous with beautiful women, kisaeng and court ladies.

Early Japanese documents indicate that the Japanese learned to manufacture and apply cosmetics from the Paekche Kingdom. However, there are no records offering specific details about the cosmetics used by the Paekche people. They did, however, maintain the tradition of the Mahan people, who wore their hair long. Paekche men wore their hair up in a topknot called *sangt'u*. Married women braided their hair in two braids, which were fashioned in side buns. Unmarried women wore their hair in two braids tied with long ribbons. A Chinese document states that the Paekche people wore white facial powder but no rouge, in direct contrast to the makeup widely used by Chinese women. The Paekche people preferred light, elegant makeup. The Mahan people were fond of round pieces of jade, which were used to adorn clothes and were bound together in necklaces.

In Paekche, hairstyles, clothing and makeup were indicators of gender and social status. This tradition was also observed by the Koguryŏ people. Koguryŏ courtiers wore silk, gold and silver for official meetings. High-ranking officials wore rectangular headgear called *tugŏn* while lower-ranking officials wore *chŏlp'ung*, a peaked hat made of thin silk. According to the *History of the Later Han*, the Koguryŏ people enjoyed dressing in clean clothes and often gathered for plays and music. They dressed according to their status and profession and also distinguished between daily attire and costumes for special occasions. The Korean *History of the Three Kingdoms* (*Samguk sagi*) describes female dancers and musicians painting rouge circles on their foreheads and coloring their lips and cheeks. Rouge was clearly a mark of certain professions. During the Koguryŏ period, rouge was made of cinnabar. It must have been of high quality, because Koguryŏ's rouge-making technology was envied by the Chinese.

There is substantial evidence that rouge was used by women of all classes. A portrait found on a mural in a tomb in Susan-ri, which is thought to date from the fifth or sixth century, shows a noble woman wearing a crown-like hat and rouge on her cheeks and lips. A female servant depicted on the walls of the Tomb of the Twin Pillars (*Ssangyŏng Ch'ong*), dating from the Koguryŏ period, is also wearing rouge. Both women's eyebrows are augmented with ink.

Koguryŏ relics reveal a variety of hairstyles from that period. In one style, hair from the back of the head is wound around the sides and fastened at the forehead. Another features a chignon low at the back of the head. Others show a portion of the hair left to hang beside each ear with the rest of the hair tied in a low ponytail at the back of the head. ◆

These blue and white porcelain bottles and containers from the late Chosŏn Dynasty were used to store cosmetic oils and powders.

Embroidery and the Lives
of Korean Women

Huh Dong-hwa

Embroidery is the art of thread. The art form developed out of the human desire to enhance the beauty of clothing. It also serves the very practical function of identifying rank or social status. Siberian shamans decorated their ritual costumes with strips of cloth and bird feathers that indicated their social rank and position. Embroidery was also one way human beings, with their limited powers, encountered the Absolute. In each embroidered stitch were prayers, hopes and desires to be fulfilled. Buddhist embroidery represents the epitome of religious sentiment in Korean embroidery. In this way, embroidery is special because it reflects the human desire to embellish and make more beautiful, and at the same time expresses a variety of hopes and desires. It is not surprising that every culture has its own unique embroidery tradition, from Europe's tapestries to the needlework of China, Egypt and Africa.

Korea's embroidery culture encompasses everything from formal costumes to items used in everyday life. Embroidery was used in aristocratic circles and among the common people. Its brilliant and refined colors accented the traditional restraint of everyday life. While it began as the simple piecing together of fabric, embroidery gradually developed into a highly sophisticated form of ornamentation. It had its very public aspects in the worlds of politics, fine arts and intellectual pursuits but was also part of the cloistered lives of women. In fact, it was one of the few ways Korean women could express their aesthetic inspirations and dreams. Needlework allowed women the freedom to express their innermost feelings through bold colors and forms.

Korean embroidery is outstanding for its matching of colors, dyeing techniques and sculptural and tactile qualities. This dynamic form of expression was based upon the individual sense of beauty that flowed through the heart of each woman. It embodied Korea's sense of tradition and the unique qualities of the Korean people. Embroidery's shortcoming—its fragility—has been overcome to a certain extent by the development of preservation techniques and the compilation of documentation related to the art form.

In Korean society, the ability to weave cloth and sew was considered a womanly virtue. It is through women's efforts that embroidery developed as an art form. Long ago, embroidery was considered a fundamental aesthetic and was part of the basic education all women received. It was thought that women could cultivate a noble personality while stitching and could pray, through their needlework, for riches, respect and lives of splendor for their families and themselves. Embroidery was also a way to relieve stress and develop patience and a spirit of service.

Traditionally, embroidery was a complicated process in which a single woman was responsible for picking the mulberry leaves to feed the silkworms, spinning, winding and dyeing thread, and embroidering designs that she designed herself. After many years each woman developed her own style and became an anonymous master in this field. Today we are able to appreciate these hidden artists in their remarkable creations and diverse themes and symbolism. Clearly the history of Korean embroidery tells the story of Korean women's lives.

The earliest forms of Korean embroidery are thought to have been created approximately 10,000 years ago when stone and bone

THE MUSEUM OF EMBROIDERY

Symbols from nature are central to the embroidered screen shown in detail here. A palanquin (opposite) decorated with embroidery and silk tassels (Museum of Korean Embroidery).

needles were first used. In other words, embroidery naturally developed when people began to sew fabric together with thread. All art originates in human needs. At times art is used for incantatory purposes, as an expression of social status or for practical purposes. Art changes and develops in response to regional and social differences. The development of embroidery as an art form was closely linked to the development of thread, and as fabrics developed, embroidery evolved from a means of patching or mending to the exquisite art form we know today.

Unfortunately, ancient examples of Korean embroidery have yet to be unearthed. We can only guess at what early embroidery was like from brief descriptions found in ancient reference texts. According to the Qin Chinese *History of the Three Kingdoms* and the *History of the Later Han* hemp and mulberry trees were being cultivated and silkworms raised in contemporary Korea. The *History of the Three Kingdoms* noted that the Puyŏ people, a tribal group active in the region of the Sungari river basin in Manchuria around the second century B.C., favored white clothing and clothes made of unpatterned and patterned silk, embroidered silk, and woven fabric made from animal fur.

As Korea developed from a collection of tribal states into a society ruled by a privileged class, a dynastic system was founded. The royal family and aristocrats held positions of status and economic power and ruled the common people, who were producers. The royal family and aristocrats used their clothing to symbolize their rank. Rigid dress codes permitted them to

embellish their clothes with gold, silver and embroidery, while the common people were denied this privilege. Embroidery became an important part of all ornamented costumes. The demand by the privileged classes for needlework encouraged the development of a variety of techniques and styles of embroidery.

Actual embroidered pieces from the Koguryŏ Kingdom have yet to be discovered. However, remnants of murals found in old tombs depict costumes from this era and suggest that Koguryŏ also enjoyed a rich embroidery culture. One such mural, dating from the end of the fourth century or the early fifth century, depicts costumes made of colored silk. Chinese histories describe the Koguryŏ people wearing hats made from materials akin to white, blue and sheer silk. They also wore formal costumes made of embroidered and patterned silk. The Chinese *History of the Three Kingdoms* contains a contemporary scholar's description of Koguryŏ costumes: "Members of the Koguryŏ court wore embroidered clothes with gold and silk ornamentation when attending official ceremonies." We can infer from this that embroidered clothing was commonly worn by members of the upper class in Koguryŏ.

The Paekche Kingdom was known for its elegant culture. It came into contact with Chinese culture later and more gradually than Koguryŏ. According to the Chinese *History of the Three Kingdoms*, "On an auspicious day in early May, [officials] held their morning meeting. They wore purple clothes with wide sleeves over blue pants. Their hats were decorated with flowers

143

and birds embroidered in gold. The outfit was completed with leather belts and shoes."

It is difficult to know what role embroidery played during the Shilla Kingdom. Among the artifacts recovered from Kyŏngju's Tomb of the Heavenly Horse in 1973 was clothing fabric embroidered with gold thread. However, we have no actual examples of Shilla embroidery. In the Korean *History of the Three Kingdoms* (*Samguk sagi*), compiled in 1145, and other historical records, references are made to Shilla's embroidery. As early as the rule of King Soji (479-500), common people were using embroidered brocade. In 650 Queen Chindŏk (r. 647-654) embroidered a poem praising the Tang emperor as a gift for the emperor. The queen embroidered over 100 Chinese ideograms herself, suggesting the importance of embroidery in her kingdom.

The Three Kingdoms saw the flourishing of Korea's traditional embroidery. During this time nature was the predominant influence on needlework designs. Official costumes were adorned with images of clouds, magical herbs, bamboo and other objects from nature. Abstract geometrical designs were also introduced at this time.

During the Three Kingdoms period, Japan absorbed a great deal from Korea's material and intellectual culture. Embroidery was no exception. Historical records indicate that Paekche embroidery techniques were transmitted to Japan around 340. This is confirmed in an embroidered curtain, now a Japanese national treasure. The curtain is said to be based on a picture drawn by Kasŏil of Koguryŏ, and the figures depicted on the curtain are dressed much like figures in Koguryŏ wall paintings. Originally the curtain was three meters square but part of it has been lost.

By 668, Shilla had conquered Paekche and Koguryŏ to form the first unified state on the peninsula. Not only did Shilla expand its territory, it also enjoyed new wealth and could support an aristocratic class that lived a life of ease and extravagance. Goods and clothing styles from Tang China were the fashion. The simple and unrestrained tastes of the Shilla people were replaced by glory and splendor. The central government was forced to issue restrictions on extravagant lifestyles more than once. In one ban on conspicuous consumption issued by King Hŭngdŏk (r. 826-836) in 834, everyday necessities such as fabric and houses were regulated according to hereditary status based on Shilla's bone-rank system. Regulations were also enacted on the use of embroidered silk, high-quality fabrics and embroidered screens. Women of the highest rank at that time, *chin-gol*, were forbidden from wearing wool and embroidered or patterned silk.

Embroidery was used in new ways during this period. While it was most commonly used on clothing, embroidery was also used to decorate palanquins, various vessels, fans and common household items. A historical record describing court entertainment in 807, during the reign of King Aejang, tells of dancers in blue costumes, musicians in red and singers in clothing decorated with painted pictures holding embroidered fans.

In Unified Shilla, Buddhism was firmly established as the state religion. Buddhist culture and Buddhist embroidery flourished as a result. The wife of King Chŏnggang (r. 886-887) embroidered an image of the Buddha in memory of her hus-

band's deceased parents. Ch'oe Ch'i-won, esteemed scholar-official and writer, praised her work this way: "This piece of dyed and embroidered fabric appears to be suspended like a shimmering cloud high in the air. The virtue exemplified in this effort shines blindingly." Wonhae, a Buddhist nun famous for her painting and embroidery, assisted in this work. Her embroidery skills must have been magnificent, because the Koryŏ king Myŏngjong (r. 1170-1197) is said to have worshiped before a portrait of the Shilla monarch Hŏn-gang (r. 875-886) embroidered by Wonhae.

Buddhism remained the state religion during the Koryŏ Dynasty. Buddhism was an intimate part of the lives of the people and a major influence on embroidery. Only a few embroidered works from the Koryŏ period have survived. All are based on Buddhist themes.

Aristocratic extravagance was a serious problem during the Koryŏ Dynasty. Monarchs were forced to issue edicts regulating consumption on numerous occasions. In 1043, during the reign of Chŏngjong, a royal order was issued prohibiting anyone living outside the capital of Kaesŏng from wearing embroidered dragon or phoenix designs or gold leaf on their clothes. In 1144, King Injong decreed that "extravagant practices, embroidered silk clothing and vessels made of gold or jade will be strictly regulated." Yet the aristocrats do not appear to have changed their habits. The trend toward extravagant lifestyles suggests that the upper classes were dedicated to the pursuit of pleasure. Elaborate and highly sophisticated embroidery on clothing was a sign of this trend.

In *An Illustrated Account of Koryŏ*, Xu Jing, a 12th century envoy from Song China, describes the embroidery used to decorate ceremonial objects. According to Xu, guards carried fans embroidered with dragons and flower patterns. Xu describes numerous types of ceremonial fans including the *pallisŏn*, a fan decorated with two dangling pieces of red silk with a mythical horned animal embroidered in its center. These fans were carried by the royal guards when the king went on royal excursions. The guards also carried silk curtains embroidered with figures of ducks and lotus blossoms to shelter the king during outdoor performances.

Embroidery skills were so developed during Koryŏ that a new art form, *sudo*, embroidered "paintings," was created to satisfy the demand for embroidered works. These "paintings" varied in composition, size, patterns and materials. A masterpiece in this genre is *Sagye pungyŏngdo*.

Embroidery also flourished at Buddhist temples. Several embroidered surplices have survived from the Koryŏ Dynasty. One worn by the state preceptor, Taegak (1055-1101), a Buddhist master and fourth prince of King Munjong, and an embroidered altar cover with a dragon design are on display at Sŏnamsa Temple in Chŏllanam-do province. The Chŏnju Municipal Museum in Chŏllabuk-do province is home to an embroidered sutra cover from the Koryŏ period.

During the Koryŏ Dynasty, women appear to have enjoyed a great deal of freedom. It was common for women of all classes to visit temples. They also had the right of inheritance. Daughters and sons received equal shares of inherited property, providing women with economic security they did not enjoy under other regimes. If a woman had three or more sons who passed the state examinations, she was awarded 30 sacks of rice. In addition, widows could remarry, even if they were from the upper class. Women married to members of the *sŏnbi* gentleman-scholar elite or officials were expected to play an active role in securing their husbands' promotions. Wives often approached high officials to ask for their help. Yet these strong-willed women were objects of criticism during the Chosŏn Dynasty, which took over from Koryŏ in 1392.

The *Administrative Code of Chosŏn* (*Chosŏn kyŏngguk-chŏn*) of the Chosŏn Dynasty, which defined the structure and function of government, forbade women of the *yangban* elite from stepping beyond the four gates of the capital of Seoul for picnics and from visiting Buddhist temples. A woman was only accorded social status through her husband's position. The positions of royal concubines and the wives of high officials were strictly regulated, and when her husband died, a woman lost her social status if she remarried.

The lives of Chosŏn women in general were narrowly circumscribed, confined to household tasks, especially those that kept them inside their homes. Women were legally prohibited from looking at men who were not family and could not leave their homes without their husbands' permission. In order to avoid men's eyes when they did leave home, women rode in palanquins or, if they were from the upper class, wore a thin black hood that covered the head and face. Women from the lower classes wore a long cape-like garment that covered them from head to toe. These strict rules extended into life in the home. Men and women lived in separate quarters, and women were not allowed to enter the men's quarters.

Women did not receive formal education. Women with an intellectual bent who were daughters of sŏnbi households sometimes learned to read and write from their grandfathers or fathers or learned over the shoulders of their brothers when they received their lessons. Poetry, writing and painting were strictly prohibited for women. *Kisaeng*, professional entertainers who were generally from the lower classes, received training in some of the arts and letters in order to entertain their male patrons.

A few women did leave outstanding calligraphy, painting and literary works behind. But they were exceptions. Fewer than 20 are known to history. Among the most prominent were the daughters of sŏnbi households such as Shin Saimdang (1504-1551) and Hŏ Nansŏrhŏn (1563-1589) along with the kisaengs Yi Mae-ch'ang, Ch'uk Hyang and Hwang Chin-i.

The common theme that runs through the poetry and painting of Chosŏn women is the writer's surrounding environment. The outside world was a forbidden world. Women had no experiences of nature and so produced few landscape paintings or poems dealing with the outside world. Shin Saimdang painted objects from the garden—birds, flowers, insects and the "Four Gentlemen" (plum blossoms, orchids, chrysanthemums and

An embroidered wrapping cloth (Museum of Korean Embroidery)

bamboo), which were classic themes during the Chosŏn Dynasty. Her themes and subjects were quite varied. Song Si-yŏl, the eminent Confucianist and scholar-official (1607-1689), was the first to introduce Shin Saimdang's mastery of flower and insect paintings to the world. Many anonymous paintings of this genre are thought to be the work of Shin Saimdang. She was also an outstanding embroiderer. An eight-panel black silk screen on which she embroidered flowers, butterflies and other insects is in the collection of the Dong-a University Museum.

My home is one thousand li away
over mountains one upon another.
But I yearn to go back day and night,
in sleep or awake.
The solitary moon over
Hansongjŏng pavilion
A streak of wind past Kyŏngp'odae beach,
Seagulls scatter from the sand
and again gather together.
Fishing boats sail in and out on the sea.
When could I ever again tread
the path to Kangnŭng
To sit beside my mother and sew with her.
(Kim Huran, "Shin Saimdang: Perfect Woman and Artist,"

Shin Saimdang is remembered today not because of her own artistic achievements but because she was the mother of Korea's most illustrious Confucian scholar, Yi I (Yulgok). She was a model daughter, daughter-in-law, wife, housekeeper and mother. Yet, according to her son, there were times when she asked a servant girl to play the kayagŭm and wept as she listened.

The work and life of poet Hŏ Nansŏrhŏn (1563-1589) demonstrate even more clearly the hardships of a talented woman during the Chosŏn Dynasty. The titles of her poems—"Lotus Pond" and "Moonlight"—tell of the cloistered life she led. She wrote virtually nothing about a woman's happiness. Her works are filled with sorrow and the frustration of women who suffered. The following poem, entitled "Poor Woman," talks of a woman's loneliness as she threads her needle on a cold winter night.

She is not bad looking,
Her sewing and weaving are good;
But she was born in a poor family,
So the matchmakers all ignore her.

Through the night she weaves without rest.
Ppi-gŏk, ppi-gŏk the loom creaks
unsympathetically.
She has woven one bolt of cloth,
It's for the neighbor girl when she marries.

Till her fingers are stiff with cold,
She cuts the cloth with scissors
To make dresses for other girls' weddings
But year after year she keeps to her empty room.
(translated by Suzanna Oh)

Hŏ had a difficult marriage and personal life. Her husband was unfaithful, she lost her two children at an early age, her father and brothers were forced into political exile, and she died at the age of 27. Still she managed to write despite the many hardships she faced. Before she died she is said to have burned a roomful of poetry manuscripts.

The kisaeng Ch'uk Hyang was renowned for her paintings of bamboo and famous enough to merit praise on her family's ancestral tablet, a rare feat for a woman. Born to a humble family, she used her inborn talents and profession to engage in sophisticated, intellectual conversations with scholars. Among the thousands of kisaeng active during the Chosŏn Dynasty, she was the one recognized by the contemporary literary community. According to the *Administrative Code of Chosŏn*, kisaeng were exempt from restrictions on clothing and accessories and the strict rules prohibiting contact between men and women.

While women were responsible for seeing to their family's basic necessities in the areas of food, clothing and housing, they were forbidden from participating in public life. Aside from a few women who had opportunities for intellectual pursuits, the only outlet for creative expression was needlework. For example, the embroidery of fans was an art form developed almost entirely by women.

Most extant examples of traditional embroidery come from the Chosŏn Dynasty. Of these, the great majority is from the latter part of this era. By its very nature, embroidery is extremely difficult to preserve and restore. Much of Korea's embroidery was lost during invasions, wars or natural disasters such as fires. Thus most extant works are from the latter part of the Chosŏn Dynasty.

At the beginning of the Chosŏn Dynasty only the upper-class yangban families could afford to make or own embroidery, but by the end of the period the art form had spread throughout society. The market for embroidery had grown. Not only did the yangban's numbers increase as people bought into the class after it was decimated by invasions and internal uprisings, but the newly wealthy merchant class became an important presence, eager to buy the trappings of the Chosŏn elite.

In 1454, during the reign of King Tanjong, a dress code that required embroidered insignia indicating court rank on the back and chest of official uniforms was instituted. Round insignia were worn by members of the royal family. They were decorated with images of mythical beasts thought to have divine powers. Civil officials wore insignia decorated with birds, which symbolized the literary arts, while military officials wore images of beasts, which symbolized the martial arts. The system was revised on several occasions until 1871, when a crane design was uniformly adopted as the symbol of civil officials and a tiger for military officials.

The court's embroidery needs were served by the *Subang*, an embroidery workshop operating within the palace walls. Court maids under the age of ten were selected for training as embroidery specialists. They spent their lives at the craft and created works of unparalleled skill. These women served all the embroidery needs of the royal household, from costumes to everyday necessities. Most of their work remains anonymous. Yet it embodies the essence of traditional Korean art. The royal embroidery workshop also employed dye specialists who prepared thread and fabric. The dedication and skill of the craftswomen and dye specialists of the Subang produced the magnificent works we enjoy today.

The embroidery of the common people was less sophisticated but no less impressive in form and content. These works often portrayed scenes from daily life or nature. Their simplicity and honesty no doubt influenced the folk paintings of this era.

Embroidery was an essential art form for Chosŏn women. Young women often hired a seamstress to teach them embroidery before their wedding in order that they might prepare suitable gifts for their in-laws.

Embroidery reached its pinnacle during the Chosŏn era and began to decline after Japanese colonization and the influx of Western culture in the 20th century. Young Korean women studied embroidery in school during the Japanese occupation but only Japanese techniques and style. As a result, the traditional primary colors were replaced by neutral tones. Thread also changed, from the traditional twisted silk thread to untwisted thread.

The use of embroidery also changed during this period. In traditional society, embroidery had generally been used on clothing or to embellish everyday items, but during the Occupation period the emphasis was on the creation of works of art. The tradition of young women of marriageable age learn-

Butterflies (left) and pairs of birds (right) symbolize marital love and fidelity in embroidered screens and costumes. Below, an embroidered Buddhist screen (Museum of Korean Embroidery).

ing to embroider and preparing gifts for their in-laws did continue, however.

After Korea's liberation in 1945, Western culture took the country by storm. Traditional embroidery was influenced by French styles and underwent another series of changes. Today embroidery is taught to girls for one semester, at most, in middle or high school, but the course focuses on Western techniques and styles. Traditional embroidery has nearly been lost in the modern era, but as interest in things Korean increased during the 1970s, a movement to revive and systematize the study of traditional embroidery was begun. ◆

Clothes, Ornaments and the Artisans Who Make Them

Kim Yoo-kyung

Throughout their country's long history, the Korean people have created and worn clothes that fit their physical and cultural characteristics. Their traditional costumes clearly reflect the Korean national character, the traditional love of bright, clean lines, and the climatic conditions of the Korean peninsula.

The traditional costume most familiar to us today is the *hanbok*. Its colors, lines and silhouette have changed with Korean society. Today Korean clothing conforms to modern tastes and yet remains firmly rooted in tradition. In this article, we examine the development of Korea's unique sartorial tradition and how traditional fabrics and costumes are made and worn today.

Women of the Chosŏn Dynasty were ingenious when it came to enhancing the beauty of their clothing, hair and general appearance. Among their many ornaments were *pinyŏ*, sticklike hairpins often decorated with dragon heads or jade flowers, bright *taenggi* hair ribbons, and rings made of amber, agate or jade. Perhaps most varied are the *norigae* pendants hung from the sashes of jackets or breast bands of skirts. The pendants usually consisted of decorative knots known as *maedŭp*, colorful tassels and tiny objects, such as glass bottles, symbolic animals and flowers, or ornamental daggers. Originally used to protect a woman's chastity, these tiny knives became another form of personal adornment.

No traditional costume would be complete without *pŏsŏn*, white "boot-socks" padded with cotton for warmth and comfort, and *kkotshin*, intricately embroidered leather shoes. These time-honored accouterments along with *top'o* robes, symbols of traditional male dignity still worn by the conservative clans of the Andong region, demonstrate the beauty and wisdom of Korea's traditional costumes and ornaments.

Hwang Son-bi, a maker of shaman costumes, Pak Yong-ki, a maker of ornamental knives, and Hwang Hae-bong, a maker of flower shoes (left to right)

Ch'ŏne

Ch'ungmu, on the southern coast of Kyŏngsangnam-do province, has long been famous for its quilting. Nowhere is the beauty of this tradition more evident than the Ch'ungmu quilted baby carrier, or *ch'ŏne*. The baby carrier, a coverlet used to carry a baby on one's back, is unique for the brilliant contrast between its finely quilted black background and bright pink or red details.

First, the outer covers, one black and one red or pink, are sewn together, then a layer of cotton wadding is applied and carefully quilted in tiny stitches. The baby carrier is embroidered with auspicious peony or bat motifs, and a bright border of pink or red is applied along the edges. At the top of the baby carrier, which is folded over to support the infant's head, a strip of white quilted fabric is applied, much like the crisp white collar on a traditional hanbok.

While this might seem sufficiently flamboyant, the Ch'ungmu chŏne goes one step further: at the center of the back, just below the baby's head, an ornamental rear apron, or *husu*, is attached. The husu is a rectangular piece of red quilted fabric covered with intricate embroidery depicting the ten longevity symbols (*shipchangsaeng*). The edges of the rectangle are finished in fine embroidery and the corners are decorated with tassels of bright thread, often in the five basic colors representing the five elements forming all cosmic matter. The husu is only used on special occasions—for example, a baby's first outing, first birthday or other important events.

In the olden days, women made their baby carriers by hand at home, but today the tradition is being carried on by one woman, Yi Chŏng-nyŏn, a former embroidery teacher who runs a quilt shop in downtown Ch'ungmu. The ch'ŏne require such careful stitching, she only makes one or two each year. In fact, she has only made about two dozen in her career.

Ornamental Knives

Hardly threatening, *changdo*, the small ornamental knives generally worn as pendants by upper-class women dur-

ing the Chosŏn Dynasty, are tiny treasures, miniature works of art. Still, it makes one wonder: Where else in the world do ordinary women carry knives as fashion accessories?

Of course, there is more to fashion than appearances. Chosŏn women chose to carry knives, a universal symbol that transcends sex, for a reason. Chastity was of the utmost importance to women during that era and, although the carefully crafted knives were hardly savage weapons, their beauty did not detract from their effectiveness.

In modern society, the changdo is little more than a fashion accessory, but it was once a powerful symbol of traditional values and the Confucian spirit, with a history of several thousand years. While the *ch'ilchido* ("seven-branched") knife manufactured by Paekche craftsmen in 369 is beautiful and mysterious, ornamental knives from fifth-sixth century Kaya and intricate gold daggers and sheaths found on ceremonial belts in Shilla tombs dating to the seventh and eighth centuries represent the epitome in decorative knives. The Kaya knife consists of two large knives with four smaller knives, each measuring 15 centimeters across and 20 centimeters in length, attached to the sheath. This knife may well be the archetype for the Chosŏn changdo.

Changdo attached to gold ceremonial belts from a somewhat later period of Shilla appear to have been used for decoration, much like the jade commas and gold fish so often found on such belts. In the Koryŏ Dynasty, government officials

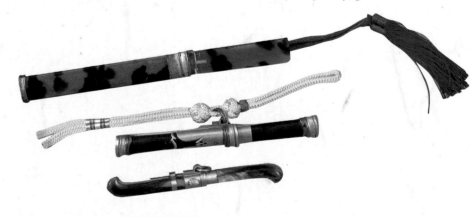

A ch'ŏne *baby carrier (left) from Ch'ungmu and ornamental knives from the Chosŏn Dynasty (above)*

149

carried two small daggers with their calligraphy brush. The changdo thus came to be associated with artistic and literary pursuits. Women soon began to wear them as chest pendants reflecting social stature and breeding.

Pak Yong-gi, designated a "human cultural asset" in the field of changdo-making, lives in Kwangyang, Chŏllanam-do province, part of the territory of the Paekche Kingdom. Through his dedication and expertise, he carries on the Paekche changdo tradition. Kwangyang has long been famous for its iron and gold as well as its many blacksmiths skilled in the smelting of these metals, so it is hardly a coincidence that the Kwangyang Iron and Steel Mill is located there today. Pak makes some 500 different kinds of changdo, using a variety of precious metals, such as gold and silver, as well as jade, mother-of-pearl and horn, to decorate their sheaths.

Pak took up his craft at the age of 17. When making a changdo, the tempering of the blade is critical. Too hard and it will break; too soft and it will bend. It takes a carefully trained craftsman with extensive experience to make a perfect knife.

Pak hones the blade with meticulous skill, making certain it is perfectly straight and unmarked. Changdo blades vary from 5 centimeters to 30 centimeters in length. Determining the correct proportions for the blade and handle is one of the craftsman's most important tasks. And fitting the sheath to the knife with such precision that only a single sheet of paper fits between them is another measure of the craftsman's skill.

"It's all a matter of experience. It can't

be learned any other way. You have to keep an eye on the steel as it heats in the fire. At just the right moment you plunge it into a vat of water mixed with yellow mud. It takes more than 200 different tools to make a single knife," Pak explains.

Flower Shoes

There is nothing so lovely as an elaborately embroidered *kkotshin*, literally a "flower shoe," peeking out from the flowing skirt of a hanbok. In traditional society, young girls waited breathlessly for their fathers to return from market, hoping they would bring a pair of kkotshin, boat-like leather shoes embroidered with floral designs. Even today kkotshin conjure up images of joyful holidays and young brides dressed in colorful bridal outfits.

The kkotshin tradition is carried on by a family in Seoul. The family has dedicated itself to the craft for five generations. The late Hwang Han-gap, of the third generation, made several pairs of these shoes for King Kojong of the Chosŏn Dynasty to wear during royal ancestral rites. Hwang's son and grandsons have carried on the tradition ever since.

Rubber shoes were introduced in the 1920s, but before they became popular, leather shoes were the preferred footwear. The late Hwang said that in the old days he was so busy at the end of the year, before the New Year's celebration, that he often had no time to sleep. Photographs from the final days of Chosŏn show peddlers seated behind piles of leather shoes on straw mats in the market. And beside these peddlers sit boys, shod in straw shoes, selling what look like sashes and hair ties.

After rubber shoes became popular in the 1930s, kkotshin craftsmen had little work. It wasn't until Koreans developed a renewed taste for the traditional that Hwang Hae-bong, of the fifth generation of the Hwang shoemakers, took up the business again. He learned the skill in his twenties, following in the footsteps of his grandfather who had been designated a "human cultural asset" in the field. Today he completes several dozens of pairs each month.

"The kkotshin's charm lies in its graceful lines and the way it turns up at the toe. There is no right or left foot at first, but the shoes mold to the feet after some wear. It takes seventy-four steps to complete one shoe. There's the embroidery, the preparation of the glue and the lining. And then there's getting all the materials together. I still have some wild boar needles. I've tried to find more, but I haven't found any."

Kkotshin are usually decorated with embroidered plum blossoms, peonies or the ten longevity symbols. The sole is made of cow leather. The quality of the shoe is determined by its stitching. The threads are left unknotted on the inside of the toes and heel so the wearer may adjust the stitching as necessary.

Hwang notes one important change in modern times: Feet have gotten larger. Visit any museum and you will see tiny leather, bronze and silk shoes worn by Princess Tŏkhye and other well-heeled personages of the Chosŏn Kingdom.

References to kkotshin are found in historical records from the Chosŏn Dynasty. One tells the sad tale of Queen Shin, wife of King Yŏnsan-gun (r. 1494-1506). The queen was a kind woman, unlike her brutal husband, but she was deposed and forced from the palace

when Yŏnsan-gun's half-brother took over the throne in 1506. Her embroidered shoes kept slipping off as she escaped the palace at the crack of dawn, so she finally ripped the silk coverings off and used them to tie the shoes to her feet.

Padded Socks

The crisp white line of a padded sock, or *pŏsŏn*, is essential to the overall effect of the traditional hanbok. It hardly shows, but the pŏsŏn is its most charming and effective when seen on a carefully upturned ankle in the stately Buddhist nun's dance.

Pŏsŏn are an important part of everyday life as well. They add to the beauty of the hanbok, and the quality of their stitching reflects on the class background of their wearer.

The paper pattern used to make a well-fitting pŏsŏn was an essential feature of every woman's trousseau in traditional society. In fact, the well-bred woman's trousseau included a special cloth bag to hold her pŏsŏn pattern, and careful attention was taken to make the pattern itself as pretty as possible. The paper patterns of court ladies, known for their elegance, became models for all paper patterns. The Bridal Pŏsŏn Shop in Seoul's Ch'ŏngjin-dong has a collection of some 20 different pŏsŏn patterns obtained from women of the Chosŏn court.

Pŏsŏn are made of four layers of white cotton fabric between which thin layers of cotton wadding are quilted. Each time the pŏsŏn are washed, the wadding must be removed and requilted. The sewing and washing of pŏsŏn were perpetual tasks for all Korean women just a generation ago. Children's pŏsŏn were often adorned with embroidery along the instep or tassels at the toe. The pŏsŏn of women from respectable families were expected to fit perfectly and often took as much effort to put on as the old Western-style corsets.

With the growing popularity of Western-style clothing over the last several decades, pŏsŏn have fallen out of favor. Gone are the days when a young bride had dozens of pairs made for her trousseau. Shops specializing in pŏsŏn-making all closed by the end of the 1980s, and most of the factories manufacturing the rubber shoes worn with pŏsŏn closed in the 1990s. Pŏsŏn-making has become a minor cottage industry, and the old pŏsŏn shops are a thing of the past. Still, pŏsŏn live on because connoisseurs of traditional fashion recognize the importance and charm of the quilted socks.

Karakchi

Like changdo, *karakchi* rings were more than simple decorations—they often symbolized self-defense to the traditional Korean woman. At first glance, they appear to be simple feminine adornments, but in the past they sometimes proved to be lethal.

Karakchi come in pairs. One is worn on each hand, and when the two hands are clasped, the rings lock together. Paradoxically, these rings are always worn with the most elaborate attire.

The most dramatic example of their power was an incident during the Japanese invasion of Korea in the late 16th century. Non-gae, a renowned *kisaeng* (female entertainer) in the town of Chinju on the southern coast, used her karakchi to kill a Japanese general in the defense of Chinju Fortress. She lured the amorous invader to a cliff above the Namgang River, embraced him and dived into the water with her rings locked together.

Non-gae's story has been passed down in poetry, song, dance and stories and remains very much alive in the hearts of the people of Chinju. Visit Chinju Fortress where Non-gae dived off the cliff and the locals will be happy to describe how the kisaeng locked her arms around the evil Japanese general and how Chosŏn sailors beat him with their oars as he floated down the river. The rock from which Non-gae jumped is a favorite photo opportunity for tourists, young and old.

In the shamanic *salp'uri* dance as performed by the Chinju master, Kim Su-ak, there is an act called "For Non-gae," in which Kim wears many rings. According to legend, Non-gae wore a ring on every finger so she would not lose her grip on the Japanese general. Practically speaking, it seems unlikely that a 19-year old girl like Non-gae could carry a full-grown man to his death, but clearly the rings represent the power of the young woman's will. No doubt her rings were made of metal, not the easily broken jade as so many karakchi are.

Non-gae and karakchi remind all Koreans of the beauty and strong will of the ideal Korean woman. Thanks to Non-gae, the ring was much more than a fashion accessory. Today we find many silver and jade rings in the antique markets of Insa-dong and Chang-anp'yŏng in Seoul, reminders of this remarkable tradition.

Gold Leaf Appliqué

In Seoul's Tapshimni lives a family that is carrying on the gold leaf appliqué tradition for a fourth generation. The family of Kim Tŏk-hwan has been applying gold leaf to fine garments for more than 100 years.

"My great-grandfather was a purchasing agent for the royal court in the final years of the Chosŏn Dynasty. He often had trouble finding enough gold brocade for large court ceremonies. The boats or caravans carrying the fabric he had ordered from China were sometimes late, so he decided that it would be easier to manufacture it here in Korea. I'm the fourth generation of Kims to

make gold leaf appliqué fabric."

The gold appliqué is applied with woodblocks carved from finely grained pear tree wood in more than 100 patterns: Chinese ideographs with auspicious meanings, pomegranates, gourd-shaped bottles, "heavenly" peaches, flowers, phoenixes and dragons. In fact, the patterns are so detailed, there are even male *and* female phoenixes.

Gold leaf appliqué is a complicated craft. One must know not only what thickness of glue to prepare for each fabric but also the elaborate rules governing the use of different patterns on different garments. Poor judgment can produce truly vulgar results. One does not learn what kind of pattern to use, where or how, in a single afternoon. "Just a few decades ago, old women

from aristocratic families brought in full court garments and asked me to do this and that," Kim recalls. "They often told me the stories behind the clothes, but nowadays, people think money buys everything. They think you can stick a dragon, a symbol reserved for the king, on anything! And I don't get anyone bringing in old court clothes. I guess the well-bred ladies have all died."

Every wall of Kim's house is covered with hair ribbons, skirts, court robes, ceremonial jackets and traditional black silk hats, all carefully appliquéd with imitation gold made of tin and copper. Garments appliquéd in real gold can be prohibitively expensive. A 2-meter hair tie used in wedding ceremonies requires about one-half tael (over six ounces) of gold.

Top'o

The men's hanbok is a classic garment adding to the dignity and style of its wearer. Whenever there is an important family ceremony in the old *yangban* households of the Andong area, particularly those of the Neo-Confucian scholar-officials Yi Hwang or Yu Sŏng-nyong, the men of the family wear *top'o*, the most distinguished version of the man's hanbok. In fact, Andong is the place to go if you want to see hanbok as they were traditionally worn.

The top'o is like the *turumagi* overcoat except its sleeves are wider, it has an extra layer of fabric in the back, and it is usually made of fine Andong hemp cloth.

I realized just how dignified and reserved Andong men are when I attended an ancestral memorial rite held at the home of

the direct descendent of Yi Hwang on October 26, 1979, the day President Park Chung-hee was assassinated. All the men of the family gathered, visiting the ancestral grave site and performing the many complicated ceremonies. Every one of them was dressed in a top'o and turumagi and carried a short walking staff. They have been wearing the same outfit for generations. The few gentlemen not dressed in the traditional attire hung back and did not participate in the solemn rites. There wasn't a single woman in sight, not even the women of Yi Hwang's immediate descendants. It wasn't until the rites were finished and the participants had sat down for a drink of wine left from the ceremonies that one of the men said, "What's this I hear about the president dying?"

I went to another ancestral memorial rite held at the family home of Yu Sŏng-nyong in 1992. The porch of the inner-

Men dressed in hemp top'o attend an ancestral rite in Andong.

most building was covered with bronze ritual utensils. Women were piling small ceremonial tables with food, and the men of the clan, dressed in the traditional top'o, turumagi and ceremonial hats, were waiting around the outer men's quarters.

I once heard a telling story about the Yu clan from Lieutenant Colonel Yi Won-sŭng who served in the Andong area in 1990. During a visit to the Yu clan's home, Yi pointed out an error in the display of a military artifacts related to the revered Yu. A few days later two dozen of the older members of the Yu clan invited Yi to the family shrine and asked him to write an article on Yu's military philosophy. "It has been 400 years since our ancestor Yu Sŏng-nyong wrote his wartime memoir, *A Record of Penitence and Warning* (*Chingbirok*), but no one has written a commentary on it. The absence of a modern-day

analysis of his philosophy is a matter of great shame for us," the old gentlemen explained. Everyone of them was dressed in the traditional top'o and wearing a horsehair hat.

"I've never seen anything so solemn and dignified. I could hardly refuse them," Yi recalled.

Mumyŏng Cotton Fabric

Ten cotton seeds smuggled out of Yuan China in 1363 by a Koryŏ official, Mun Ik-chŏm, gave root to the Korean cotton industry that has since provided fabric and clothing for the Korean people. Once so popular and universal that it was as good as currency, *mumyŏng*, homespun and woven cotton, disappeared with the mechanization of the textile industry. The first machine woven cotton fabric was produced by Kyŏngsŏng Textile Co. in 1919 and sold

under the brand name Vega, a name borrowed from the heavenly weaver who freed earthly weavers from their looms.

In the late 1960s, belatedly recognizing the impending extinction of the homewoven mumyŏng tradition, the government searched the country for mumyŏng weavers and discovered the family of No Chin-nam in Naju, Chŏllanam-do. No was designated a "human cultural asset" as the nation's only practitioner of mumyŏng weaving.

In 1946, when No Chin-nam married and came to her husband's village in Naju, all 40 households were engaged in cotton farming and weaving. She herself had woven all the mumyŏng for her trousseau before she married at age 20. Every man and woman in her husband's 14-member three-generation family was involved in cotton weaving by the time they were 10 years old, and until the

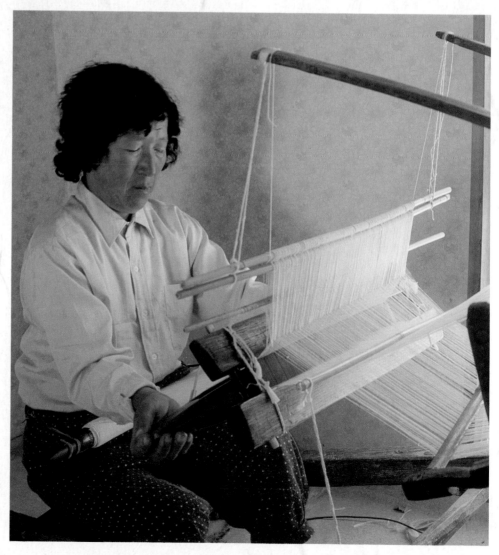

youngest left home to get married, all the family's fabric needs were satisfied on their own loom, which the family figures to be more than 100 years old.

Mumyŏng was made in varying textures depending on its use and was sometimes quite thick for use in Western-style suits. No Chin-nam recalls her family farming yellow and white cotton before the Korean War. With dyed black yarn, she sometimes wove tricolor mumyŏng. Her village in Tashimyŏn was reputed to produce the finest mumyŏng. However, as machine woven cotton gained popularity, the villagers began hauling their looms to the village dump on the hill. The only reason the loom in No Chin-nam's home survived was that she had sisters-in-law requiring trousseaus well into the 1960s. The soil of their village was suited to cotton farming and the fabric she wove was of better quality than the machine-made fabrics available at the market.

Unlike ramie and hemp weaving which still defy mechanization, cotton weaving has became completely mechanized over the past century. The country's last remaining loom was saved just in the nick of the time after the marriage of No's youngest sister-in-law. The old loom is so worn today that it is accorded the care reserved for a national treasure when it is moved to Seoul or other cities for weaving demonstrations. The wooden parts of the loom and spinning wheel are quite rare and not easily replaced.

These days, No weaves only a couple of bolts of mumyŏng each year for demonstration purposes. Occasionally, she produces some special orders for textile artists. Meanwhile, the descendants of Mun Ik-chŏm, who introduced cotton to Korea, established Mokhwa (Cotton) Girls' Commercial School whose school badge features a cotton boll in bloom.

Hansan *Moshi*

The production of *moshi*, ramie cloth, is an age-old process that hasn't changed much in modern times. Ramie plants are cut, their bark is split into fibers with the hands and teeth, and the fibers are mounted on looms. The oldest extant ramie garment was made in 1326.

Finely woven ramie is likened to cica-

da wings. Modern designers describe the fabric as an art in itself. When asked the Korean idea of beauty, the image of a woman wearing an immaculate ramie dress automatically pops into the mind of every Korean.

A courteous old gentleman dressed in a ramie ensemble, complete with a ramie coat and wide-brimmed horsehair hat, is a daunting presence on a hot summer day. For women, too, ramie clothing is a luxury to be worn from Tano, the fifth day of the Fifth Moon, to the beginning of autumn.

Home to two expert weavers recognized as "human cultural assets" and an authentic beater craftsman, Hansan in

Sŏch'ŏn, Ch'ungch'ŏngnam-do province is the center of ramie weaving in Korea. Ramie is sensitive to dry, cold air, so the workshops are partially underground. Ramie fibers are acquired by chewing the tip of the bark into hair-thin strands. These strands are then twisted into thread.

The finest ramie fabric measures 31 centimeters wide. The warp consists of 900 strands of two-ply fiber. About 20 skilled weavers produce fine ramie in the Sŏch'ŏn area. A market specializing in ramie goods is held every five days in Hansan. Usually only two of the approximately 200 bolts on sale are of the finest quality.

When age has dulled their teeth, weavers split the bark with their fingernails but these fibers are not up to the Hansan standard as the resulting fabric is almost as coarse as hemp. Hansan moshi is famous because fabric from other regions cannot match its fineness.

Ramie can last more than 30 years unless it is exposed to cold air which causes its fibers to break. Imported Chinese ramie, on the other hand, is of a single ply and the fiber is not smooth. As a result, the fabric looks worn out after a single season.

In recent years Hansan moshi has attracted the attention of international designers. However, making the fabric is hard on weavers' teeth and many suffer from arthritis after years working in the damp workshops. Efforts to mechanize ramie weaving have not been successful, however. According to local people, "Machines don't agree with ramie."

Hemp Weaving

Hemp is another fabric that has frustrated mechanization efforts. Hemp weaving techniques have changed little since the dawn of civilization. Much heavier and better fitting than ramie, hemp is used for top'o robes and shrouds. It is also popular for summer clothing because it is cheaper than ramie and is thus produced and used in greater quantities.

Andong in Kyŏngsangbuk-do is the place to go to see how hemp weaving is done, and, better still, to see people who know how to wear hemp clothing with flair and pride. Grandmother Pae Pun-yong of Kŭmso-dong, Andong, has been designated a provincial "intangible (human) cultural asset" by the Kyŏngsangbuk-do government. She learned weaving as a small girl. At the time there were no schools or factories for rural women, so a girl learning hemp weaving at home was as natural as a girl going to school today.

Pae Pun-yong works on a loom made by her husband 50 years ago. A few changes have been made to accommodate today's somewhat thicker hemp fibers, but weaving is still done by hand. Pae alternates between four and five reeds when she weaves because the reeds determine the texture of the hemp fabric. In the past, some hemp was woven so fine that a whole bolt would fit in a single bowl, but such fabric is no longer produced because it requires special fibers and "demonic" skill.

Pae Pun-yong and her daughter-in-law do all the work themselves: from sowing hemp seeds in the spring to harvesting, cleaning and bean-starching the fibers, and finally weaving on the loom. Between them they weave about ten bolts a year to sell at the Andong mar-

Pae Pun-yong weaves hemp (top). Her daughter-in-law examines hemp fabric (above). Hemp thread in a shuttle (right), and the finished product (below).

ket, which opens every five days, and at a hemp exhibition hall that opened recently.

In 1992, I overheard three old ladies from Pae's village gossiping while shelling beans. They complained that girls these days know nothing about stitching top'o coats for their future fathers-in-law and have to order the garments from professional seamstresses. Hemp coats and skirts for parents-in-law are still an essential part of every Andong girl's trousseau, especially since the fabric can be put to other uses later.

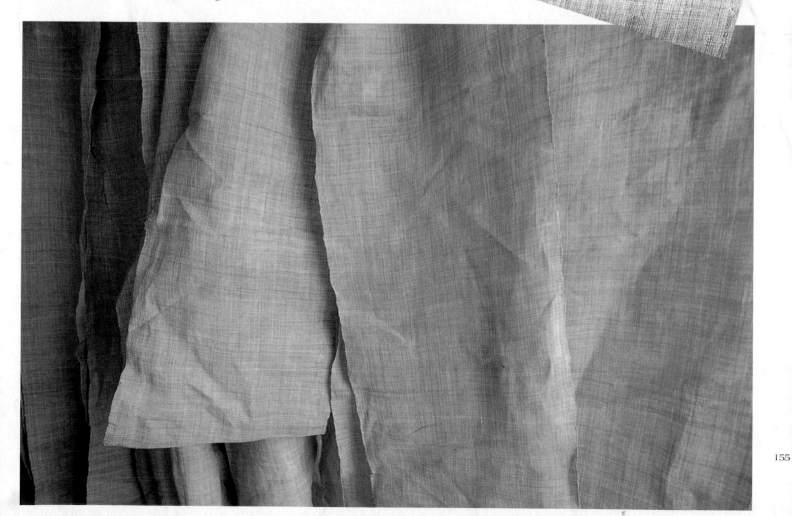

Mourning Clothing

Sangbok, traditional mourning clothing, graphically represented Confucian ideals during the Chosŏn Dynasty when scholars embraced the *Family Rites* of Zhu Xi, the Chinese Neo-Confucian (1130-1200), as a golden rule to live by. Even today, sangbok is the Korean garment that most closely resembles traditional styles.

Controversies over mourning customs and clothing vividly illustrate the importance of Confucian values in Chosŏn life. In 1488, Ch'oe Pu (1454-1504), an official stationed on Chejudo Island, was sailing to the mainland to attend his father's funeral when his boat encountered a storm. After drifting on the Yellow Sea for 15 days, Ch'oe's party washed ashore in China. Ch'oe and his crew were taken captive by the Chinese who mistook them for Japanese pirates. Although Ch'oe did not speak Chinese, he could communicate with his captors in writing as most educated Koreans at the time understood and wrote Chinese characters.

The Chinese officials were greatly impressed with Ch'oe's gentlemanly demeanor and learning, especially his knowledge of family rites and the seriousness with which he followed them, and the Ming emperor decided to award him with a gift. One of Ch'oe's servants went to the palace and received the award on Ch'oe's behalf because he was still in mourning for his father. Ch'oe himself had to thank the emperor for the gift, but palace etiquette prohibited the wearing of mourning clothes in the palace. His discourses with Chinese officials epitomize his adamant beliefs on loyalty and filial piety. Eventually, it was agreed that he would wear a court outfit within the palace grounds but change back to his mourning attire the moment his audience with the emperor was over. Ch'oe Pu's account of his experience in *A Record of Drifting at Sea* (*P'yohaerok*) presents an unequivocal picture of the rigid sangbok culture of Chosŏn Korea.

Even more dramatically revealing is the controversy that erupted over the mourning period to be observed by King Hyojong's mother, the Queen Dowager Cho upon his death in 1659. Hyojong was her second son by King Injo. He had ascended the throne because his older brother, Crown Prince Sohyŏn, died prematurely. The dowager had already mourned her first son's death for three years as required by Confucian protocol. A great dispute erupted in the court, already troubled by factional strife, as the Westerner (*sŏin*) faction including Song Shi-yŏl, a prominent Confucianist and powerful official, insisted the dowager observe a one-year mourning period because Hyojong was the second son. The Southerner (*namin*) faction, led by Yun Hyu and Hŏ Mok, argued for a three-year mourning period because the second son succeeded to the place of the first. Eventually, the Westerners prevailed but that was only the first round of the controversy.

The debate originated in the two factions' differing interpretations of Confucian rites, but it also reflected a preexisting power struggle that had raged between Crown Prince Sohyŏn and his brother Hyojong who disagreed over diplomatic policy toward Qing China.

Adding fuel to the controversy was the objection by the poet Yun Sŏn-do, who had tutored Hyojong when he was still a prince, that "a one-year mourning period would demote the king and thereby weaken the line of royal succession." This made the question a political issue rather than a simple disagreement over mourning rituals. Yun Sŏn-do was eventually exiled, but the dispute spread across the country with local Confucianists sending endless depositions to the court.

The conflict worsened when Hyojong's queen died in 1674. Again the two factions collided head-on over the question of whether the Queen Dowager should mourn for the period required for a first daughter-in-law or a second daughter-in-law. The Southerners emerged victorious from this second round and took control of the government. Their victory also meant that ritual

theory, which had dictated the mourning procedures for King Hyojong was wrong and the annals of the king had to be rewritten. The dispute stretched on for 15 years.

In more recent years, Yi Ku, the son of the last crown prince of the Chosŏn Dynasty, wore the heaviest and most complicated sangbok, *ch'amch'oebok*, while mourning the death of his grandmother the Empress Yun in 1966, the death of his father in 1970 and the death of his mother in 1989. The garment was of the same style as the one Sunjong, the last king of Chosŏn, wore at the funeral of his father, Kojong. The use of such a cumbersome costume so many years after the downfall of the kingdom demonstrates Korea's strict mourning customs.

On a November day in 1992, I journeyed to Munp'yŏng-myŏn, Naju, Chŏllanam-do to visit the indigo dye master Yun Pyŏng-un. The dyeing of yarn and fabric deep blue with an extract of *tchok*, or indigo plant, was an integral part of daily life until a synthetic chemical process was invented in Germany in 1897. In recent years, however, a small group of people have been trying to revive indigo and other natural pigments in Korea.

The lower reaches of the Yŏngsan-gang River near the southwestern coast were the last stronghold of indigo dyeing. The craft thrived here until the Korean War thanks to the region's fertile soil, warm, sunny climate, ideal for growing indigo, and an abundance of oyster shells, which served as an essential oxidizing agent. Almost all Yŏngsanp'o households were once engaged in indigo dye production, and the dyeing of fabrics thrived in the neighboring Naju. Yun Pyŏng-un's grandfather and father did dyeing work, and by the time the Korean War broke out, Yun was helping as well. His early experiences helped him when he decided to revive the craft in 1983. However, the indigo fields had long since been turned into paddies, and indigo seeds were hard to come by.

The indigo dye-making process begins with the harvesting of indigo plants. They must be cut in early morning before the summer sun dries the dew. The plants are stored in a jar and turned over exactly 24 hours later. Oyster shells are burned on a pile of wood, covered by straw mats, then pulverized, sieved and added to the jar of indigo. As the oyster powder is stirred into the jar, the indigo juice changes from yellow to jade green to green to blue, and froth rises like a cloud. At the end of the oxidation-reduction process, the indigo settles to the bottom of the jar and jells. The jelly is saved, moved to another jar and diluted in water mixed with wood ash. The jar is kept inside while the solution seasons into dye.

I scheduled my visit in November because Yun was waiting for cooler weather and had plenty of ash from heating his home. It is a fussy business waiting for the solution to mature into dye after ash has been added. The jar must remain covered, and no one who is "impure" should come near it. "Tchok dye is an uncanny thing," Yun says when I ask how the oxidation-reduction process works.

"Blue skirts and blue bed covers were essential to a bride's trousseau before the Korean War," recalls Yun. "You couldn't marry off your daughter if you didn't have tchok to dye the fabric. It was only used for silk, linen, ramie and hemp. My father used to keep 40 dye jars and dye hundreds of skirts. The dyeing process was usually repeated eight times, but sometimes he would dip the fabric ten times for a deeper blue. I have provided indigo fabric to some 400 people from across the country since I began my business."

Indigo dyeing has not yet been recognized as a cultural tradition deserving state protection. Lack of governmental support makes Yun dubious about the future of his specialty. Han Kwang-sŏk, another dyer operating in Pŏlgyo, Chŏllanam-do, grumbles that, "People come to buy indigo fabric as rarely as a dragon appears in a dream."

Indigo dye master Yun Pyŏng-un of Naju, Chŏllanam-do province with some of his creations

The costumes of the royal family and their retainers were rich in symbolism. Clothing was an indicator of rank in the highly stratified society of the Chosŏn court. The cut of a garment and the colors and designs on emblems, chest and shoulder bands and ornamental aprons symbolized rank and the aspirations of the wearer.

When engaged in official duties Chosŏn kings wore red silk robes decorated with cloud patterns. Golden dragons were embroidered on the chest, shoulders and back. The dragons' five claws symbolized the supreme power of the monarch. In 1897 these red robes were adopted as the official garment of the crown prince as King Kojong declared himself emperor of the Taehan Empire, instead of king of Chosŏn. The emperor's new robes were yellow.

Kings and courtiers wore wooden boots made of black silk and lined with thick flannel. A double-crested crown was worn with the royal robes. It had two small vertical "wings" at the back to distinguish the king from court officials who wore hats with horizontal wings. Beneath the royal robe, the monarch and princes wore chŏgori jackets, vest, and pants of fine silk.

The queen's ceremonial robe was also made of red silk until 1897 when the newly named empress wore yellow. The ceremonial robe, or wonsam, was made of glossed silk embroidered and embossed with clouds and phoenixes. The ceremonial emblem depicted a phoenix until 1897 when a dragon design was used to represent the empress. The wide sleeve bands which hung to the floor were striped with bright yellow, blue and white.

Beneath the queen's ceremonial robe was a blue silk robe embroidered with hundreds of peacocks. An inner gown, a silk brocade underskirt and loose pants were also worn beneath ceremonial robes. Ceremonial aprons hung down the front and back of the outer robe, together with decorative pendants made of jade.

When wearing a ceremonial robe, the queen wore blue silk shoes made of glossed silk. Her hair was arranged in an ornate hairdo using silk hair bands, jeweled hair pins, wigs and hair ribbons. For

The Empress Yun (1894-1966), consort to King Sunjong, Korea's last monarch, as a sixteen-year-old in 1909 (left) and in her later years (above).

formal occasions, Chosŏn queens, princesses and noble ladies had their hair braided and twisted with silk ribbons, then arranged in a chignon, enhanced with a false hair-piece, and held in place by elaborate hair pins.

The ceremonial robes of Empress Yun (left), the last queen of Chosŏn, demonstrate the use of Chinese characters, color and decorative symbols. Her robes were

159

decorated with gold-leaf patterns made by pressing carefully carved woodblocks dipped in glue onto fabric, then pressing thin gold leaf over the glue. Elaborately embossed fabric was also used to enhance the dignity of the empress. ◆

Chajŏk-yongpo, a king's ceremonial robe (below), and an embroidered hwal'ot ceremonial top coat (bottom) with a close-up of it (opposite)

Beauty of Traditional Korean *Hanbok*

Kum Ki-sook

Today most people do not consider the *hanbok*, Korea's national costume, suitable for daily wear. They prefer to wear it on special occasions, to social gatherings and seasonal festivals. Still, for many modern Koreans, wearing a hanbok is a way of showing pride in their cultural heritage.

Like any national costume, the hanbok is a reflection of the nation's climate and artistic sensibility. A study of the hanbok can thus provide insight into the Korean character.

The hanbok basically consists of two parts: a top and a bottom. The woman's hanbok is composed of a *chŏgori*, a bolero-like blouse, and a skirt, or *ch'ima*. A vest (*paeja*), jacket (*magoja*) and overcoat (*turumagi*) may be worn over the outfit. Hood-like headgear, such as the *ayam* or *chobawi*, may complete the ensemble.

The man's hanbok is similarly composed of two main pieces: a chŏgori and trousers called *paji*. While men may or may not wear a vest or jacket over the chŏgori, traditional etiquette requires them to wear an overcoat, or turumagi, outside the home.

In traditional society, hanbok styles and designs reflected the wearer's gender, profession and social status as well as individual preferences and lifestyles. Ceremonial clothes for weddings, funerals and other important occasions were most diverse. This was especially true of costumes worn by royalty and court officials. However, it is the basic two-part outfit for daily wear that has long been favored by Koreans, regardless of class or profession.

Like Korean art, the hanbok is characterized by flowing lines and curves. The chŏgori is especially rich in subtle curves—in the collar, the underside of the sleeves, the hem and the front opening, all of which are sometimes highlighted with dark lines. The silhouette of the dress also has curves that undulate as the wearer moves. The ties and folds of the dress create more flowing lines.

A straight silhouette was the fashion in the mid-16th century, but it gave way to voluminous curves by the mid-18th century. This style then evolved into more moderate, natural curves in the late 19th century. Flowing, supple lines have consistently characterized the hanbok throughout the centuries, however.

In *tang-ŭi*, ceremonial jackets worn by court ladies during the Chosŏn Dynasty, the curve of the front opening veers outward sharply as it meets the curve of the hem, emphasizing the beauty of reversal. The sharp angle formed at each corner is a common aesthetic found in all forms of Korean art. In fact, curves are apparent not only in clothes but also in the eaves of traditional buildings, in dance movements and in handicrafts and painting. They are even present in classical melodies. The curved line cannot be overemphasized when discussing the hanbok's beauty.

Empty or open space is a characteristic common to all Korean art. The blank areas on the surface of a porcelain jar, free of any ornamentation, complement its beauty. The blank areas in a painting inspire the viewer to fill the canvas with empathy. The same holds true for the hanbok. As it covers most of the wearer's body, the hanbok abounds in open surfaces. Women's skirts and men's coats and robes

The combination of lines and color make the traditional hanbok a work of art.

Hanbok *from the Chosŏn Dynasty (above) and the evolution of the garment (below)*

Mid-16th century	Mid-18th century	Late 18th century	Mid-19th century	Late 19th century

have especially large unadorned areas. Koreans have traditionally favored plain fabric for clothing. When a garment is decorated, it is usually with patterns woven into the fabric rather than embellishments applied after sewing.

Contrasting colors on the collar, underarm panels, cuffs and sashes are sometimes used to enhance the beauty of the woman's chŏgori. At the same time, pleats along the upper rim of the skirt create long, fluid lines which, shifting as the wearer moves, serve as an additional decorative element.

These open surfaces allow for great versatility as testified to in many anecdotes. When a woman soiled a skirt that she had borrowed from a neighbor, Shin Saimdang (1504-1551), the famous painter-poet, painted a grapevine on it, thus solving the woman's dilemma for she could sell the skirt at a high price and reimburse the owner with cash. Men often painted on the skirts of their mistresses as an expression of their affection. In fact, it was the dream of every *kisaeng* (professional woman entertainer) to have her skirt painted by a gentleman friend.

The Koreans were long known as the "white-clad people" because of their predilection for white. White was used in men's and women's clothing because it contrasts well with black hair. In fact, today's sartorial experts concur that Koreans are best complemented by combinations of black and white. They reason that the contrast becomes Koreans because the tonal values of their hair color and skin color differ so radically.

In traditional society, the preference for white clothes was so excessive that the government often promulgated special orders to ban white cloth, but the people responded by dyeing their clothes the palest blue, ivory or gray. The frequency of government prohibitions suggests that people continued to wear white, despite government orders.

White has been favored in many cultures but the persistence with which Koreans adhered to the color sets them apart from other peoples. The powerful attachment to white is believed to be closely related to the Korean people's innate love of purity in material and spirit. The Korean predilection for white should be understood as a spiritual matter rather than as a visual preference.

On the other hand, combinations of strong colors are also evident in the hanbok. A yellow chŏgori over a red skirt and a green chŏgori over a blue skirt were the ideal combinations.

Commoners generally wore primary colors for seasonal festivals and ceremonial occasions such as weddings, but members of the privileged classes wore them anytime. The ruling class preferred primary colors because they were flattering. Of the five cardinal colors, yellow symbolized the emperor and empress, and red, the king and queen. The color of a woman's ceremonial dress was determined by the class and position of her spouse.

Complementarity characterizes the combinations of primary colors used in the hanbok. Green against red and yellow against blue, for example, are attractive because of their bright, eye-catching contrast. In ceremonies and rituals, garments of such colors attract attention to the main participants.

Primary colors were also believed to ward off evil spirits. Bright colors were auspicious. *Saektong*, a combination of five basic colors, was favored for wedding gowns, festival clothes, children's clothes and for the ritual costumes of shamans. Saektong chŏgori and saektong turumagi were also quite popular.

Primary color schemes are frequently found in embroidery. For example, wave and rock patterns on ceremonial gowns and pouches were embroidered with layers of different colors to accentuate the primary values. Harmonious combinations of primary colors can also be seen in women's ornaments and accessories.

One attribute of the hanbok is that it conceals almost the entire body. In the Chosŏn Dynasty's Confucian society, where the greatest virtue for men was integrity and for women chastity, clothing reflected social values. Men avoided being seen outside without the proper attire, including a hat, and women hid their faces with overcoats when they stepped beyond the confines of their homes.

Women wore layers of clothing because of the Confucian edict that females must never reveal their flesh to others. Under their skirts, they wore baggy pants over three pairs of increasingly smaller bloomers and a loin cloth. The layers of undergarments resulted in a voluminous lower body. To make their skirts even more voluminous, upper-class women wore two kinds of underskirts for formal occasions.

By concealing most of the body under layers of fabric, the hanbok subtly highlights the beauty and grace of the female figure and titillates the viewer's imagination.

An example of bold exposure is the baring of breasts. Given the excessive preference for male heirs in Chosŏn society, women were

This ceremonial tang-ŭi jacket was worn by court ladies in the Chosŏn Dynasty.

understandably proud at giving birth to a son. They proudly bared their breasts to nurse a child, deliberately provoking the envy of other women. In this sense, the direct exposure of the body can be understood as a status symbol.

From the mid-Chosŏn period, hanbok fashions became more revealing, at least in terms of exposing the wearer's undergarments. Genre paintings from this period show women wearing hiked skirts which revealed a glimpse of baggy bloomers. This must have been quite shocking to those dedicated to the strict dress code of old. This provocative show of undergarments is believed to have been an exhibitionistic gesture. Similar exhibitionism is described in detail in *The Tale of Ch'unhyang* (*Ch'unhyangjŏn*), the popular romance of a kisaeng's daughter and the son of a government official. As Ch'unhyang rides a swing on a late spring day, "her red skirt billows and her white silk bloomers flap in the southeasterly wind." This reference to undergarments must have been titillating to those raised on staid Confucian values.

Photographs taken in the closing years of the Chosŏn Dynasty show that revealing a glimpse of bloomers was in vogue at that time. These shifts in fashion were obviously the result of changing social values and ethics. They were also part of the process by which some undergarments developed into clothes for outer wear.

Movement was an essential part of the hanbok's beauty. This is evident in the chŏgori's long sashes, hair ribbons, tassels attached to pendants and other personal ornaments that undulated as the wearer moved.

Fluttering sashes and ties were as integral to the everyday dress of the Chosŏn Dynasty as hair ornaments and pendants worn on the chest. Ornamental knots (*maedŭp*) and tassels on pendants mirror the line and motion of the chŏgori and skirt. Pendulous tassels, popular during the Chosŏn Dynasty, were used to decorate many items such as perfume pouches, small ornamental knives and bags.

Ornamental pins with moving parts were also popular as evidenced by their use in bridal crowns and other headgear and hair decorations. Tiny ornaments were attached to thin wires, causing a fluttering effect when the wearer moved. This is yet another manifestation of the undulating line, a visual expression of the Korean people's quest for the natural beauty of movement.

The hanbok is replete with symbolism in its colors, patterns and ornaments. At wedding

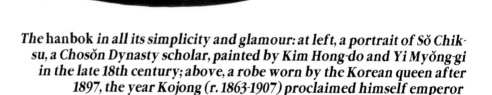

ceremonies, for example, the groom's mother always wears cool blue or green and the bride's mother wears a warmer pink or coral.

In the traditional hanbok, the purple collar of a woman's chŏgori symbolized her husband and the blue cuffs her sons. If an older woman wore a chŏgori with a purple collar and blue cuffs, she was regarded as truly blessed. The combination of green chŏgori and red skirt was reserved for brides. An unmarried woman wore a yellow chŏgori and red skirt for seasonal festivals.

Patterns on fabrics were not only decorations but also expressions of the wearer's wishes. Peonies embroidered on a bridal gown symbolized the desire for wealth and honor. The lotus flower, symbolizing nobility, was a popular motif for embroidered folding screens used in women's quarters during summer. Bats and pomegranates symbolized fertility. Since axes represented sons, pregnant women often wore ax-shaped pendants. Decorations featuring dragons, phoenixes, cranes and tigers were reserved for the privileged classes because they symbolized royalty and high rank.

More common and straightforward expressions of wishes were Chinese characters or motifs designed on the basis of these characters. The character *pok*, meaning "good fortune," and *su*, meaning "longevity," were used extensively.

In fact, practically every pattern used in the hanbok had some symbolic meaning. Similarly, ornaments functioned not only as decorative complements to clothes but also practical and supplicatory devices. For instance, perfume containers, needle cases and small knives were ornamental and functional. Tiger claws were

The hanbok in all its simplicity and glamour: at left, a portrait of Sŏ Chik-su, a Chosŏn Dynasty scholar, painted by Kim Hong-do and Yi Myŏng-gi in the late 18th century; above, a robe worn by the Korean queen after 1897, the year Kojong (r. 1863-1907) proclaimed himself emperor

decorative and also protected the wearer from evil spirits, while bat decorations were pretty to look at and auspicious because they symbolized fertility and good fortune.

The diverse aesthetic elements of the hanbok embody the Korean sense of beauty. The shape and flowing lines are derived from the Korean preference for natural beauty and the desire to be in harmony with nature. The careful contrast of black and white, the use of blank spaces, combinations of primary colors and varied symbolism developed as an expression of the wearer's personal character and desires as well as the values of the larger society. The aesthetic framework of the hanbok is based on the Korean preference for naturalness, a desire for supernatural protection and blessings, and a Confucian-inspired dress code. ◆

FOOD AND DRINK

Koreans have long been famous for their love of food and drink. Ancient Chinese histories tell of the Koreans' fondness for good food and wine as early as the Three Kingdoms period (1st century B.C.-A.D. 7th century), and the superabundance of restaurants, drinking establishments and cooking schools in modern Korea suggests that the Korean love affair with food and drink lives on today.

The history of Korea's dietary culture is the focus of Yun Seo-seok's essay; she surveys the introduction and use of Korea's most basic foods. Kang In-hee considers dietary customs, emphasizing the importance of Confucian values, family and community tradition and solidarity, and the Korean veneration for nature in Korean food customs.

Food plays a central role in traditional rites of passage. Professor Park Tae-sun looks at the symbolic role of food and table settings in traditional rites. Yim Jae-hae considers the significance of holiday foods, suggesting that holiday food customs developed out of a desire to supplement the daily diet and heighten the festive atmosphere.

Culinary expert Han Pok-jin provides a survey of traditional foods and table settings, while Kim Manjo offers a history of kimchi, that ubiquitous Korean side dish, and an analysis of its nutritional value.

The kitchen was traditionally a woman's domain. Lim Young-ju explains how kitchen furnishings and food vessels remain close to the Korean heart because they symbolize the love and care given to the preparation of daily and ritual food in traditional society. Kim Kwang-on echoes this sentiment in his survey of the history of the kitchen and customs related to the kitchen and cooking utensils.

The alcoholic beverages traditionally enjoyed by the Korean people are little known in the West. Professor Lee Hyo-gee offers a history of alcoholic beverages and distilling techniques, while Professor Yoo Tae-jong examines ten traditional wines still being made today. Creamy *makkŏlli* and the ever-powerful *soju* are perennial favorites, but as modern Koreans rediscover their cultural roots, flavored wines and regional speciality liquors are gaining new popularity. Choi Seung-beom concludes the discussion of drink with his history of drinking customs, offering a firsthand look at the influence of Confucian and Taoist values on drinking in East Asia.

Looking Back on Korea's Dietary Culture

Yun Seo-seok

The natural environment is a decisive element in the foundation of a nation's dietary culture while political, economic, social and cultural trends contribute to changes and further development in diet. Once dietary habits have evolved, they become a central part of the culture to be carefully handed down through the generations.

Korea started growing cereals from the mid-Neolithic Age. In some parts of the country rice was grown from around 2000 B.C. Korea remains a rice-producing nation today. Beans were grown from the beginning of Korean history along with various cereals, and after the introduction of rice, cereals appropriate to each region were still grown. As a result, rice, beans and other cereals became the staples of the Korean diet. Among the earliest cereals were foxtail (Italian) millet, Chinese millet, and kaoliang (African millet). Barley was introduced only after rice farming began, and wheat much later, around the first or second century.

Because the Korean peninsula is situated at the intersection of cold and warm currents and has plenty of large rivers, it is blessed with an abundant supply of seafood. From early times Korea's extreme seasonal changes encouraged the development of various methods for processing fermented foods, such as *chŏtkal*, fermented seafood. Koreans were also skillful hunters and established a tradition, rarely seen in agrarian societies, of preparing meat dishes.

Thus the everyday diet of rice, soup and shared side dishes evolved. The table setting showed a clear distinction between the main and subsidiary dishes. With four distinct seasons and climatic differences, the food of each region varied greatly. This variation was most apparent in side dishes consumed on a daily basis. Processed foods that could be preserved, such as soy sauce, kimchi, fermented seafoods and pickled radish and cucumber, were also consumed from ancient times.

The preparation of special holiday foods has been popular throughout Korean history. In traditional society, the preparation of special foods reinforced the holiday's significance and the need to devote oneself to farming tasks in ordinary times. It also fostered a spirit of cooperation, solidarity and harmony among village residents and family members.

These traditions developed over time, through a process of trial and error and finally refinement. The history of a dietary culture is, in many ways, the history of a people.

Basic Traditional Foods

Grains

As stated previously, Korea began to farm cereals such as foxtail millet, Chinese millet, kaoliang and barnyard millet from the mid-Neolithic Age and rice from about 2000 B.C. Excavations of

Pungent toenjang tchigae, bean paste stew

a Neolithic residential site at Chit'am-ni, Pongsan in North Korea's Hwanghae-do province, dating to approximately 3000 B.C., have yielded stone farming tools and grains of foxtail and barnyard millet. Rice grains, together with foxtail millet, have been discovered in peat beds dating to 2100 B.C. at Kahyŏn-ni, Kimp'o, Kyŏnggi-do province and at a residential site dating from the latter part of 3000 B.C. in P'yŏngyang.

Korea is situated in a temperate monsoon belt which provides an ideal environment for rice cultivation. As a result, rice became the staple of the Korean diet very early. Though small in area, the Korean peninsula has a varied climate. In regions not suited to rice farming, other cereals were grown. This regional variety stimulated the development of a dietary culture based on the mixing of rice and other cereals.

The development of specialized farming tools was essential to a flourishing of agriculture. In Korea, the Iron Age took place from about 300 to 100 B.C. Stone farming tools were replaced by ironware during that period. Tools made of iron have been excavated from Kujŏng-ni in Kyŏngju, Kyŏngsangbuk-do province, Yean-ni in Kimhae, Kyŏngsangnam-do province and Wiwŏn, P'yŏng-an-do province, which is in North Korea.

It was only during the Three Kingdoms period that rice became a staple of the Korean diet. The three kingdoms of Koguryŏ, Paekche and Shilla all promoted land reformation, expanded irrigation systems and actively propagated the use of iron farming tools. Rice became a staple when the necessities for rice farming, such as oxen for pulling plows, became available.

Of the Three Kingdoms, Paekche had the best climate for rice cultivation, while Shilla was better suited to barley farming and Koguryŏ to foxtail millet. In the Unified Shilla period, with the development of farm implements, the opening of new land to cultivation and the enhanced productivity that resulted from these improvements, rice became the main cereal.

Barley, wheat, foxtail millet, Chinese millet, beans, red beans, mung beans, African millet and buckwheat were also grown. It was during the reign of China's

emperor Wu (141-87 B.C.) that minister Zhang Qian introduced wheat to China from Central Asia. Records show that wheat was introduced to Japan from Korea around the fourth century. Thus it seems likely that wheat was introduced to Korea around the first century with the coming of the Iron Age.

Barley is thought to have come to Korea earlier than wheat, but the exact date is unknown. Barley cultivation was concentrated in southeastern Korea and came to be a staple together with rice. Though P'yŏng-an-do and other parts of northern Korea had a relatively good climate for growing wheat, it was generally produced for family consumption and not on a large scale. In the 1930s, land cultivated in wheat amounted to only half that of barley nationwide. Wheat has never been a staple in the Korean diet.

Seafood, Meat, Fruit and Vegetables

Seafood, meat, fruit and vegetables were widely consumed from early in Korea's history. By the Three Kingdoms period, shipbuilding skills had developed and fishing was an important source of food. Although there is no way of knowing all the seafood and fish consumed in ancient times, middens discovered in Kimhae on the southeast coast contain evidence of at least 30 different varieties, including clams, abalone, oysters and mud snails. Midden excavations in Pusan's Tongsam-dong and at Unggi in Hamgyŏngbuk-do province have yielded the bones of sea bream, mackerel, pike and shark, as well as remains of

sŏnggae, a type of echinoderm. Since the confluence of currents off Korea's shores attracts many varieties of marine life, we can assume that other fish and sea creatures were also eaten.

Koreans have enjoyed seaweed since ancient times. Historical records indicate that some varieties were particularly valued and exported to the Parhae Kingdom and to China.

Korea is not geographically suitable for the raising of livestock on a large scale, but hunting was common, and cows, horses, pigs and chickens were raised in small numbers. The Koguryŏ people were famous for their hunting skills in that kingdom's largely mountainous terrain and consumed much game including roe deer, wild boar and deer. The people of Shilla raised some livestock on nearby islands, catching the animals whenever the need arose. The Paekche people also raised some livestock and poultry, but horses and cows were generally used for transportation and in farming, and hens were kept for their eggs and not consumed indiscriminately. Pheasants, on the other hand, were a more common source of meat.

Fruit and vegetable consumption also dates to ancient times. While pinenuts and chestnuts were noted local produce, pears, peaches and hazelnuts were also popular. Lettuce, eggplant, gourd plants, radishes and yams were some of the many vegetables cultivated. Yams appear to have the longest history, dating to ancient times, while lettuce was brought from China by a Shilla envoy. This envoy was said to have paid a great deal for the lettuce so it was called the "vegetable worth a thousand pieces of gold." The Shilla Kingdom actually had a gardening law governing vegetable and fruit cultivation. Many varieties of wild greens, such as bamboo shoots, kubi, a kind of grass, bracken, tŏdŏk roots, a relative of ginseng, and broad bellflower were also gathered and consumed.

Cooking Methods

The grain-based diet of Korea developed from misu karu, a powder made of several roasted grains, to roasted rice cakes, steamed rice cakes, steamed rice, and finally, boiled rice. This development mirrored improvements in implements for hulling, pulverizing and cooking.

During the Three Kingdoms period, various mortars and pestles, millstones and treadmills were used to hull and grind grain. Earthenware steamers were used to cook food. An earthenware steamer is the oldest extant relic unearthed at a seashell midden dating to the Bronze Age (1000-300 B.C.) in Najin

on the east coast of North Korea. Third-century Koguryŏ wall paintings depict food being cooked in an earthenware steamer. Of course, bowl-shaped earthenware pots were also used in cooking from the early days of farming in Korea, but food cooked in a steamer is of much better quality. Many foods were cooked in steamers: mixtures of rice, millet, soybeans, red beans, barley, barnyard millet and sorghum in various combinations, steamed rice cakes (sŏlgi, chŭngp'yŏn) and plain glutinous rice cakes. Fried rice cakes or kaoliang pancakes were also consumed.

It was in the final years of the Three Kingdoms period that cast iron kettles were used regularly to cook rice. Since rice is easy to prepare, it became an everyday food. A wide variety of rice cakes was developed for celebrations and rituals.

Fermented and Preserved Foods

Wine and soy sauce are Korea's most common fermented foods. From the early days of farming, grain was used to make wine. Rice wines and other grain-based wines became traditional drinks. Soy-based sauces, or chang, made from

processed beans were used everyday as a source of protein. It is not known when chang was first made but it is thought to coincide with the introduction of bean cultivation. Wine- and chang-making techniques were perfected during the Three Kingdoms period and introduced to Japan.

Many seasonal foods were processed and stored for use at other times. In order to retain their freshness and nutritive value they were fermented or preserved. Fermented vegetables consumed during the Three Kingdoms period can be divided into several categories: those preserved in salt water, those preserved in a mixture of salt, wine and rice porridge, and those preserved in soy sauce or soy paste. These foods were the predecessors of today's kimchi. Fermented food made with salted seafood came to be known as chŏtkal.

Koreans developed their fermentation skills quite early. Fermented foods were part of the basic diet during the Three Kingdoms period. This fact has been confirmed from the inclusion of many types of hae (a general term for fermented vegetables and seafood) in the record of gifts sent to the bride of the Shilla king Shinmun on the occasion of their marriage in 683. The flavor of fermented food is so ubiquitous in the Korean diet that it deserves to be recognized along with the five basic Korean tastes, sweet, salty, sour, bitter and spicy.

Meals consisting of a main food and subsidiary side dishes developed gradually from the introduction of farming in the Neolithic period through the late Three Kingdoms era. Rice with various grains became the main dish, and soy

sauce, kimchi and fermented seafood were standard side dishes, adding taste and nutrition.

From its founding in 918 the Koryŏ Dynasty actively encouraged the development of farming by adopting a salary land (nokkwajŏn) system, which allocated land to current office holders, and by offering tax benefits on land newly cleared for farming. Regulations were placed on emergency rice reserves and the price of grain in order to encourage rice production. As a result, techniques for making wine, rice cakes and rice pastries became more sophisticated, and the production of rice wine became a popular custom.

Steamed chestnut rice cakes, steamed mugwort rice cakes, pancakes made with glutinous rice and kaoliang and yakshik, chewy bars made of glutinous rice mixed with honey, jujubes and chestnuts, were some of the rice cakes enjoyed during the Koryŏ Dynasty. Chestnut rice cakes were made from a mixture of ground chestnuts and rice flour steamed with honeyed water. Since rice flour is not naturally glutinous, it was pressed through a sieve, thus aerating it, and mixed with honey water to hasten the cooking process. This method is still used to this day.

Radish, turnips, lotus roots, taro, leeks, dropwort, lettuce, hollyhock, green onions, water shields, garlic, shallots, cucumbers and eggplants were cultivated during the Koryŏ Dynasty. Mountain greens and wild mushrooms were consumed as well. High-quality radishes and pears were grown for use in "water kimchi" in which vegetables were pickled in salt water. Koryŏ's pickled vegetables were fresher and the nutrient composition superior to the fermented vegetables eaten during the Three Kingdoms era. The method of preservation was also quite scientific. Aromatic vegetables, such as lettuce and small green onions, were used for ssam, rice or meat wrapped in vegetable leaves, one of Korea's simplest and most well-balanced dishes.

In the early years of Koryŏ, everyone, from the lowest commoner to the king, refrained from eating meat because of the influence of Buddhism. Slaughtering techniques were crude, and at one time the slaughter of cattle was actually

Hearty beef-based soups

banned. As a result, meat dishes were not popular until the mid-Koryŏ period when high-quality cattle were raised on ranches on Chejudo Island. Among the best-known meat dishes from Koryŏ were *sŏlya myŏkchŏk*, roasted prime ribs, and *sŏllŏng t'ang*, bone and tripe soup. Pork, lamb, chicken, pheasant and swan meat were also consumed.

Korea's tea culture reached its peak during the Koryŏ Dynasty. A "tea village" was formed near Mt. Chiri-san to grow tea, and fine teas were imported from China's Song Dynasty. At court, a tea chamber was established for the brewing of tea, and during national ceremonies, such as *yŏndŭnghoe*, the light festival on the 15th day of the first lunar month when wishes were offered to the Buddha, and *p'algwanhoe*, the "Festival of the Eight Vows," when thanks were offered to local gods, tea rituals were performed and refreshment tables prepared.

This tea culture was soon institutionalized, and *Hangno tadam kunsa*, a mobile force in charge of preparing tea, was founded to serve tea to the king on official trips.

Sweets and pastries developed with the tea culture. They varied widely in ingredients and preparation. Among them were: *yu-milgwa*, fried honey cookies; *yu-gwa*, fried cookies made from glutinous rice; *tashik*, small pressed cakes made of powdered grains, herbs or pollen; *chŏn-gwa*, candied fruit or roots; and *kwap'yŏn*, jellied fruit. Yu-milgwa were most popular during the Koryŏ Dynasty. They were served at wedding feasts and with tea when entertaining guests.

Several kinds of rice wine were enjoyed during the Koryŏ Dynasty. *Ch'ŏnju* was a clear strained wine. The introduction of *soju*, a distilled liquor made from fermented yeast and rice, in the latter part of the Koryŏ Dynasty, signaled the rise of distilled drinks. Distilleries began to crop up around the kingdom, and numerous varieties of wine, such as *p'odoju*, grape wine, *ch'angp'oju*, iris wine, *hwanggukju*, chrysanthemum wine, *chukyŏpju*, bamboo leaf wine, and *ogap'iju*, root-bark wine, were consumed.

Agricultural techniques were further developed during the Chosŏn Dynasty, and many different grains were cultivat-

ed. From the beginning of the dynasty, practical farming texts, such as Chŏng Cho's *Straight Talk on Farming* (*Nongsa chiksŏl*, 1429) and Shin Sok's *Compilation for Farmers* (*Nongga chipsŏng*, 17th century), contributed to the advancement of farming techniques specifically suited to the Korean peninsula. In the 17th and 18th centuries, numerous agricultural tracts, such as Yu Hyŏng-wŏn's *Treatises* (*Pan-gye surok*, 17th century), the *Augmented Supplement to Farm Management* (*Chŭngpo sallim kyŏngje*), a farming reference text published in 1766, and *Sixteen Treatises on the Development of Nature and the Comforting of the People* (*Imwon kyŏngje shimnyuk-chi*), written by Sŏ Yu-gu (1764-1845), a scholar-official who specialized in agricultural administration, were published. Irrigation was extended from the mid-Chosŏn Dynasty, and improved rice planting methods were promoted on a national scale. With these improvements and the increased use of oxen, the cultivation of rice and barley became easier.

During this period, 69 varieties of rice, 15 varieties of foxtail millet, eight varieties of soybeans, seven varieties of red beans and four varieties of barley were cultivated. Cowpeas, peas, buckwheat and corn—which had been introduced in the 1700s—were also grown.

It was also during the Chosŏn Dynasty that chili peppers, pumpkins, potatoes, sweet potatoes, tomatoes and other foreign foods were first introduced. Chili peppers and pumpkins are thought to have been introduced from Japan before or after the Japanese invasion of Korea in 1592. However, in Japan there is a belief that the chili pepper was brought from Korea. In either case, the chili peppers grown on the Korean peninsula, unlike those originally introduced, were uniquely sweet and hot, a mixture of chili and paprika. This distinctive flavor is largely responsible for the unique taste of Korea's traditional food.

The cultivation of sweet potatoes developed over a period of some 100 years after their introduction by Cho Ŏm (1719-1777), who sent seeds to Pusan from Taema Island on his way to Japan as a correspondent in 1753. They have since been widely grown and consumed. Potatoes were introduced from China in

the 1800s and cultivated with relative ease in the northern regions.

Fishing techniques were further refined during the Chosŏn Dynasty, and as the consumption of seafood products rose and a barter economy developed, fishing grew rapidly as an industry. The principal catches of the large-scale fishing industry during this period were croaker, herring, cod and anchovies. Seaweed and sea tangle were popular local produce from ancient times, and now sea laver was cultivated as a major product. Laver was raised and processed on Wando Island off the southwest coast from the mid-Chosŏn Dynasty.

Sea produce was dried, processed in salt water or fermented, and distributed countrywide. Korea's most famous marine product is Alaska pollack, which is considered best when it is dried in January. Records indicate that some 140 kinds of fermented or preserved seafoods, including fermented croaker, salted dry croaker and salted oysters with chili pepper were consumed during the 17th century.

Beef, pheasant, chicken and pork were also widely eaten. Beef raised on Chejudo was especially tasty and noted for its quality. Roe deer, deer and bear's feet were also considered delicacies. These meats were usually dried as jerky, roasted (*ku-i*), steamed (*tchim*), or boiled for soup.

During the Chosŏn Dynasty, food reserves were kept for medical research and famine relief. *Kuhwang ch'waryo*, a treatise written in 1554, lists 851 foods which were stockpiled for famine relief. *Exemplar for Korean Medicine* (*Tongŭi pogam*), written by Hŏ Chun in 1613, gives a detailed explanation of foods related to medical research.

In more recent times, the traditional Korean diet has undergone many rapid changes. Today almost all foods are available in every season. Foreign foods are widely available, and food preparation techniques have also diversified. Fermented foods once made at home are often mass-produced. Restaurants provide more opportunities for dining out. With these unprecedented changes, we look forward to new developments in the Korean diet, but we must also work to provide traditional foods suitable for our modern lives. ◆

Traditional Dietary Customs

Kang In-hee

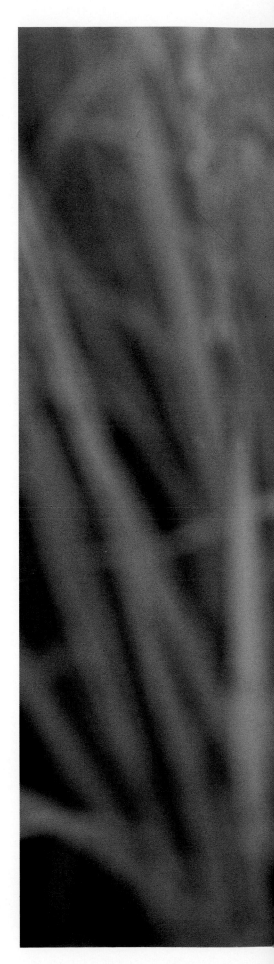

Korea's traditional dietary customs are evident in everyday foods, the foods eaten on special occasions, the foods eaten outside the home, and the foods preserved for later use. While modern Koreans have embraced many foreign food trends, their indigenous dietary culture is a fascinating window on their traditional culture.

Rice, or *pap*, has been a staple in the Korean diet since the Neolithic era. It is eaten in many forms: boiled alone or together with other cereals, such as barley, beans, millet, soybeans, barnyard millet and sorghum.

The traditional extended family averaged 20 members, which meant that rice had to be cooked in large quantities without scorching. First, it was carefully washed to remove sand, stones and husks. Then, after spreading the rice evenly in the kettle, water was added. The level of water was adjusted by placing the palm flat on top of the rice. Water was added until it reached halfway up the back of the hand. The cooking fire was stoked high until the rice boiled. When the water was almost completely absorbed, the fire was allowed to die down, and the rice slowly absorbed the steam. At this point, new fuel was thrown on the fire and burned slowly for watery or soft rice. However, if drier rice was desired, the fire was allowed to keep burning high so that the water and steam evaporated more quickly.

"Two-tiered rice" was prepared when there were elderly or infirm people in the household. One side of the rice kettle was raised higher than the other so that the rice on the lower side would be softer and more watery. Rice cooked in this manner was tastier and rich in gluten. While this obviously had something to do with the quality of the rice, the kettle and method of cooking also played important roles. The heavy kettle lid raised internal pressure, producing sticky and glutinous rice.

Traditional superstition said that luck escaped if the scoop used to serve cooked rice faced the outside of the house. To scoop cooked rice correctly, the uppermost layer was scooped into the bowl of the eldest member of the household first, always facing the inside of the house.

Men's rice bowls were called *chubal* while women's were called *pari.* In winter, brass bowls were used. Porcelain was used in summer. Chubal were rather tall with the top wider than the bottom, which was round and deep. Pari were shorter with a round and flat shape. The lids of these bowls were proportioned such that they could be used to measure rice to be cooked.

The task of scooping cooked rice into so many bowls at each meal was not easy for the traditional daughter-in-law. "Hardships of Life with the In-laws," a Chosŏn-era folk song, points to the difficulties of serving rice.

> Chili peppers may be hot,
> But life with the in-laws is hotter still.
> Oh, how hard it is to scoop rice
> Nice and even into the bowls!

Common people usually cooked a combination of rice and other grains. White rice was placed in the center of the pot and less valuable grains on the bottom and side. The daughter-in-law carefully served the white rice to senior members of the family, saving the softer rice from the middle of the pot for revered elderly family members.

Rice was always accompanied by subsidiary dishes. Vegetables, meat, fish and seafood were prepared in soup, *tchigae* (stew), *chŏn-gol* (casserole), steamed dishes, dishes simmered in soy sauce and

sugar, roasted dishes and *chŏk* (roasted meat or fish on skewers). Seasoned greens, dried slices of radish or cucumber seasoned with soy sauce, fermented seafoods and kimchi, fermented vegetables, were also served at most meals.

Soup and kimchi have always been the basic components of any Korean meal. Side dishes are shared while the main food, rice or noodles, is served individually. Side dishes complement the main food and serve as an important source of nutrients. The taste of side dishes varies with each cook, though the same ingredients and condiments may be used. A cook who turns out delicious food is said to have a "tasty hand." But cooking skills are not acquired overnight. More often than not, cooking expertise was passed down from mother-in-law to daughter-in-law or from mother to daughter. During the Chosŏn Dynasty, the eldest daughter-in-law went through arduous training under her mother-in-law in order to acquire the "tasty hand" passed down as a family tradition. When the daughter-in-law's skills fully developed, the mother-in-law entrusted her with the keys to the pantries where the most important foods, rice in particular, were stored. In this way, family traditions were kept alive through the generations. This system of passing down cooking methods from generation to generation contributed to the formation of unique eating habits in each household and to the creation of regional specialties.

Traditional Korean meals were served on low tables, carried to the diner who sat on the floor. When serving her elders, the housewife or servant was careful to carry the table above her waist, with her head slightly bowed to those seated. She placed the table on the floor several steps from the diners, and then, kneeling, carefully slid the table to them. After politely encouraging them to enjoy the meal, the server removed the lids from the bowls. While the elders were having their meal, the daughter-in-law remained seated next to them to help them with the various dishes so that they were not inconvenienced in any way. When the meal was nearly finished, she returned to the kitchen to prepare tea brewed from the scorched rice on the bottom of the rice kettle.

Scorched-rice tea is fragrant and

savory. The last few spoonfuls of rice were mixed with this tea and consumed with the remaining side dishes. The tea was drunk for taste and to facilitate washing up after the meal.

Koreans customarily ate three meals consisting of a main dish of rice or noodles and side dishes. However, workers who performed hard physical labor or farmers during the busy seasons often had four or five meals a day. Even today, in rice-planting season, farmers have breakfast at dawn, and then around ten in the morning have *saech'am*, a mid-morning snack, followed by lunch at about one in the afternoon. Then at four in the afternoon, between lunch and dinner, another snack is served. Dinner is usually served after the day's work is finished.

Special occasions call for special dishes. In traditional society, rice cakes were the favorite special dish. Rice cakes were generally consumed in autumn and winter. With the harvest over and rain falling, people could not go out to work in the fields. And with the abundance of newly harvested rice, the preparation and consumption of rice cakes became a tradition.

On long winter nights, Koreans roasted *injŏlmi*, flat glutinous rice cakes, which were made in large quantities, on a grill over the brazier kept in the main room. The roasted rice cakes were dipped in *choch'ŏng* (sweet grain syrup) or sometimes in ripe persimmon.

Rice cakes were always shared with neighbors. Rice cakes made on special holidays or for household or village rituals were called *pan-gi*. These rice cakes were stacked on a wooden plate and passed among neighbors and relatives. The sharing of pan-gi was called *pan-gi sari*. Under the extended family system, proper pan-gi sari was an important criterion for a virtuous housewife and daughter-in-law. Moreover it was an important factor in maintaining good relations with relatives and neighbors.

Special dishes, aside from rice cakes, included noodles, hot and cold, grilled wheat cakes, thick grain porridge and dumplings, which were cooked differently depending on the season. Among the favorite porridge dishes were pumpkin porridge, red bean porridge, mung bean porridge and seafood porridge. *Sixteen Treatises on the Development of Nature*

and the Comforting of the People (*Imwon kyŏngje shimnyuk-chi*), a mid-Chosŏn agricultural tract, describes a special porridge enjoyed more for its fragrance than taste. Fallen petals of the Japanese apricot were gathered, then boiled in melted snow and mixed with cooled white rice porridge.

Foods eaten outside the home, at work, on picnics and on trips are another important culinary genre in Korea. The term *ture pap* refers to food eaten outdoors while working in the fields. Laborers gathered in a circle at the edge of the field to share a meal brought out from a home in the village, most often that of the owner of the field. The term derives from *ture*, community cooperation among villagers who take turns helping each other with farm work during the peak farming seasons.

During the spring rice-planting and autumn harvest season, ture pap was taken to the fields four or five times a day. Noodles were the most common main dish. Sometimes rice was cooked as described in this farming song.

Why don't you beat the rice
in a mortar, missus.
Better make plenty of rice mixed
with barley,
Soup and lettuce
with hot soybean paste.

Side dishes, generally consisting of fresh green vegetables, such as lettuce to wrap around rice with hot soybean paste, and rice mixed with barley were frequently carried to the fields in large quantities.

Hungry workers were happy to eat anything and there was no special formula for ture pap. Milky white rice wine, or *makkŏlli*, was a must, however. Makkŏlli was traditionally included with the morning snack, which was sometimes called the "wine snack."

Farmers whetted their appetites before the meal with makkŏlli drunk from a hollow gourd, and after the meal they drank to clear away the aftertaste. Once their tongues were loosened by the alcohol they often sang work songs in chorus.

Food consumed in the mountains or while working in the fields was called a "field meal." Rice and wine were the most

common components of these meals. Grilled meat was also prepared as an appetizer to go with the drinks. On outings, the upper classes were often served *kujŏlp'an*, a collection of nine vegetables, meats and eggs, sautéed separately and arranged in a nine-compartment serving dish. Diners wrapped these ingredients in small flour pancakes or ate them one by one like other side dishes.

In traditional society, flower-viewing outings were a popular upper-class diversion. These outings usually took place on the third day of the third lunar month or on the ninth day of the ninth lunar month. Among the foods associated with these outings were flower pancakes eaten while admiring the seasonal blooms. Glutinous rice flour, cooking oil and a frying pan were taken along to prepare the treats under the trees. The tradition of eating outdoors reflects the Korean desire to bond with nature and is one of the most obvious examples of nature's important role in Korean dietary customs.

Hanghan was another food associated with travel. It generally consisted of roasted cereal flour. Cereals were washed carefully, then dried, roasted and ground into a fine powder. This powder was easy to carry and could be mixed with water along the road to satisfy hunger. It is still popular today in the form of *misu karu*, a powdered drink made of several roasted grains.

Bran cakes or rice balls the size of a fist were also prepared for short trips, as they did not stay fresh on longer journeys. Dried fish or meats were convenient side dishes for such meals. However, these were hanghan for the well-to-do. Ordinary people carried soybean paste cakes as side dishes. The round, flat cakes were made of diced green onions and garlic and salty soybean paste. After mixing these ingredients the cakes were spread on the lid of a pot in the yard and coated with sesame oil. They were salty, yet tasty, and easy to carry and keep on extended trips.

Preserved foods have long been an important part of the Korean diet. These foods were usually processed when the ingredients were in abundance. In Korea, the custom of preserving food developed over centuries. Typical preserved foods are *chang*, soy sauce and other soy-based

pastes.

Chang-making is one of Korea's oldest dietary customs. Originally it involved the production of soy-based condiments, but after the introduction of the chili pepper during the mid-Chosŏn period, spicy soybean paste, or *koch'ujang*, was also made. Chang was the basic seasoning for food, and the earthenware jars in which these condiments were stored were treated with great care. Traditional houses had raised stone terraces on which these storage jars were kept. Soy sauce was kept in a large jar, a middled-sized jar was used for bean paste, and a small jar for koch'ujang. The outside of each jar was cleaned daily, and the contents were

A typical Korean meal (top), cold noodles from the northern provinces (upper left), yakshik, glutinous rice mixed with chestnuts, jujubes and pinenuts (above), and hwajŏn, rice cakes decorated with sliced jujubes (upper right)

aired on clear days to prevent mold from forming on the surface of the condiments.

The chang-making process began with the preparation of soybean mash at the end of the tenth lunar month. The mash was dried in the sun and ready to be used by the beginning of the following year. Soy sauce was made from the end of the first month until early in the third month. An auspicious day was picked for this important event. People tried to avoid Shinil, the "Day of the Monkey," which was thought inauspicious, as well as a day on which any woman of the household was menstruating.

The winter kimchi-making was another important household event. Cabbages and other vegetables were pickled, processed and stored when vegetables were plentiful in order to provide valuable nutrients during the long winter months when fresh vegetables were scarce. This process, called *kimjang*, was performed in early winter, usually before the first snow.

Kimjang required many hands. Traditionally, sisters-in-law, relatives and neighbors each picked a different day for kimjang and took turns helping each other in a cooperative practice called *p'um-ashi*. Salted cabbages and leftover ingredients were also shared, and samples of freshly-made kimchi were handed out as a gesture of gratitude to the helpers. Women from poorer households helped as many households as possible in order to collect kimchi and the ingredients necessary to make their own kimchi.

Korea's traditional dietary culture is characterized by several distinct features. First, courtesy toward elders was always important. Elders were served first and when possible, with a better quality rice. No one could eat until the elders had been served. Respect for elders was an essential virtue.

Second was the sense of family tradition. Recipes and special cooking methods were handed down from generation to generation, thus perpetuating the unique taste of each household's meals. In addition, regional specialities were recognized and appreciated.

Third was the sense of community. Special dishes were shared with neighbors and relatives, just as happy occasions and grief were shared. Similarly, the exchange of labor in the form of ture and p'um-ashi reflects the strong cooperative spirit in which the community took precedence over the individual.

Finally, Koreans have long savored refined and poetical pursuits. The custom of working and eating together derived from a spirit of generosity and a refined sense of community. Meals were often followed by drinking and singing, and the tradition of picking flower petals to make flower cakes while on flower-gazing expeditions encouraged a closer relationship with nature. These are the underlying values of the traditional dietary culture, the foundation for a rich and rewarding cuisine. ◆

Clockwise from top left: Glutinous rice cakes with beans; kujŏlp'an; kyŏngdan, stuffed hand rolled rice cakes; and jars used to store soybean paste and other condiments

181

Life's Milestones:
Ceremonies and Food

Park Tae-sun

Birth has always been considered an act of grace and a mystic phenomenon. We all know that human beings are conceived and given birth to by their parents, yet the mystery and wonder remain. The belief that human beings were born by divine will was common in ancient times because people wanted an explanation for the mystery of life.

Koreans shared this belief in life's divine dimension and regarded life as extremely precious. They marked events in their lives, giving each special meaning. From this arose ceremonies celebrating life's milestones: coming-of-age, marriage, death, and memorial services after death. In Korea, these ceremonies were called the "four formalities" and remain important events in Korean life.

Although birth was not included in the four formalities, it was extremely important. The actual birth itself, the third day of life, every seventh day up to the 49th day, the hundredth day and the first birthday were all celebrated. Many families continue to hold these ceremonies.

Birth rituals actually begin before the birth itself. Just before delivery, three bowls of rice and three bowls of soup are placed on a table. Helpers rub their hands in supplication to Samshin or Sanshin, the goddess of childbirth, who governs pregnancy, safe birth and child rearing. Samshin is also called Samshirang or Samshin halmŏni (birth grandmother) depending on the region. The table honoring Samshin includes plain white rice, seaweed soup and water drawn from a well at daybreak. After the helpers pray, a senior family member or neighbor, usually the mother-in-law, prays for the mother's health and the baby's longevity, rubbing her hands as she recites. This prayer is called pison, a compound of pilda ("to pray") and son ("hand"). After the baby is delivered, plain white rice and seaweed soup are served to the mother.

On the third day after delivery, the mother washes herself with boiled sagebrush water and the baby with warm water for the first time. Three bowls of plain white rice and three bowls of seaweed soup are prepared and set on a table for Samshin and pison is performed again. It is only from the third day that others can see the newborn.

Every seventh day up to the 49th day of life, a special ceremony is held. Those days are called ire, with the prefix of the number, one to seven, added. Thus ch'o-ire is the first of the seven days, tu-ire is the second, se-ire is the third, and so on until mangjong-ire, the "last" ire. On each of these special days, early in the morning, plain white rice, seaweed soup and sometimes rice cakes are served, and pison is performed. Then the relatives gather to bless the baby.

Sometimes the food is shared with neighbors. The royal family and wealthy people made large quantities of rice cakes from glutinous kaoliang and gave them to passersby at the main and rear gates of their households on these special days. This custom was called inbushim, the "cleansing of impurities."

After the final seventh day ceremony, all taboos are rescinded. The kŭmjul, "taboo ropes" hung across the gate of the house announcing the birth of a child, are removed. Family members are allowed to visit the homes of people who have had recent deaths in their families. The mother can do ordinary housework, and the baby can be taken outside.

The one-hundredth day after the delivery is called paegil, literally "one hundred days." A special ceremonial feast is held. In the morning, plain white rice and seaweed soup are prepared for Samshin, and pison is performed for the last time. After the mother has eaten the rice and soup, the food for the banquet is arranged on a table.

A variety of rice cakes are served for paegil: steamed white rice cakes, which represent purity and cleanliness; glutinous kaoliang rice cakes and glutinous rice cakes coated with mashed red beans, which represent endurance and strong will; rice cakes steamed on a layer of pine needles, which represent

Rice cakes and other homemade sweets are served at all special rites and celebrations.

generosity; and stuffed rice cakes, which represent a full mind. Each cake is made for longevity, purity and divinity. It is important that at least 100 people partake of the cakes so that the baby will enjoy a long life.

The neighbors and relatives in turn present the child rice and string, symbols of longevity and good fortune. The paegil party is meant to bless the child and prevent misfortune which may hinder the baby's growth.

The first birthday is called *tol*. It is more elaborate than the paegil party. The main foods are rice cakes and fruit. The four kinds of rice cakes served at paegil are prepared again. *Kyŏngdan*, steamed rice cake balls rolled in cinnamon, bean flour or powdered sesame are served in colorful displays. "Rainbow" rice cake, or *mujigae ttŏk*, is also prepared in the hope that the baby will have many accomplishments, as varied as the colors of the rainbow.

The first birthday includes a special custom called *tolchabi*. On a low table various items are arranged: rice, rice cakes, cookies, money, thread, books, paper, a writing brush, and a bow and arrow. For girls, a pair of scissors and a ruler take the place of the bow and arrow. The baby is formally dressed in a traditional costume and encouraged to take hold of anything he or she likes. The baby's future is told by the item chosen. Money and rice indicate wealth. Thread symbolizes longevity, and books or a brush represent scholarship.

Again the party food is shared with relatives and neighbors, who usually give presents with blessings. Traditional gifts are

KUNG-JUNG FOOD RESEARCH INSTITUTION

The first birthday predicts the baby's future and brings family members and neighbors together.

thread, clothing, money, gold rings, spoons and chopsticks, bowls and toys.

Every birthday is celebrated with the sharing of food with relatives and neighbors. As with paegil and tol, tables for Samshin and for the household god (*sŏngju*) who takes care of the house are prepared in the main living room, and prayers are offered for longevity and good fortune. The person celebrating his or her birthday eats the food placed on the table for Samshin.

The Korean term for "birthday" varies according to the person concerned. The usual term is *saengil* which refers to the birthdays of younger people. *Saengshin* is the term for elders, and *t'anil* or *t'anshin* refers to the birthdays of respected Buddhist monks and royalty.

After the first birthday the next important milestone in a Korean life is the coming-of-age ceremony, generally held between the ages of 15 and 20 for boys and at 15 for girls. A boy's

parents must not have lost any of their own parents or close senior relatives during the previous year; otherwise the ceremony is postponed. Traditionally, Korean boys of 15 were supposed to have a knowledge of two Confucian classics, the *Analects* of Confucius and the *Book of Filial Piety*. The boy was expected to understand the manners, ways and teachings of the sages. Only after the boy had mastered these teachings was the ceremony performed.

Though relatively rare, the ceremony is still held today. The ceremony is usually held in the first month of the lunar calendar. The ceremonial table is relatively simple with wine, dried meat, marinated meat and boiled meat. Relatives and guests are served additional food, however, such as noodles, rice cakes, other meats, wine and fruit.

The sixtieth birthday, *hoegap*, is a landmark in any Korean life. Celebrations are usually organized by the person's offspring. The banquet is magnificent. The main ceremonial table, *mangsang*, is placed in front of the parents. Another large table, also for the parents, is prepared separately. The offspring carefully fill a cup with wine, offer it to the parents and bow in pairs before them. Meanwhile, there is dancing and music, and drinking songs are sung by guests or performers. The senior guests are carefully looked after and served wine and side dishes.

Traditionally, marriage could only take place with the recognition and acceptance of the two families involved. Marriage was seen not as the union of two individuals but as the union of two families, which were thus brought together in a close and lasting relationship.

In traditional Korean society, the act of marriage consisted of four steps set forth in *An Inquiry into the Four Ceremonies* (*Sarye p'yŏllam*), a treatise written during the rule of the Chosŏn king Sukchong (r. 1674-1720).

The agreement to marry, or *ŭihon*, is the first step in the marriage process. The family of the boy sends a letter proposing marriage to the girl's family, along with another letter in which *saju*, the "Four Pillars" (the year, month, day and hour of birth) of the bridegroom-to-be, are written. After receiving the saju, the girl's family sends a letter agreeing to the marriage and another giving the dates for the delivery of the wedding chest prepared by the groom's family and for the marriage ceremony.

The delivery of the wedding chest filled with blue and red silk cloth and marriage documents by the bridegroom's family is called *napp'ae*. The cloth was usually meant for two sets of traditional costumes for the bride-to-be. Sometimes, hair ornaments or bracelets were sent instead of silk. Farmers were more practical. They usually sent cotton seed, chilies, charcoal and seaweed.

Ch'inyŏng is the final stage of the wedding ceremony in which the bride is received at the bridegroom's house. Originally, the bridegroom went to the bride's house on horseback and gave a pair of wild geese carved from wood to the bride's family. Then, he brought the bride to his home in a palanquin to hold a ceremony in which bows are exchanged. Later, the giving of wooden geese, *chonan*, and the ritual exchange of bows, *kyobaerye*, was held at the bride's home.

In more modern renditions of the traditional wedding, a marquee is set up, and a wedding table is prepared in the center of the main room or yard. Usually, branches of pine and bamboo, chestnuts, Chinese dates, red beans, rice, a live hen and cock, a candle stand, blue and red thread, and a cup are placed on the table.

The bridegroom stands to the east, and the bride to the west. The bride bows first, then the bridegroom returns the bow. They repeat their bows and share a cup of wine three times. That is the end of the ceremony.

On the wedding night, the couple meet in private. A drinking table called *chuansang*, or *inyŏnsang*, "table of the bond of affinity," is set up in their room. Only after the table is taken away do they retire.

The next morning the couple bows to the bride's parents and other senior family members. Usually on the third day the couple leaves the bride's house for the bridegroom's house.

The presentation of the new bride to the bridegroom's parents for the first time is now called *p'yebaek*. The bride offers wine and slices of dried beef or steamed chicken as a side dish. The mother-in-law then casts Chinese dates or chestnuts into the bride's skirt, wishing prosperity and many sons for the new couple.

Three days after the couple's arrival at the bridegroom's house, the bridegroom visits the bride's house again. In earlier times, the bride visited her home only after eating the food of the first harvest at her new home. This visit was called *kŭnch'in*, "seeing one's parents." When the bride returned to her in-law's house, a party was held with the neighbors.

Funerals are the most serious ceremonies

because they deal with the dead and their spirits. The Korean funeral is a complicated process starting with the moment of death and continuing for up to two years. After two years have passed annual memorial ceremonies are held. Each rite related to the passing of a family member involves the preparation of ritual food for the deceased and a feast for relatives and neighbors attending the rites.

Ancestral spirit tablets are kept in an ancestral shrine called a *sadang*. Though most of these shrines have disappeared, the sadang was rich in family history and served as a reminder of family ties over the last several hundred years.

In the past, when someone died, his or her spirit was served food at the mourning shrine every morning and evening for a full two years. The meal was prepared in the usual way with special bowls, chopsticks and a spoon reserved for the deceased. The meal had to be served as if the person were still living in the house. Special food, with extra dishes, was offered on the new moon and full moon, and the cook was expected to devote herself to the preparation of the meals. When all was ready, a ceremony was held. Vigorous keening was important.

On the deceased's birthdays, the food and ceremonies were more elaborate. Wine, fruit, dried or seasoned meat, soup, skewers of fish and meat, rice cakes, cold rice drink, white rice, soup and greens were served in special dishes. The food was cut in large pieces or cooked whole. Decorations were simple and colors modest.

After the second anniversary of the death, or *taesang*, the mourning shrine was dismantled and the mortuary tablet was enshrined in the ancestral shrine, which contained the mortuary tablets of ancestors from four generations.

Seasonal memorial rites, or *shije*, are held quarterly in the middle month of each season. A Fire or Pig Day is chosen and a service is offered to four generations of ancestors. The appointed day is announced at the ancestral shrine three days in advance. Shije is held in the main room of the house.

For ancestors five or more generations back, the descendants gather once a year, usually during the tenth lunar month, and hold a memorial rite at the burial mound. Offerings are prepared by a tenant farmer who tends the fields. The oldest grandson of the main family supervises the rites, called *myoje* ("grave side rites"). Myoje is similar to the four seasonal services. Before the ceremony com-

Hours are spent making rice cakes for birthdays and other rites and celebrations, then still more time and patience are required for the careful stacking of the final product.

mences, a smaller ceremony honoring the mountain god is held. Participants stand in order of their relationship to the deceased and according to seniority from the left of the burial mound.

When the rite is over, family members eat the food used in the service and talk about their ancestors and family affairs.

In the Kyŏnggi region, services are held at burial mounds on every festival day, such as Hanshik (the 105th day after the winter solstice) and Ch'usŏk (the Harvest Moon Festival on the 15th of the eighth lunar month). The services are relatively simple. Offerings are limited to fruits of three different colors, dried, marinated meat and rice cakes steamed on a layer of pine needles on the Harvest Moon Day, or rice cake soup on New Year's Day.

At midnight on the memorial day after two years of mourning, a ceremony called *kije* is held by the descendants. A special table is set up in the main room, and the mortuary tablets are brought from the shrine. The tablets are set up together or separately depending on family custom.

Food offerings are arranged according to strict rules. The mortuary tablets are placed to the north. Close to the tablets, a cup of wine, cooked rice and soup, seasoned meat on skewers, soup again, seasoned vegetables and fruits are placed. Red fruits are placed to the east and white ones to the west. Chinese dates, then chestnuts, pears and fresh or dried persimmons are placed in that order from the west in the front row. Skewered fish is placed to the east and skewered meat to the west. Slices of dried, marinated meat are placed to the west and a cold drink made from fermented rice is placed to the east.

Human life is a series of events from birth to death. Suffering and pleasure follow the natural succession of prosperity and poverty, success and failure. Koreans believe these events are predetermined by the will of the heavens. Traditionally they held ceremonies to honor the spirits of their ancestors and pray to gods of nature, such as the mountain god and the goddess of childbirth. They believed that an innocent heart and deep devotion were essential to ensure the success of these ceremonies. They offered prayers, performed purifications of the mind and the body, and took extra care in choosing materials and preparing the food. Thus the food and the rites embodied the pure intentions of the Korean people which in turn influenced the dietary culture of Korea. ◆

186

Food offerings are arranged according to strict rules for ancestral memorial rites and funerals. Above, preparations for a memorial rite; right, the ritual offerings of a yangban clan. Below, a funeral procession and the meal served to the "messengers of death." According to popular Korean belief, food is prepared for the three messengers as an incentive to guide the dead on a comfortable journey to the underworld. Three bowls of rice, three pairs of straw shoes, and three packets of "travel money" are offered.

Holiday Customs and Food

Yim Jae-hae

In all cultures, there are two categories of cuisine: everyday food and occasional food. Everyday food is usually simple, wholesome and relatively inexpensive. Occasional food includes anything eaten as a snack or delicacy as well as food consumed during special holidays or festivals and at ritual ceremonies. This food is usually more difficult and costly to prepare but much loved by the people.

In Korea, the daily fare is simple. It generally consists of plain rice, soup and a few side dishes, everything following the seasons carefully. Festival food, on the other hand, is more complicated. Often special dishes are prepared with costly ingredients not readily available. Dried vegetables and fruits as well as special cakes are central to festival food. Traditionally, everyone looked forward to holidays because special foods were served. The food was a symbol of the celebratory atmosphere and a means of supplementing the daily diet.

Plain boiled or steamed rice is central to daily meals but not on special occasions. If rice is served, it is usually glutinous rice, rice cakes or red-bean porridge. At ancestral memorial rites or parties, ordinary rice is consumed, but many special foods, such as rice cakes, fruits, and various side dishes, are also served.

Traditionally, each holiday and rite had its own foods and customs. Rice cake soup (*ttŏkkuk*) was served on New Year's Day, glutinous rice or five-grain rice (a mixture of any five of the following cereals: millet, soybeans, red beans, barley, barnyard millet, and sorghum) on Taeborŭm, the first full moon of the year, azalea pancakes on the third day of the third lunar month, steamed rice cakes mixed with tender zelkova leaves on the eighth evening of the fourth lunar month, cakes made of rice flour and mugwort paste during the Tano Festival (the fifth day of the fifth lunar month), grilled wheat-cakes at the Yudu Festival (15th of the 6th lunar month),

crescent-shaped stuffed rice cakes on Ch'usŏk (Harvest Moon Festival on the 15th of the eighth lunar month), chrysanthemum pancakes on the ninth of the ninth lunar month, and red-bean porridge on the winter solstice.

The tradition of specific holiday dishes was not the result of personal choice or temporary desire. On the contrary, these customs evolved quite naturally over a long period of time. There are good reasons for preparing a specific kind of food at a specific time of the year. Many food traditions originated in seasonal and agricultural activities. Rural people naturally consumed food soon after it was harvested. These seasonal foods were part of their everyday diets and were incorporated into special dishes.

Barley and wheat are harvested in summer, so Koreans naturally ate boiled barley and noodles in the summer months. In autumn, rice and foxtail millet are harvested and used in seasonal foods.

Side dishes are no different. In spring, wild mountain greens are favorite side dishes, while in summer, vegetables grown in the fields, such as lettuce and cabbage, are consumed. Of course, foods made of seasonal ingredients are not always holiday foods. Still, a cake made with rice flour and mugwort paste, a spring favorite, is a special holiday dish if it is enjoyed on special days or during a given holiday. Thus, in certain regions, a seasonal dish becomes a holiday food.

Naturally, traditional holidays are not ordinary days. On New Year's Day, Koreans pay their respects to their ancestors. The first full moon of the year is a day to offer tribute to the village gods, and the Tano Festival in the fifth lunar month is a time to pray for a bountiful harvest. On Ch'usŏk, Koreans offer freshly harvested crops to the gods before consuming them. As such, these four special days are unique in the year, a time for special rituals and games. On these days, Koreans take a rest

Ch'usŏk, the Harvest Moon Festival, is celebrated with crescent-shaped rice cakes (top) and seasonal specialities such as taro soup (left) and skewered mushrooms (right).

from everyday chores, hold ancestral memorial rites or perform rites honoring the village god. During festivals, the whole village plays special games. People wear new clothes, eat delicious holiday food, and visit their relatives and neighbors to exchange greetings.

With this break in routine, it is only natural that special foods replace the everyday fare. There are several reasons for making special dishes on traditional holidays.

The significance of the holiday is brought to life and its function emphasized by special food. Holidays, such as New Year's Day and Ch'usŏk, are for honoring ancestors, praying for a rich harvest or performing exorcisms to prevent natural disasters. In order to perform these holiday ceremonies properly, we must prepare a variety of food offerings. On Taeborŭm, we cook rice with five different grains to bring about a bumper crop, and on the

New Year's Day brings the exchange of formal greetings (top) and rice cake soup (below).

KUNG-JUNG FOOD RESEARCH INSTITUTION

winter solstice, we cook and mash red beans into a porridge to drive ghosts away. Just as it would not seem like Ch'usŏk or New Year's Day if we did not perform ancestral memorial rites, it would not feel like Taeborŭm if we did not eat five-grain rice. In order to bring the holiday tradition alive, we must have dishes appropriate to the occasion.

Holiday dishes made with the crops and wild greens of a particular season supplement the daily diet. All foods are most nutritious when consumed during the season in which they are harvested. Thus holiday foods contribute to good health. For instance, the mugwort paste used in rice cakes during the Tano Festival is thought to be medicinal. Mugwort is a wild green plant known to provide energy and is widely used in traditional Oriental medicine. Its effects are said to be best at the time of the Tano Festival. Thus it is a Tano custom to gather

mugwort, dry it to make a medicine, and use its tender leaves to make rice cakes. On Ch'usŏk, it is customary to eat freshly harvested rice, make rice cakes and rice wine from it, and consume fresh autumn fruits and vegetables, thus taking advantage of the season's bounty.

Delicious foods reserved for special occasions also heighten the festive atmosphere and the importance of a special day. Traditional holidays provide relief from tedious daily chores. People wear their good clothes, play games and eat delicious food. In this way, the holiday is truly enjoyed.

Special holiday dishes also help reduce the workload of the housewife who must receive and feed many relatives and guests. Often holiday foods, such as rice cake soup and red-bean porridge, are easier to prepare and serve in large quantities and require less washing up afterward For

Taeborŭm, the first full moon of the new year, is celebrated with five-grain rice, seasoned vegetables, nuts (below) and noisy fireworks (above).

example, on New Year's Day, ancestral memorial rites are held at the home of the eldest son in the clan. Not only do relatives come to pay respects to their ancestors, but many neighbors call to offer their respects to the household's senior members. Rice and ritual side dishes are prepared for the memorial tables but guests are served rice cake soup, the New Year's holiday dish. Vast quantities of white rice cake are prepared beforehand, and when the need arises, the housewife simply boils soup stock prepared in advance, adds the sliced rice cake and garnishes, and serves. With garnishes of meat and scallions, and a bowl or two of kimchi, no other side dishes are needed. Dishwashing is easy too for each guest uses only one bowl, a spoon and a pair of chopsticks.

The same is true for red-bean porridge, the holiday dish of the winter solstice. Rice is added to a soup made from strained red

191

beans and boiled, then glutinous rice cakes the size of birds' eggs are added. The porridge's red color is believed to drive evil spirits away. Plenty is made, feeding the family and friends for several days after the holiday. It is simply reheated before serving and requires few side dishes.

Every holiday has unique significance. More often than not, various meanings are attached to it. Holiday dishes also have several meanings which help define the holiday in people's minds. In fact, holidays would hardly exist if not for the ancient customs and cuisines associated with them.

Holiday dishes serve many purposes. They play an important role in sacrificial rituals, for example. Special care is taken in the preparation and offering of the food at ancestral memorial services or in rites honoring household gods. Foods offered during ancestral rites should be white. The rice cake soup served at the New Year's Day ritual and rice cakes at Ch'usŏk rituals are always white. Rice is also the basic ingredient in holiday dishes because it was long considered a sacred grain. Ghosts, including the spirits of deceased family members, like white and shun red. For this reason, the red skin of beans was peeled off for use in rice cakes offered to ancestors. The only grain used in these ritual foods was rice because other grains would make the food less white and less delicious to the spirits. As the family wanted the spirits of their ancestors to enjoy the food, they made it appealing to them.

Some holiday foods served in rites are used to predict the outcome of the coming harvest. The five-grain rice consumed on Taeborŭm is a good example. Many ceremonies in supplication for a good harvest are performed at this time because it is the first full moon. Rites honoring the village god ask for a rich harvest, and the outcome of games, such as tug-of-war, which involve the whole village, predict the result of the harvest. It is only natural that the foods eaten on this day are connected with these rituals. Five-grain rice or glutinous rice are eaten in hopes of promoting a bountiful harvest in all grains and offered, with brief prayers, to the household god, the goddess governing childbirth, as well as the kitchen god and family gods.

Five-grain rice and wild greens are given to oxen on special days to predict the performance of all crops. The outcome of the impending harvest is predicted by the order in which the ox consumes the food. For instance, a good harvest of grains is anticipated if the ox eats the rice first. In some regions, holiday

food is placed in front of the ox shed in the hope that the ox will stay healthy and accident-free.

Taeborŭm is also marked by the *pokssam* tradition. Pokssam literally means "wrapping luck." Cooked white rice is wrapped in sheets of dried seaweed or laver, or occasionally castor-bean leaves, taro leaves or jelly greens. These rice bundles are then eaten in the belief that the meal will bring a bountiful harvest. The more that is eaten, the better the harvest.

Holiday dishes also drive away evil spirits and ward off misfortune. The red-bean porridge of the winter solstice is the best example of this tradition. Malevolent ghosts are thought to come out on the winter solstice because it is the longest night of the year. Naturally many customs associated with ghosts are performed on this day. Red frightens ghosts, so red-bean porridge is the main holiday dish. The Chinese share this tradition on the winter solstice. According to a Chinese folk tale, there once was a silly man who, for no apparent reason, was afraid of red beans. He died on the winter solstice to be reincarnated as an evil ghost spreading illness everywhere. From that time on, red beans and red-bean porridge have been scattered through villages to frighten the repulsive ghost away.

Some people believe this is why Koreans eat red-bean porridge on the winter solstice, but the custom most likely began as a ritual to prevent the appearance of ghosts on the longest night of the year. A bowl of porridge is placed in every room, on the open wooden-floored room or veranda at the center of the

KUNGJUNG FOOD RESEARCH INSTITUTION

Red-bean porridge for the winter solstice

house, in the barn, and at the shrine of the village god. The rest is consumed by the family and neighbors.

Some foods are thought to prevent accidents or natural disasters. When a person's fortune indicated that he or she would be harmed in water, wrapped rice was thrown into a well in the middle of the night. People who thought they had an especially unlucky year went around the neighborhood, begging for grain. Then a small amount of the grain was wrapped in window paper and hung on a rope between two pine trees on the first full moon, thus warding off misfortune. This ritual originated in the belief that vengeful gods or ghosts could be appeased with good food.

Among the holiday dishes cooked with gods and ghosts in mind are those said to be good for health or to bring a whole year of good luck if eaten on a specific day. Red-bean porridge eaten on the winter solstice was said to help maintain good health throughout the year. Rice cake soup consumed on New Year's Day was thought to prevent headaches. Its preventive effects were enhanced by a candle lit on the fireplace while the soup was being prepared.

On Taeborŭm, the first full moon, roasted peas, walnuts, ginkgo nuts, chestnuts and other hard nuts are cracked open with the teeth and eaten. The practice is thought to strengthen the teeth. The nuts are also believed to prevent boils and swelling in the coming year. The day starts with a cup of unheated rice wine, dubbed "hearing enhancing wine," in the belief that it clears the ears. On this occasion women drink with men, a rare occurrence.

In midsummer when the weather is very hot, many foods thought to strengthen the body are consumed. People perspire heavily, lose their appetites and are thus susceptible to illness during Pok-nal, the three seasonal divisions of the lunar calendar that mark the hottest summer weather. *Samgyet'ang*, chicken soup made of a chicken stuffed with ginseng, Chinese dates and glutinous rice, and croaker stew are thought to fortify the body against summer's heat.

Special holiday foods also remind us of the holiday's significance. As they eat rice cake soup, New Year's Day celebrants reflect on the fact that everyone is a year older. "How many bowls of rice cake soup have you eaten?" is a polite way of asking how old a person is. It is even said that a person does not really age if he or she has not had a bowl of rice cake soup on New Year's Day.

Other holiday dishes also bring the meaning of the holiday to life. The red-bean porridge of the winter solstice serves the same purpose as the rice cake soup of New Year's Day. From ancient times, the winter solstice was called the "small" New Year's Day because it was the year's shortest day and marked the beginning of longer daylight hours. The red-bean porridge eaten on this day was a sign that one was a year older, just like rice cake soup on New Year's Day. Some people say that the number of round rice cakes in your porridge should match your age.

Some foods are traditionally forbidden on certain holidays. One avoids these foods to prevent misfortune. These taboo foods are not forbidden throughout the year, only on certain days. For example, on the first Chicken Day of the new year, hens are not slaughtered for consumption. On Taeborŭm, it is customary not to mix rice with water or to make porridge for breakfast. If rice is consumed in this way, weeds will grow thick in the fields. If glutinous rice is mixed with water and consumed on Taeborŭm, one can expect a sudden shower while on the road.

On the eve of the first moon and the following morning, one should avoid drinking cold water or eating scorched rice or ground chili pepper. Otherwise, you may be stung by a bee or another insect. These customs were probably established to correct bad eating habits.

Holiday food is largely for sacred rites or for consumption on a special day. Sacred food was prepared and offered to benevolent gods, including village gods and household gods. Offerings were made for a good harvest and the well-being of the family. Food was also offered to ancestors. Special dishes were prepared for ghosts that might bring misfortune or diseases. Foods that evil ghosts disliked were also placed at strategic locations to protect the household.

Holiday food for human consumption can also be divided into two categories: holiday dishes that protect health and ward off illness, and dishes that help us reflect on the significance of the holiday and heighten the festive mood. The former makes us sound in body while the latter makes us sound in mind. As such, holiday dishes offer several benefits. From the religious point of view, they help ease our minds and give us hope for a brighter future. From the nutritional point of view, they provide nutrients and make eating a pleasure.

The rise of mass-produced food products and improved food distribution systems has diminished some of the holiday spirit by providing many "seasonal" foods throughout the year. The adoption of the solar calendar and Western holidays has also undermined many traditional holidays. Special holiday foods not only compensate for our excessive consumption of additives and preservatives found in "instant" foods but also help us

A simple offering of fruit and rice cakes at a village shrine

maintain a balance of nutrients. Holiday dishes also whet the appetite, adding variety to our diets.

Equally important is the seasonal aspect. Holiday food generally consists of produce that has been harvested at its peak and so has the greatest nutritional value. And we must not forget its spiritual significance. The preparation of holiday dishes to be used as offerings at rituals, the subsequent sharing of the food with neighbors and relatives in the belief that one will receive luck, and the cooking of dishes thought to prevent misfortune and diseases put people in a spiritual frame of mind and prompt them to think about the relationship between gods and humanity. If we eat a specific holiday dish believing that by doing so we will have good fortune and remain healthy, then, through the power of faith, the effects are, to some extent, obtained. This placebo effect cannot be ignored for it certainly contributes to our spiritual well-being. ◆

Traditional Foods and Table Settings

Han Pok-jin

A careful look at traditional Korean food reveals close cultural links between Korea and other Asian countries. Korea's dietary culture shares many characteristics with the food cultures of China and Japan. For example, all three are based on rice. However, despite these similarities, the food and customs of the three countries have developed in quite different directions. Let us look at the foods Koreans have eaten for centuries, cooking methods and customs associated with the serving of food.

Main Dishes

Rice

When rice is the main dish, it is called *pap*. Pap is generally plain white rice, though other grains are often added. The grains are boiled in water, then steamed in the resulting vapor until thoroughly cooked. Vegetables, seafood or meat are sometimes mixed with the rice. *Pibimbap* is steamed rice mixed with seasoned vegetables and meat and topped with hot soybean paste.

Porridge

To make porridge, or *chuk*, whole grains or milled grains are boiled with plenty of water until they are thoroughly cooked and the mixture becomes thick and smooth. Vegetables, meat, fish or shellfish are sometimes added to the mixture. Nuts and beans are also used for porridge. They are ground fine, then boiled to create a smooth gruel. Nut and bean porridge are generally eaten for breakfast, as a special treat or as a palliative for the sick or elderly. *Miŭm*, a thin rice gruel often given to patients, is made of whole grains of rice, which are boiled in water, then pressed through a sieve.

Noodles

Noodles are usually eaten as a simple and light food at lunch time. They are generally made of wheat, buckwheat, or arrowroot and can be divided into three categories: warm noodles in hot soup, cold noodles in cold broth or clear kimchi broth, and noodles mixed with vegetables and meat, much like pibimbap, without any liquid.

A humble noodle lunch (left) and a meal fit for a king (right)

Dumpling Soup and Rice Cake Soup

Dumpling soup (*manduguk*) and rice cake soup (*ttŏkkuk*), like noodles, are served as a simple main meal. On New Year's Day, every Korean family prepares rice cake soup to offer to its ancestors. It has been the first meal of New Year's Day since early times. Rice cake soup is made of sliced white rice cake boiled in meat stock and garnished with scallions, shredded meat and eggs.

Dumplings (*mandu*) consist of a thin pastry skin, which is filled with a variety of ingredients, such as minced meat, kimchi, bean curd, bean sprouts and other vegetables, nuts, meats and seeds. Dumpling soup, dumplings boiled in beef broth and topped with a garnish of scallions, is a winter favorite.

Side Dishes

Soups

Soup is the most important side dish when the main dish is rice. Korean cuisine features many soups: clear soups, thick bean paste soups, meat stock soups, and chilled soups. Soups can be made with shellfish, vegetables and seaweed as well as meat. The meat is usually used to make a stock, then vegetables are added. When possible, especially with beef, all parts of the animal, including the bones, intestines, and blood, are used.

Soups are seasoned with salt, soy sauce, soybean paste and hot soybean paste. During the hot summer months, chilled soups made of cucumber, seaweed, and sea tangle are often eaten.

Stews

Korean stews, or *tchigae*, are served in a common pot and are thicker than soups. Classic tchigaes are soybean stew, hot soybean stew and clear stew. Soybean stew is best loved by Koreans. The taste differs with the soybean paste

Tchigae

Sliced boiled pork (p'yŏnyuk)

and ingredients added. Main additions are bean curd, fresh chilies, beef, anchovies and a variety of vegetables. Hot soybean stew uses fish, bean curd and many vegetables. Clear soup is seasoned with *chŏtkal*, fermented seafood, and includes bean curd, daikon radish and shellfish.

Chŏn-gol

Chŏn-gol is a casserole of seasoned meat and vegetables, fried individually, then placed in an attractive mold and boiled with meat broth. It is cooked on a small stove at or near the table. Restaurants have special tables with stoves in the middle for the diners' convenience.

Steamed Foods

Koreans steam food by boiling it in broth or cooking it over steam. Both processes are called *tchim*. In the former method, meat, such as pork or beef, is boiled over a low fire for a long time until it is very soft. The latter method is usually used to cook fish, shellfish or shrimp on a steamer over boiling water.

Sŏn is a kind of tchim, in which the main ingredients are vegetables and bean curd. Among the vegetables prepared in this manner are zucchini, cucumber, cabbage and eggplant. Secondary ingredients, including minced beef and scallions, are often added.

Fresh Vegetables

Any kind of fresh, seasonal vegetable can be mixed with seasoned soy sauce, hot soybean paste or mustard to make *saengch'ae*, a zesty salad. Sugar and vinegar are added to create a fresh sweet and sour taste. Daikon radishes, lettuce, cucumber, and *minari*, or dropwort, which is similar to parsley, are most commonly used in saengch'ae. Sometimes seaweed, cuttlefish, shellfish or shrimp are parboiled and mixed with the dressing and vegetables.

Seasoned Vegetables

Seasoned vegetables are called *namul* or *sukch'ae*, which means "cooked vegetables." They are Korea's most popular side dish. No meal is complete without a variety of them. Green vegetables are parboiled in hot water and seasoned with various ingredients. Other vegeta-

Seaweed soup

bles, such as bracken, royal fern and bell-flower roots, are parboiled, seasoned and stir-fried. Namul should contain enough sesame oil and sesame powder to be soft and tasty. Some fresh mountain vegetables are seasoned with hot soybean paste mixed with vinegar. *Chapch'ae* is a dish of mixed vegetables, to which thin cellophane noodles and a little beef are added.

Gentle parboiling reduces the bulk of the vegetables and destroys less nutrients than other cooking methods. Sesame oil is an important seasoning which helps absorb oil-soluble vitamins. Sesame powder also adds nutrients.

Hard-boiling

Many of Korea's everyday shared side dishes are "hard-boiled" in a mixture of soy sauce and sugar. First the meat, seafood or vegetables are boiled in water. Most of the water is then drained and replaced with a sweet soy sauce solution. The food is then slowly simmered to create *chorim*, which can be kept for a long time.

Ch'o is sweeter than chorim. The food is boiled, then starch paste is added to thicken the sauce. Ch'o seasoning is not as strong as that of chorim. The most popular ch'o is made with mussels.

Pan-Frying

Meat, fish or vegetables are often sliced, seasoned with salt and pepper, then breaded in flour and egg batter before frying in a shallow pan. Foods prepared in this manner are called *chŏn*. Pan-fried fish is called *chŏnyuŏ*. *Chŏnyuhwa* means "flowers pan-fried in oil." These are the seasonal flower cakes fried and eaten by aristocrats and royalty on flower-gazing expeditions.

Chijim is similar to chŏn. Various vegetables are drenched in flour and fried in a small quantity of oil. No egg is used. P'yŏng-an-do province is famous for *pindaettŏk*, pancakes made of ground mung beans and chopped kimchi, scallions and pork. Pindaettŏk are a kind of chijim. Tongnae in Kyŏngsangnam-do province is known for its spring onion and seafood pancakes, which are served sizzling at the table.

Broiling and Grilling

Broiled or grilled foods are called *ku-i*

Chŏn-gol, *a casserole of seasoned meat and vegetables boiled with soup stock, can be made with a variety of ingredients.*

or *chŏk*. Meat, fish, vegetables and mushrooms are seasoned or marinated, then put on skewers. *San-chŏk* is made from raw ingredients, which are marinated. After skewering, the food is broiled or grilled. *Nurŭm-chŏk* consists of pre-cooked skewered food. *Chijim nurŭm-chŏk* is made of raw ingredients which are skewered, then dipped in flour and egg batter before being cooked in a fry pan.

Raw Fish and Meat

Hoe is raw or slightly cooked meat or fish. It is eaten with seasoned soy sauce, seasoned hot soybean paste, green mustard paste, or a mixture of oil and salt. The soft parts of beef, fresh fish, such as

croaker, flatfish or pomfret, oysters or sea cucumber are used. Some kinds of white fish, octopus, squid and shrimp are parboiled and chilled before being serving.

Pickles

Garlic, garlic stalks, sesame leaves, radish and cucumber are sometimes pickled in soy sauce, soybean paste or hot soybean paste to make *changatchi*. Before serving, the pickled vegetables are cut into slices and sometimes mixed with sesame oil, sesame powder and sugar for a more pungent side dish.

Sliced Boiled Meat

P'yŏnyuk is made by boiling a large cut of beef or pork. After it is fully cooked, the meat is compressed under a heavy stone. The result is firm meat, which is cut into thin slices and eaten with seasoned sesame sauce or fermented shrimp sauce. P'yŏnyuk can be made from any part of the animal.

Jellied Side Dishes

The tough parts of the cow, such as the leg, muscle, or skin, are boiled for a very long time. The meat is discarded and the broth is poured into square molds, then cooled to make *chokp'yŏn*, "cow's hoof jelly." The jelly is sliced or cut into small pieces and served with seasoned soy sauce.

Muk is made from starch extracted from mung beans, wheat or acorns. It is eaten like chokp'yŏn, or mixed with pungent greens, scallions, soy sauce, sesame oil and sugar and served like a salad.

Fried "Flakes"

T'ui-gak are dried flakes of kelp, sprouts of the tree-of-heaven or walnuts that have been roasted and salted. *Pu-gak* are made by frying potatoes, chilies, sesame leaves, laver or the leaves of the tree-of-heaven, after they have been thoroughly dried.

Beef or Fish Jerky

Jerky, or *p'o*, is meat or fish marinated in a soy sauce solution, then dried. Fish p'o is sometimes prepared by drying the whole fish or by drying slices marinated with soy sauce. Pollack p'o is dried without seasoning.

197

Fermented Vegetables

Kimchi is unique to Korea and the most important accompaniment to any meal or snack. Cabbage and radish kimchi are most common. Chinese cabbages and radishes are salted, seasoned with spices, such as chili powder, scallions and garlic, and left to ferment. When properly fermented, kimchi is slightly sour due to the presence of lactobacillus. The spicy chili stimulates the appetite and helps digestion. A small amount of chŏtkal, fermented seafood, is often added to supply protein and flavor.

Fermented Seafood

Chŏtkal is made from raw fish, shrimp or shellfish mixed with salt and seasonings. Proteins and nucleic acids are hydrolyzed, freeing the amino acids and giving chŏtkal its peculiar smell and taste. Shrimp chŏtkal and anchovy chŏtkal are generally used in kimchi. Chŏtkal made from pollack fry, cuttlefish, shellfish or oysters are used as side dishes.

Rice Cakes

Korean rice cakes, or ttŏk, fall into two general categories by cooking method. They are either steamed, or first steamed, then fried. Ttŏk can be further categorized by the method of preparation: some are pounded with a wooden mallet and others are shaped by hand.

Steamed Rice Cakes

Grains are ground, mixed and steamed to make shiruttŏk. There are two kinds of shiruttŏk: layered and unlayered. Shiruttŏk with layers has powdered red beans, mung beans or sesame between the layers of rice powder or glutinous rice powder. Shiruttŏk without layers is soft and chewy.

Fried Rice Cakes

To make fried rice cakes, or chŏnbyŏng, glutinous rice is kneaded with hot water, shaped, then fried. In some cases, seasonal flowers or leaves are placed on top before the cakes are fried to create hwajŏn, "flower pancakes."

Chu-ak are stuffed rice cakes, filled with sesame-seed powder or Chinese dates mixed with honey. The cakes are shaped into half-moons, then fried and coated in honey.

Pukkumi are made of glutinous rice powder or kaoliang powder kneaded in hot water, shaped into thin pancakes, stuffed, then fried.

Pounded Rice Cakes

Injŏlmi is made from regular rice or glutinous rice, which has been steamed, then ground in a mortar or a small stone mill while still hot. Water is added to make rice cake dough, which is cut into shapes and rolled in powdered sesame, bean flour, mung bean flour or other

Top, stuffed rice cakes; middle, yu-milgwa, fried cakes dipped in honey; bottom, chŭngp'yŏn. Right, a dessert table of tea, fruit and confections

flours. Sometimes mugwort is added, which gives a natural green color to the cake.

Shaped Rice Cakes

Glutinous rice or kaoliang powder is kneaded in hot water to make dough, which is then rolled into small balls. The balls of dough are boiled in hot water and coated with bean flour, powdered sesame or cinnamon to make kyŏngdan.

Songp'yŏn are half-moon shaped rice cakes stuffed with sweet bean paste,

sesame seeds or chopped or powdered chestnuts. The dough is made by kneading rice flour with hot water, shaped into circles which are folded around a spoonful of filling. The rice cakes are then steamed on a layer of pine needles. Songp'yŏn are part of every Harvest Moon (Ch'usŏk) celebration.

Yu-gwa

Yu-gwa are made of glutinous rice flour. They are kneaded, shaped, cooked, dried, fried in oil, then covered with various coatings, such as sesame, black sesame, chopped pine nuts, grains of boiled white rice or ground glutinous rice. Ground cinnamon or angelica plant powder is sometimes added. Yu-gwa are also known as *kangjŏng*, *sanja* and *kwajul* and can be divided into several categories according to shape and coating.

Yu-milgwa

Most representative of this type of confection are *yakkwa*, cakes made of a flour batter kneaded with sesame oil, honey, wine and ginger juice, then fried and dipped in honey. Yakkwa come in different sizes and shapes. *Mandugwa* are stuffed yakkwa.

Sukshilgwa

Sukshilgwa literally means "cooked fruits." Chestnuts or Chinese dates are boiled in honey to create candied fruit, or *ch'o*. Sukshilgwa are also made from chopped chestnuts, Chinese dates or ginger, which are kneaded into a dough and made into shapes. These sukshilgwa are called *nam*.

Kwap'yŏn

The flesh of sour fruits, such as cherries, Chinese quince and apricots, are reduced in a honey solution, poured into a square mold and allowed to harden into jelly. The jelly is then cut into slices and served with raw chestnuts or other fresh fruits.

Tashik

Powdered grains, herbs or pollen are kneaded with honey and shaped in decorative molds. Sesame, beans, angelica plant, pine pollen and wheat flour are also used for tashik.

Chŏnggwa or Chŏn-gwa

These confections are made from citron, Chinese quince, ginger, broad bell-flower root, lotus root or ginseng, which has been boiled in honey, malt or sugar.

Yŏtkangjŏng

Grains are fermented with dried barley sprouts creating wheat-gluten. Roasted beans, sesame, wild sesame and peanuts, raw pine nuts or ground raw walnuts are mixed with the wheat-gluten, hardened and cut in small pieces to make a chewy candy.

Beverages

Hot beverages are called *ch'a*, literally "tea." Cold beverages are called *hwach'ae* or *ŭmch'ŏng*.

Nokch'a, green tea, is made of dried tea leaves steeped in hot water. It was introduced during the Three Kingdoms period, at the same time as Buddhism. However, the custom of drinking nokch'a declined during the Chosŏn Kingdom when national policy encouraged Confucianism. At that time, *sungnyung*, scorched-rice tea, and *makkŏlli*, a fermented rice wine, became the main beverages. In recent years, however, nokch'a has been revived and a growing number of people drink it on a regular basis. Other teas include those made of barley, Job's tears, corn, brown rice or wild sesame seeds. These grains and vegetables are roasted or ground,

then steeped in boiling water to make tea. Ginseng, ginger, cinnamon bark, the fruit of the Maximowiczia chinesis (*omija*), Chinese matrimony vine, arrowroot, citron, Chinese quince and Chinese dates are also used for tea.

Hwach'ae is fruit punch flavored with honey. Rice cakes, glutinous rice cakes or barley cakes are often eaten with it. Citrons, pears, strawberries, mandarin cherries, watermelon and peaches are just a few of the fruits used in hwach'ae.

Shikhye is a unique beverage made from rice and lightly fermented with dried barley sprouts. Creamy *misu karu*, which can be served hot or cold, is a powder made of several roasted grains.

It is blended in water with honey or sugar. The yellow pollen of pine blossoms (*songhwa*) is also mixed in honey to make a drink.

Table Settings

Korean table settings can be divided into two general categories by main dish or the purpose of the meal.

Pansang is the usual meal of rice, soup and shared side dishes. The table setting varies according to the number of side dishes, starting with three, and going up to five, seven, nine and 12 side dishes. The 12-dish setting, *surasang*, was reserved for kings.

A setting with three side dishes is

Tashik, *molded cakes (left), and a simple tea table (below)*

KUNGJUNG FOOD RESEARCH INSTITUTION

standard. One bowl of rice, a bowl of soup and a dish of fermented vegetables are placed with three shared side dishes, each cooked differently. The ingredients of a meal should be as varied as possible.

The vessels that hold food have special names and uses: *chubal* or *pari* for rice, *t'anggi* for soup, *choch'ibo* for stews, *kimch'ibo* for kimchi, *chaengch'ŏp* for cold water, and *chongji* for soy sauce or seasoned soy sauce mixed with vinegar.

Ideally one set of dishes, all of the same material, is used for each meal. Ceramic dishes are used in summer, and silver or brassware, which retain heat, are used in winter.

Chuksang is the table setting used for early morning meals or simple meals. The main dish is a semi-liquid food like chuk, porridge, or miŭm, thin rice gruel. The main dish is arranged with dried side dishes, kimchi with a watery sauce and a clear stew. Dried side dishes, such as slices of seasoned meat, fish or salted dry fish are good accompaniments to chuk.

Noodle soup, rice cake soup or stuffed dumpling soup is often the main dish for lunch or for a simple meal. Deep-fried fish, a dish of mixed vegetables, kimchi or white radish kimchi with a watery sauce are often served as side dishes.

The table setting for wine-drinking is called *chuansang*. Side dishes are chosen according to the type of wine served. Hot foods with broth, such as chŏn-gol and tchigae, deep-fried fish, seasoned fish or meat, sliced boiled meat and kimchi are all suitable.

Kyojasang is a large table prepared for many guests during a celebration. The main dish is noodle soup, rice cake soup or stuffed dumpling soup. Side dishes vary according to the season. Steamed vegetables, deep-fried fish, sliced boiled meat, broiled or grilled meat or fish, seasoned meat or fish and vegetables are favorites. Two kinds of kimchi are served. For dessert, various confections and a sweet beverage are served separately.

After the meal is finished, a dessert table called *tanggwasang* is prepared. Tanggwasang is also used to serve snacks to visitors. Rice cakes, confections and beverages are standard fare. ◆

Kimchi:
A Korean Original

Kim Manjo

Kimchi is a uniquely pungent mixture of fermented vegetables. Cabbage (*Brassica chinensis* or *Brassica pekinensis*) and radishes (*Raphanus sativus*) are most commonly used in kimchi today. These vegetables are combined with aromatic vegetables, sauces, salt and seasonings to create a food that nourishes the Korean soul as much as the body. In fact, kimchi provides both physiological and psychological comfort to the Koreans. On a cold winter evening, a humble meal of piping hot rice, soybean paste soup and cabbage kimchi, just taken from its earthenware jar buried in the backyard, is as satisfying to most Koreans as a banquet at a luxurious restaurant.

Kimchi has been part of the Korean diet for centuries and is prepared in as many as 300 variations, depending on region, season and personal preference. Throughout the world people have eaten some form of fermented vegetables, usually cabbage, for more than 4,000 years. Around 2030 B.C., the inhabitants of northern India brought cabbage seeds to southern China. The preservation of vegetables in brine was common in China, Mongolia and the Korean peninsula from early times. Approximately 2,000 years ago, the laborers who built the Great Wall in China were kept strong with cured vegetables. They were fed a diet of cabbage preserved with salt and rice wine. Some 1,000 years later, Genghis Khan and his troops carried this pungent dish with them into parts of the European continent. Cured raw vegetables were soon a staple of the European diet.

Early Koreans preserved vegetables in salt or vinegar and other spices. Sometimes they rubbed the surface of the vegetables with salt, or preserved vegetables in brine or *chang*, soy-based sauces made from processed beans.

Kimchi is thought to have originated from Chinese pickles brought to Korea and modified for Korean tastes some time during the

Late autumn cabbages (above) are destined to become kimchi (right) to help Koreans make it through the long winter months when fresh vegetables are scarce.

KUNG-JUNG FOOD RESEARCH INSTITUTION

Nabak *kimchi* (above), made from sliced turnip, is easy to make.

Unified Shilla period. Among the writings of the Koryŏ scholar Yi Kyu-bo (1168-1241) is a reference to the pickling of homegrown radishes in brine for use during the long winters. This dish may have been a precursor to *tongch'imi*, sliced pickled radish in refreshing salty liquid that modern Koreans still enjoy.

The spicy red kimchi we eat today has been a part of Korea's dietary culture since the 17th century. Red chili peppers were introduced to Korea by Portuguese traders during China's Ming dynasty (1368-1644). A cookbook from 1670 describes pickled mixtures of wild greens and pickled gourd melons but makes no reference to the use of chilies.

One historical record describes 11 types of kimchi at the end of the 17th century. The first historical mention of chilies' use in kimchi was made in 1766. Whole-cabbage kimchi

and other spicy red varieties appear to have gained popularity during the middle of the Chosŏn Dynasty. At that time, chilies were added for taste, without knowledge of their preservative or nutritional qualities. In recent years, chilies have become essential ingredients for almost all kimchi. They have been found to inhibit the growth of undesirable microorganisms that form during the fermentation process.

Prior to the introduction of red chili peppers, kimchi was preserved in salt, vinegar and spices. Without modern farming techniques or refrigeration, a few earthenware jars of kimchi were the only source of juicy vegetables available for much of the year. Vegetables were often dried for use in winter, but these were less flavorful and lost nutritional value over time.

The addition of fish or shellfish paste

(*chŏtkal*) to enhance fermentation and flavor may have begun during the 1800s. Sometimes abalone shells were also added to the jars to reduce acidity. Salt was used to produce lactic acid.

The first scientific study of cured vegetables was made by Dr. James Lind in the 1700s. He undertook this study to discover why Dutch sailors, who carried tons of cured vegetables in the holds of their ships, did not contract scurvy as often as their English counterparts. His research showed cured vegetables to be anti-scorbutic, that is to say they prevented vitamin C deficiencies. From his research, Lind learned that cured and fermented vegetables not only supply the body with vitamin C but also help the body utilize and assimilate vitamin C. Historical records also indicate that Captain James Cook made certain his sailors were fed a daily portion of cured cabbage to prevent scurvy when they set sail in the 1770s.

The great Russian biologist Elie Metchnikoff (1845-1916) studied several ethnic groups in Russia and the Austro-Hungarian Empire and discovered they enjoyed superior health, living long and vigorous lives. Metchnikoff found that one of the most important factors in their longevity was a diet rich in lactic acid, and concluded that these people's consumption of brine-preserved vegetables was the main source of lactic acid in their diets.

The first English-language research paper about kimchi fermentation was presented at the second International Conference of Food Science and Technology, held in Warsaw in 1966. The paper concentrated on the maturation period. Since then approximately 500 papers have been published in English,

The cook's hands are thought to add a special flavor to kimchi.

Korean and other languages. Most consider the physical and chemical nature of kimchi fermentation, storage and ingredients, but several have dealt with the history of kimchi and cooking techniques. Today research projects funded by the Korean government, universities and private companies focus on the development of new technologies, such as mechanization and automation to enhance efficiency and packaging techniques to extend shelf life.

Ch'onggak *kimchi made from small native turnips*

At present, more than 60 firms produce kimchi in South Korea. Each South Korean consumes an average of 18 kilograms (40 pounds) of kimchi every year. While the exact volume of kimchi production and consumption in North Korea is not known, we can assume it is similar to that of South Korea, because the northern Korean provinces have long been famous for their delicious kimchi. The kimchi of P'yŏngyang and Kaesŏng are considered gourmet delights. North Korean kimchi was prized in Ming and Qing China as well.

Today the most popular varieties of kimchi are made with Chinese cabbage, also known as Napa cabbage or lettuce cabbage, daikon radish, spring and summer cabbage, round-head cabbage, cucumber, leek, eggplant, sesame leaves and scallions. However, almost any vegetable, cultivated or wild, can be fermented to make kimchi.

Kimchi varies by ingredient and prepara-

tion method. For example, cabbage and radish kimchi are pickled in brine or cured with spices and seasonings. They can include soy sauce and soybean paste or chili paste; chŏtkal; rice wine or *soju*, a distilled grain beverage; malted rice or rice or fruit brews.

Proper storage is crucial to flavor and nutritional value. Kimchi must be kept at a constant temperature, around 5 degrees Celsius, to prevent freezing or excessive fermentation. It lasts four to six weeks at this temperature. Traditionally, earthenware kimchi jars were wrapped in straw and buried to ensure a constant temperature. Care must be taken to prevent air from entering the storage vessel because this will cause the kimchi to sour. The proper concentration of salt—approximately 3 percent—is also a key factor in good kimchi.

Kimchi enhances the taste of other foods and has 42 milligrams of vitamin C per 100 grams, more than half the U.S. recommended daily allowance. The capsaicin from kimchi's red chili peppers is rich in vitamin E, which works with vitamin C as an antioxidant. Capsaicin also prevents oils in the chŏtkal from turning rancid.

Kimchi is high in fiber, necessary for proper digestion, and is rich in minerals and vitamins, including thiamine, riboflavin, calcium and iron. It is also surprisingly low in calories, with only 33 calories per cup.

The people who first practiced preserving vegetables in brine did not understand the microorganisms that dominate the fermentation process. Many species of microorganisms, such as lactobacilli, are found throughout nature. Few permeate leaves, however. Most remain on the surface of the vegetable. If a cabbage is ground up, placed in a sanitary container and left at room temperature, bacteria naturally present in the plant cells colonize rapidly, quickly lowering the pH, thereby creating an acidic environment that ferments vegetables.

In this environment, beneficial microorganisms, including *Lactobacillus plantarum* and *Lactobacillus brewis*, proliferate. Through enzymatic actions, these microorganisms convert the sugars and starches naturally present in vegetables into lactic and acetic acids. These acids are natural preservatives. This process maintains a slightly acidic environment conducive to the further proliferation of beneficial microorganisms.

It is important to maintain the proper microecological balance in the human digestive tract. The consumption of fermented vegetables such as kimchi is one of the best ways of doing this. Vegetables ferment as lactobacilli convert natural starches and sugars into lactic and acetic acids, which then create an environment in which more beneficial lactobacilli can proliferate.

Kimchi-making has long been the test of Korean homemakers' culinary skills. While kimchi's basic flavors derive from salt, lactic acid fermentation, garlic, ginger, scallions, red pepper and chŏtkal, the "hands" of each cook provide their own unique flavor. Women in traditional society also recognized the important role that their brightly colored and flavorful kimchi played in everyday life. This perception remains strong today.

While no two individuals have exactly the same food preferences, people tend to share general preferences. To a large extent, these individual and collective food tastes have contributed to the formation of food patterns and habits, which may be linked within a broader food culture. Food patterns form the basis for communities, and if they are shared by enough people, they become a distinguishing characteristic of the national food culture.

Food is intimately linked to our deepest feelings. It is part of our earliest sensual experiences and the medium through which we develop bonds of love with our parents and form feelings about the world. However, food does not come to us of its own free will. A great deal of time and effort is spent creating a healthy, individually tailored diet. Each family must determine what food choices appeal to them and how to heighten the pleasure they derive from food. If there is a lesson to be learned from early childhood food experiences, it is that eating should be sensually and emotionally satisfying, as well as physiologically nourishing. Food is of profound psychological importance for all beings. People who do not have a good relationship with food typically do not have satisfying relationships with the people around them.

Eating habits are generally conditioned by geographical, cultural and ethnic history. Every food culture should therefore be viewed in terms of natural environment, geo-graphical circumstances, religious beliefs, economic status and cultural background. It is important to take into account both the physiological and emotional acceptability of foods in the general culture.

Kimchi is especially satisfying when prepared and preserved according to an old family recipe. Koreans believe that the texture, color and taste are determined by an inherited hidden wisdom mysteriously passed down from mother to daughter over the generations.

Homemade kimchi is usually seasoned with red chili pepper, garlic, ginger, scallions, salt, chŏtkal made of fermented anchovies, oysters, baby shrimp, baby squid, small swordfish or shellfish, and sometimes nuts and herbs. These ingredients are harvested,

prepared and stored from late spring until early autumn. The entire kimchi-making process, from the harvest of ingredients to serving, reflects the rhythms of Korean life. A meal of kimchi and freshly cooked rice on a snowy day stirs nostalgic memories of childhood autumns: the pleasure of running around heaps of newly harvested cabbages and radishes, the warmth of the sun, delightful aromas and a sense of abundance. ◆

Tongch' imi, *refreshing watery turnip kimchi eaten in late autumn and winter*

Traditional Furnishings and Food Vessels

Lim Young-ju

In traditional society, women spent most of their daylight hours in the kitchen. Their lives were quite literally spent among kitchen cabinets, tables and utensils, practical necessities in those days. Today these items have taken on new value to be appreciated for both their beauty and utility.

The typical kitchen had several pieces of furniture used to store food, dishes or utensils. The *ch'anjang* was a pantry cupboard with doors that was used to store leftovers and keep flies from food. The *ch'ant'ak* was a doorless cabinet with several shelves used for storing plates or bowls. A *ch'anhap* was a wooden storage and serving container with many different compartments. It usually had more than one level. *Kujŏlp'an*, octagonal wooden serving dishes with nine separate compartments, are one example of ch'anhap. *Mokpan* or *mokp'an* were tray-like wooden serving dishes. Sets of everyday dishes, or *pansanggi*, were made from wood, porcelain or brassware. Another set of dishes known as *chegi* was reserved for ancestral memorial services.

The traditional kitchen was also home to a variety of rice cake presses, or *ttŏksal*. These were used to stamp patterns onto rice cakes. Favorite press designs were pairs of fish, flowers and abstract patterns. Finally, stored in the kitchen were *soban*, small dining tables that were loaded with food and carried into the living quarters where meals were eaten.

The ch'anjang (or *ch'anbang*, which literally means the "room where side dishes were made") stood in one corner of the kitchen. Cast-iron cooking pots, glazed pottery for storing food, wine flasks, unglazed earthenware bowls and brass and porcelain bowls were stored here. In another part of the kitchen was the ch'ant'ak. A *chang*, or shelved cabinet, was placed here to provide easy access to frequently used bowls and dining utensils.

Generally this cabinet had doors in the middle for the separate compartments. In some versions the front was divided into four separate sections with sliding doors. The ch'ant'ak was simple in design and generally made of rough pine boards. Each ch'ant'ak reflected regional idiosyncrasies and was as unsophisticated and loyal as a country farmer.

Among Korea's traditional vessels, *onggi*, coarse pottery with dark brown glaze, have attracted the most attention from non-Koreans, because they seem to epitomize the Korean aesthetic. Onggi come in many different size and shapes. Huge pots are used to store kimchi, while long narrow containers are used for storing *chŏtkal*, fermented seafood. Steamers for rice cakes and pots for brewing herbal medicine are also made with the same dark brown glaze. The containers are basically undecorated except for wavelike patterns and floral designs around the body and neck made with the fingers. Their casual simplicity reflects the spirit of their creators.

Brass vessels are called *notsŏnggi*. They are made by pouring molten brass onto pagodite, or figure stone, and fashioning a round lump. This lump is then heated by fire and pounded into bowls and dishes. Ansŏng in Kyŏnggi-do province was once known for making the highest quality brass. It was especially coveted by well-to-do households, the principal users of brassware. Brass vessels played a vital role in one traditional custom, the *Nallohoe*, or "stove gathering." During the tenth month of the lunar calendar, villagers gathered in one home to prepare and eat a variety of foods cooked in brass chafing dishes called *shinsŏllo*. These dishes were popular because they kept food warm.

Korean homes traditionally used an underfloor heating system called *ondol*. Most activities at home, including meals, were conducted while seated on the warm floor. For this rea-

Brass dinner set from Ansŏng, Kyŏnggi-do province

KUNG JUNG FOOD RESEARCH INSTITUTION

son, small tables, or soban, were important. The soban was used to hold dishes of food and also could be used as small dining tables. Soban settings varied with the age, sex and household rank of the diner. The tables' design also varied from region to region, so much so that most styles were named for their region of origin.

As trays, soban were used to carry food from the kitchen to other rooms. Often they were used as the main dining table. The top of the soban was essentially a tray. It could be round or polygonal. Legs varied. Some were simply straight; others were jointed like bamboo or curved in the "dog-leg" or "tiger-leg" style. Soban from Haeju in northern Korea had rectangular trays and two plank-like legs

Soban *tables (above) are used to hold and serve food. A brass rice bowl (below).*

with decorative openwork. Tables from Naju in the southern Chŏlla region are typically four-sided with a rimmed tray and bamboo joint, dog- or tiger-style legs. Tables from T'ongyŏng in the Kyŏngsang region also have rectangular trays, but their legs are more ornate, often with leafy embellishments supporting the tray. *Konggosang* are round or octagonal tables supported by a sturdy wood-paneled "skirt" with latticed holes which allow the server to see where he or she is going when carrying the table on his or her head to the fields.

Wooden furniture and utensils were traditionally made from a variety of trees including pine and Japanese white pine, white birch, jujube, chestnut, willow, wild walnut and walnut, paulownia, linden, persimmon, pagoda and wild pear. The pine, wild pear, zelkova, maple and walnut trees are prized for their solid grain. Paulownia, pine, fir, mulberry, ginkgo, zelkova and apricot trees have beautiful grain and color and are suitable for main panels in furniture. The fine grain of the pagoda and willow trees makes them popular for use in fans.

The furniture and vessels produced during the Chosŏn Dynasty tell much of that culture. There was nothing forced or excessive in the construction of these objects. They give the impression of being created with a definite internal logic. When possible, the original grain was preserved. Extraneous ornamentation was avoided.

Ceramic dishes are most commonly used today. A rice bowl (below) and a full meal (bottom).

Traditional housing reflects the fact that daily life revolved around the heated floor. Interior proportions were appropriately intimate and avoided visual burdens to the viewer.

Traditional furniture and vessels reflected the craftsmen's careful consideration of function and raw materials. Each craftsman selected his materials with care. Like traditional architects and carpenters, these craftsmen avoided using metal nails and fastenings whenever possible. Wood panels were carefully fitted together and fastened with wooden plugs or glue. Kitchen vessels were designed according to their specific function. Wood too was selected according to its intended function. Ornamentation was simple, with

Brass vessels (top) and the wooden ritual vessels and stands used in ancestral memorial rites (bottom)

It had a flat rim and was used as a mixing bowl. The i-nambak and hamjibak both had rough-hewed exteriors. Their rough surfaces gave them a special unsophisticated beauty, another facet of Korea's traditional aesthetic.

In Korea, ancestral memorial rites were an essential part of everyday life. The vessels in which offerings were placed were treated with special care. These chegi were made of wood, porcelain or brass. Wood was most commonly used. Wooden vessels were not only inexpensive and easy to acquire, they were also light and easy to care for. After a rite was finished, the ritual food offerings were placed on a wooden tray or mokpan and shared with neighboring homes. Such trays were made of thin panels of wood. Large mokpan were rectangular, and smaller ones were square.

Special wooden vessels were used on the road, for picnics and journeys. Rice and side dishes were carried in ch'anhap lunch boxes, and small gourd vessels were used to carry liquid refreshment. Ch'anhap were often made of bamboo, for bamboo was strong yet light. Bamboo vessels also facilitated ventilation and so enhanced the flavor of food. They were also extremely attractive.

The kujŏlp'an exemplifies the beauty of Korean design and food. As mentioned earlier, the kujŏlp'an is an octagonal serving dish with nine separate compartments. The dish itself is about 30 centimeters across and 5 centimeters deep. The interior is coated with red lacquer, while the exterior is often inlaid with mother-of-pearl over a black background or painted over with lacquer.

At court, kujŏlp'an cuisine consisted of julienned strips of tender meat, vegetables, rare mushrooms and egg, artfully arranged in eight separate compartments around the edge of the container. Thin pancakes were placed in the center compartment. Small amounts of each ingredient were placed on a pancake, which was then folded and dipped in soy sauce before eating.

Commoners used glutinous rice flour or flour pancakes to wrap simpler vegetables such as scallions, crown daisies, carrots, turnips and cabbages, with raw meat or fish when available.

While many traditional vessels and household items were made of wood, other materials such as paper, wicker, sedge, barley or rice straw and rush were also used. Paper had the most important role in everyday life. During the Chosŏn Dynasty, Korean paper, or hanji, was produced from mulberry bark. Not only

function overshadowing style. Solid construction and practicality were the first considerations in the manufacture of furniture and wooden vessels.

A variety of wooden objects were used in everyday life. One of the most important in a culture where rice was served at every meal was the i-nambak, a wooden bowl with a grooved interior surface. It was used for washing rice, especially removing small stones or sand.

The hamjibak was a large wooden bowl made by hollowing out a solid piece of wood.

did it have extraordinary aesthetic appeal, it was also very durable. Papermaking was a poor man's craft. Most paper was for everyday use and thus did not require careful manufacture or complicated technique. Hanji embodied the feelings of the common people, not technical perfection. In Korean folk arts, beauty is not found on the surface. It is born of function and the simple feelings of the people who made each piece.

It is important to understand the basic thinking of those who manufactured traditional paper and the fundamental forms of paper craft. In the past, innumerable household items were made of paper. Yet specific references to or research on the use and role of paper in traditional society are rare. The varied uses of paper in Korea hint at the practical wisdom of the traditional Korean. For example, because learning was universally valued among Koreans, and paper was a vital part of learning, every scrap of paper was carefully recycled.

Hanji products were used throughout Korean society from the court and gentry to the households of the common people. At first, only royal workshops produced paper to be used in government offices. Later, paper and paper products were made in households and sold commercially as well as by farming families during the off-season when they had extra time on their hands. The work of professional paper craftsmen reveals remarkable skill in detail, proportion, the use of color and design. In contrast, the paper made in homes lacked sophistication but had its own naive charm. Natural dyes were used to produce paper products of brilliant color. These were valued both as practical household items and for their decorative purposes.

Paper and paper products were used by every level of society and were especially loved by gentlemen-scholars and women. Their designs and patterns reflect the tastes of past generations. A characteristic of hanji is that along with a spiritual meaning, it eloquently expresses the feminine element of folk art. By its very nature it is soft and pliable. Products made of paper, such as small boxes and sewing kits, are simple and seem to exude more feeling as time passes.

The production of many crafts was once the responsibility of each region's governmental offices. Regional workshops manufactured and distributed household items made of hanji, as did many families in their spare time. Thus, many examples of this gentle craft are available for us to admire today. ◆

Clockwise from top: simple ceramic condiment jars; eight-sided wooden serving bowls; a carefully crafted wooden ch'anhap lunchbox; a bamboo ch'anhap; and i-nambak, wooden bowls with grooved inner surfaces for washing rice

The Kitchen

Kim Kwang-on

The kitchen is one of the most important areas in any Korean house. Not only is it important for cooking and heating, but it was the place where grain was ground in the mortar and women and girls washed up at the end of a long, hard day. The younger members of the family had their meals in the kitchen, daughters-in-law cried in frustration and anguish there, and many used the coal pike instead of a brush as they tried to teach themselves to read and write.

The kitchen was not simply a kitchen. It was a bathing room, a resting place, a school and the center of family life in traditional Korean society. For the newly married daughter-in-law, it was a place of employment, where for 20 or 30 years, from the third day of marriage, she spent her days, from morning till night, slaving like a kitchen maid. In fact, women spent most of their lives in the kitchen. The management of the household took place there as well.

The history of kitchens is second only to the history of humanity. The first Korean houses, in the Neolithic era some four or five thousand years ago, were pit dwellings protected by a straw thatch covering. There was no division between the kitchen and living area. The hearth was situated in the center of the dwelling's floor. It was dug out of the floor and paved with smooth, river stones. A ridge made of more stones or mud around the edge of the hearth kept the fire from spreading to the rest of the dwelling. The living area was around the hearth.

Kitchen "equipment" was made of stones. Clay vessels were buried in the earth to store grain. Fire served to cook the food, warm the house and give light. Smoke from the fire escaped from a hole at the top of the straw

In this large country kitchen a double-holed hearth is used for cooking and heating.

covering.

In the Bronze Age (seventh-eighth centuries B.C.) and the early Iron Age (fourth century B.C.-first century), Koreans still lived in pit dwellings. The hearth had been moved, however, to one side of the rectangular dwelling. In larger dwellings there was sometimes a hearth at the center and another one near a wall. The central hearth was mainly used for heating and the side hearth for cooking. As housekeeping became more elaborate, a separate storeroom was built, a mud chimney built into the wall conducted the smoke from the house. It was called *kok'ol* or *kkotkul.* Similar primitive chimneys could be seen in the mountain houses of Kangwŏn-do province until quite recently.

From wall paintings found in many tombs dating to the Three Kingdoms, we know that the kitchen had almost completely evolved by this period. Murals found in the Koguryŏ Tongsu Tomb dating from the mid-fourth century B.C. tell us much about kitchens in ancient Korea. The kitchen is a separate area with a tiled, sloping roof supported by eaves. On one side of the roof perches a bird. Three women work inside. One is standing in front of an earthenware steamer on the fire. She holds a large, flat spoon in her right hand and chopsticks in her left and appears to be checking rice cakes to see if they are done. A second woman is crouched down, checking the fire. A third woman arranges vessels on a round table with legs. The smoke from the fire goes out through a chimney, which is shaped like a duck's neck. The chimney is vertical against the wall.

Considering the tile roof, the size of the kitchen and the fact that it is separate from the main house, we may assume that this is a palace kitchen or one belonging to a wealthy family. The kitchen is reminiscent of the *panbikkan*, separate buildings used for food preparation, which are found in later Korean houses.

The wall paintings at the Tongsu Tomb also depict a mill and ox shed. In the mill scene, two women are working. One woman is on a one-legged treadmill and the other is winnowing grain. This single-legged treadmill was introduced from China in the mid-fourth century, which leads us to postulate that the two-legged treadmill was invented by Koreans at a later date. Other pictures portray scenes still commonly seen today. The well with a large water dipper and the ox shed housing three or four animals look surprisingly familiar.

Condiment jars occupy a place of honor in an urban neighborhood (above). This spacious kitchen and fine brass rice bowls belong to a well-heeled yangban clan (right).

Another scene shows an outdoor kitchen. Outdoor kitchens were always built near the main kitchen. Koreans still use outdoor kitchens in summer or for special occasions with many guests.

The first written reference to Korean kitchens is found in *Sanguoji,* the Chinese *History of the Three Kingdoms* dating to the third century B.C. It consists of a single sentence: "The kitchen is usually located to the

west." However simple, this record suggests that the Korean custom of situating the kitchen in the western part of the dwelling had already established itself at this time.

For Koreans, the ideal house faces south with a mountain behind it. In fact, this belief is so strong that a Korean proverb says, "A family must do good deeds for three generations to merit a house facing south." The mountain to the rear, in the north, protects the house from the harsh northeasterly winter wind. The winter sun shines directly into the house when situated in this manner. Because of these two advantages, south-facing houses were prized from ancient times.

The third-century Chinese reference to Korean houses should thus be understood to mean that kitchens were located to the west in houses facing south. Thus, when a woman scoops rice from a pot, the spoon automatically faces the inside of the house. This was the reason for placing the kitchen in the west. If, on the other hand, the kitchen faced east, the spoon would face the outside, an unfortunate, even detrimental, harbinger of the family's fortune. When the spoon faced the inside of the house, it meant good fortune. According to the

Augmented Supplement to Farm Management (*Chŭngpo sallim kyŏngje*), an agricultural reference text published in 1766, kitchens built in the southwest part of the house were thought auspicious, while a kitchen built to the northwest was considered bad luck.

The Korean word *puŏk* (kitchen) is first seen in the 1481 edition of *Tushi ŏnhae*, a Korean translation of the works of the Chinese poet Tu Fu. In the southeast and some parts of southwestern Korea, the kitchen is called *chŏngji* or *chŏnju*. These two words may derive from *chŏngjukan*, an extension of the kitchen in a *kyŏpchip*, a house with four rooms arranged in two pairs back to back.

The *chŏngjukan* is a heated *ondol* floor raised above the floor of the kitchen. There is no wall separating it from the kitchen. The *chŏngjukan* was the most spacious and warmest place in the house. Guests were received there and it was also used as a bedroom at night. Memorial and wedding services were held there, and the shrine honoring the household god was kept there. Thus, the *chŏngjukan* was the central room in the house.

One reason for using the word *chŏngji* instead of *puŏk*, the usual word for kitchen, was because food was prepared in the *chŏngjukan* in Hamgyŏng-do province. In some parts of Chŏllanam-do province, the *chŏngjukan* is called *puttumak*.

Daily necessities—an iron kettle, condiment jars, wicker basket and a cutting board—stand ready in a traditional kitchen (above). Baskets, cushions and bumpers for hanging windows and doors were made from straw (below). In the old days, a wooden scoop was used to clean ashes from the fire hole (opposite).

The words *chŏngji* and *chŏngjukan* probably derive from the culture of the Orochon tribe who lived near the Hinggan Range in Manchuria in round tents with hearths situated opposite the entrance. The area near the fire was called *malro* or *mallu*, which are similar to the Korean word for their open wooden-floored rooms, *maru*. The malro was the center of the house where the master sat. The gods were also enshrined there. From the entrance, the right side of the tent was called *juingidui*. Men sat there, nearer to the malro, while women sat near the entrance. At night, young couples slept on the juingidui. The word juingidui may have been introduced to Korea and later changed to chŏngju or chŏngji. The word chŏngju appears in a *New Augmentation of Chinese Character Styles* (*Shinjŭng yuhap*), published in 1576, and *Vulgate Elucidations of Collective Essentials of Conception and Delivery* (*Ŏnhae t'aesŏn chipyo*), published in 1608.

Since the kitchen was such an important part of the Korean home, great care was taken in choosing and preparing the soil used for its floor. According to *Farm Management* (*Sallim kyŏngje*) written by the *Shirhak* scholar Hong Man-sŏn (1643-1715), "The soil should be dug from clean earth after about a spoon of earth has been removed from the surface. Then the soil is mixed with water drawn from the well

at daybreak and perfumed."

The most important and sacred place in the kitchen has always been the hearth. Housewives tried hard to keep the hearth clean at all times. The cleanliness of the hearth was the measure of their abilities. Chowang, the kitchen god, was believed to reside in a small bowl of water kept on a shelf at the center of the wall behind the hearth. Each morning the housewife drew fresh water from the well to place there, then bowed and prayed for the health and happiness of her family.

In some places, the kitchen god was thought to reside in other places. Sometimes she (The kitchen god was generally thought to be an old grandmother *chowang halmŏni*) resided in a gourd dipper, a piece of white paper or white cloth pasted to the wall, a piece of folded paper wrapped around some dried pollack pasted to the wall, a small jar filled with rice behind a kettle, or a ket-

tle on the hearth. If she resided in the kettle, women prayed to her for an easy delivery when a birth was drawing near. In some areas, people believed the kitchen god was everywhere. They turned a kettle lid over, made their offerings to her there and prayed.

The kitchen god is believed to ascend into the sky on the 23rd day of the 12th lunar month and return at daybreak on New Year's Day. During her stay in the sky she informs the Heavens of the year's events in the household. If someone has committed an act they are ashamed of, he or she must stick rice gluten over the hearth opening on the night before the kitchen god makes her ascent. The opening symbolizes the path that the kitchen god takes to the Heavens as well as her mouth. If it is sealed with rice gluten, the kitchen god has difficulty making her ascent and even if she does manage the journey, she cannot report anything because her mouth is sealed.

In the kitchens of many Korean temples, a statue of the kitchen god is kept on the shelf above the hearth. Food is served to it every morning and evening. This custom was probably introduced from China. Not all temples have a statue, however. Some display a piece of writing instead.

Traditionally, on the eve of the first moon of the first lunar month, people stole soil from the yards of wealthy households and sprinkled it over their cooking fires the next day. This practice, called "stealing the soil of fortune," was believed to enhance family fortunes in the coming year. The family from whom the soil was stolen was thought to suffer diminished good fortune. Therefore, on that particular night, wealthy fami-

lies stationed special guards at their homes. A similar custom is mentioned in *Various Events of the Capital* (*Kyŏngdo chapki*) and in the *Korean Almanac* (*Tongguk seshigi*). During the Chosŏn Kingdom, the people of Seoul dug soil from Chongno plaza and sprinkled it at the four corners of their houses or sprinkled it on their hearths.

These customs are rooted in the belief that everything comes from the earth. Sprinkling special soil on the hearth was also a way of showing respect and honoring the place where cooking was done. Sections of the hearth that were chipped or cracked were also repaired at this time.

The traditional kettle, or *sot*, is made of iron and has a ridge around the center of its body and a lid with a handle. It goes by many different names depending on its size. The largest, *tumŏngsot*, has a wide mouth and is used to steam or boil large quantities of food for gatherings. The lid is made of two half-moon shaped pieces of wood, which can be opened and closed separately. *Kamasot* is the next largest size. It is sometimes used for cooking rice but was mainly used for boiling chopped hay for cattle. *Chungsot*, literally a "middle-sized" *sot*, and *ongsot*, a small shallow kettle, are used for cooking rice and soup respectively.

When struck, a good kettle rings true like a fine earthenware pot. An unclear tone indicates poor quality iron or a crack in the kettle. Kettles are polished by boiling water with some animal fat remaining after cooking two or three times over a low flame. The water is poured out and the kettle is rubbed, inside and out. Then fresh water is boiled three or more times to rinse the kettle. Proper care guarantees long use. Sot are also preserved by using an oiled rag to rub soot from the bottom of the kettle on the outside and lid.

The sot is a symbol of good housekeeping. When a new house is built or a family moves, the placement of the sot on the hearth marks the beginning of a new life. When a family receives a new daughter-in-law into the family, a kettle furnace is built on the threshold of the main room and the lid of a chungsot is placed upside down in front of the doorstep. The bride steps over the lid with her left foot. This symbolizes the family's hope that the new bride will be "as healthy as iron and without troubles." It was also a way of "interviewing" the newcomer who would be doing all the cooking in the future.

Sot were also believed to foretell disasters. If the sot made a "bu-ung, bu-ung" sound during cooking or the lid moved up and down to release steam, it was considered a bad omen. If the rice kettle made a noise, the master of the house would

Traditional kitchens had few cabinets. Hooks and nails were used to hang utensils within easy reach, and simple wooden shelves held rice and soup bowls.

enter the kitchen and his wife would bow to him. If, on the other hand, the soup kettle made a noise, the husband had to bow to his wife until the sound stopped.

The sot was also thought to have miraculous powers. According to the Korean *History of the Three Kingdoms* (*Samguk sagi*), when the third Koguryŏ king, Taemushin (r. 18-44), was on his way to attack Puyŏ, the capital of Paekche, he saw a woman with a sot. As he drew closer, he saw only the sot. He ordered rice to be cooked in it. Mysteriously, the rice cooked before the fire was built, and all his soldiers ate their fill.

Like the thread that always accompanies a needle, the *chugŏk*, a large wooden spatula, is the sot's constant companion. The chugŏk is used to scoop rice into bowls.

In Korea, the sot symbolizes housekeeping. Japanese housekeeping is symbolized by the big spoon. In Japan, a mother-in-law passes the family's big spoon onto her daughter-in-law when she relinquishes her housekeeping duties to her. In Korea, the mother-in-law passes the keys to the household storerooms to her daughter-in-law when she is ready to hand over responsibilities. Through these simple customs, the characteristics of the two countries are evident. Koreans emphasize the

moral obligation of housekeeping while the Japanese see the job in a more utilitarian light. In the Japanese view, the rice may be stored in the storeroom, but the person with the spoon decides how much rice goes in each bowl.

The chugŏk's mate is the soup ladle, or *kukcha*. It has a long handle so hot soup can be ladled easily. In the Neolithic era, large shells were used as ladles. As soup became more important in the Korean diet during the Koryŏ Dynasty, the ladle became essential.

Ladles were originally made of brass, but in later times, they were made of albata. Today most ladles are made of stainless steel or synthetic resin. Since 80 percent of Korean food falls in the soup category, the ladle will always be an important utensil.

Chori, bamboo strainers, are used to sift sand and small stones from rice. They are made of fine strips of bamboo woven together to form a mesh. The rice is placed in a bowl of water, "scrubbed" several times with the hands, then sifted with the chori in a back and forth motion. The chori catches the light grains of rice and leaves the heavier sand and stones.

Because it separates the good from the bad, the chori has always symbolized good fortune. A pair of chori are often hung next to each other on doors or on the walls of the main room. In traditional society, on the 14th night of the first month, peddlers sold chori tied with red string. No one haggled with the peddler over the price of these *pok chori* ("good luck chori") for a discount was thought to reduce the amount of good fortune received.

Before municipal water services were established, people drew water from a well and kept it in a large jar, or *tumŏng*, near the hearth. The tumŏng was usually made of dark brown glazed pottery. However, wealthy families had tumŏng made of iron. Both were well-polished and spotless.

Siru are steamers used to steam rice or rice cakes. The many holes in the bottom allow the steam to rise up and cook the rice or cakes. The oldest Korean siru was found in a midden in northern Hamgyŏng-do province at a site of Bronze Age remains. From this we can assume that siru have been used from the era when primitive farming was just starting.

Until recently, every household had two or three steamers. Rice cakes cooked in siru are still essential at ancestral memorial rites, parties and festivals. A ceremony without rice cakes is inconceivable. At harvest time in the tenth lunar month, when offerings are made to the spirits, both rice cakes and siru are offered.

A small siru is called *ongsiru*. At temples or shrines, unbreakable brass siru were used instead of earthenware siru. Recently aluminum siru have become popular.

An iron pan, *pŏnch'ŏl*, is used for grilling. Sometimes called *chŏkcha* or *chŏnjŏl*, it is wide and round like a Korean kettle, with handles on both sides to make it easy to lift on and off the fire. For large gatherings, the kettle lid was turned upside down and used for grilling.

The pŏnch'ŏl has probably been used in Korean kitchens from the time of the Three Kingdoms when iron kettles were also used. Firm vegetables like radish or potato were used to brush oil on the grill before cooking.

The gourd dipper, or *pagaji*, was another essential implement in the Korean kitchen. It was made by cutting a gourd in half, scooping out the flesh and drying the shell. Pagaji were most often used to scoop water but also were used to scoop uncooked rice, soya or bean paste. A dipper made of hollowed wood with a short handle was used to ladle out cattle feed. Today most gourd dippers have been replaced with plastic ones.

Gourd dippers were generally used by housewives, so a nagging woman was said to be "scratching the gourd dipper." This expression is still commonly used today. And if a person was cheated or overcharged he was said to be "wearing a gourd dipper." Among soldiers, military police are called pagaji because of their round helmets.

A *tui-ung pak* is a pumpkin gourd which has been hollowed out without being split in two. A hole the size of a fist is made near the stem, then the flesh is hollowed out and the gourd is dried. To prevent the gourd from breaking, a net of woven bamboo is wrapped around it and the net ends are joined to form a handle. Tui-ung pak absorb water and humidity so the gourds are used to store rice during Korea's humid summer months. Sometimes seeds and eggs were kept inside the gourds. Tui-ung pak were often hung from the eaves or outside the

door. Dark glazed pottery and gourd-shaped straw holders were also used to store food. Since tui-ung pak had round bottoms and were unsteady, a precarious task was often said to be "like wearing a job on one's foot."

Ttukpaegi are small, glazed earthenware bowls used for boiling or stewing. They have wide mouths, are relatively deep and are used mainly for stews made from soybean paste.

Korean housewives have always spent a great deal of time waiting for their husbands. While they wait, they watch the ttukpaegi, taking it on and off the stove, trying to keep the food hot and ready for the moment their husband returns. Thus the ttukpaegi is a sign of a woman's love for her husband. The bowls are rough and ill-finished. So when something is better than it appears people say "beanpaste tastes better than the ttukpaegi looks."

Ch'e are sieves used to sift powder or liquid. They come in different sizes. In traditional society, sieves were also used to drive away misfortune. On the 15th of the first lunar month a luminous ghost was believed to descend from the Heavens. When the ghost finds a pair of children's shoes that fit, he takes them and the owner is expected to have bad luck in the coming year. In order to prevent the ghost from taking the shoes, people hang a sieve on the outside wall of the house. The ghost will be so busy counting the holes in the sieve that he will forget to steal shoes and be frightened away by daybreak.

Some households have their own noodle machines. Kneaded dough is placed in the machine, the handle is pressed, and noodles come out the other end. Noodles are often served at large gatherings or during festivals. Therefore "eating noodles" has long been associated with getting married. Noodles were also prepared on birthdays as a symbol of long life.

In the early days, no house, not even those of the well-to-do, had a separate bathing-room. Aristocratic men hardly ever took a bath because they were reluctant to remove their clothes in front of others. Women, on the other hand, used to lock the kitchen door and wash themselves in the kitchen using water heated in the kettle.

The kitchen was also a refuge for daughters-in-law who suffered under strict mothers-in-law and cross sisters-in-law. Crouching in front of the hearth, feeding the fire, was a way to rest and recuperate. Sometimes, when the stress was too much, these poor women would break the poker in frustration.

Hungry for learning and knowledge, some women learned *han-gŭl*, vernacular Korean, as they crouched in the kitchen. They used the poker to practice writing on the earthen floor, pretending that it was a calligraphy brush.

As Korea made more contact with other cultures, the traditional kitchen changed. Traditionally it was situated near the main room but in modern houses the kitchen is usually next to the living room, which is also the center of the house. This means that most of the important aspects of family life center around the housewife.

Times have changed drastically. No longer does a woman have to sacrifice all her time to kitchen work. The kitchen is not simply a place for food preparation, it is the housewife's domain, as well as a sitting-room for family members. The kitchen has taken on a wider variety of functions and is becoming more and more convenient. ◆

A History of Traditional Korean Alcoholic Drinks

Lee Hyo-gee

Alcoholic beverages are among the oldest beverages produced by man. Primitive humans probably discovered intoxicants by accident as fermentation occurs naturally in fruit and grains containing sugar. No doubt pleasantly surprised by their effects, people began to produce and develop alcoholic beverages.

Grain was the main ingredient used in the ancient Korean people's alcoholic manufacture as agriculture was a way of life early in Korea's history. Various methods may have been used. They may have waited for the grain to ferment naturally, chewed grain so that saliva would hasten its fermentation, or soaked grain in water to make malt. A number of Korean wines and other alcoholic drinks can be traced back to a period before the rise of the three kingdoms of Shilla, Koguryŏ and Paekche.

By the Three Kingdoms period, grain wines fermented with yeast or germinated grains were already popular. In fact, historical records show that wine was an integral part of life for the people of the ancient states of Ye, Puyŏ, Chinhan, Mahan and Koguryŏ. They wined, dined and sang day and night during seasonal festivals.

The people of Koguryŏ produced a fine wine known as *chiju*, for which they earned a reputation for their fermentation expertise among the Chinese. Inbŏn, a wine expert from Paekche, introduced the technique of making grain wine to Japan and was recognized as a god of wine among the Japanese. Although ancient documents indicate that chiju and wines called *nangnangju, mion* and *yorye* were consumed at the time, there is no record of how they were made.

Techniques for producing alcoholic beverages fermented with yeast or malt were well established by the late Three Kingdoms period. Koguryŏ winemaking techniques were exported to China and led to the creation of Korean wines called *koryŏju* and *kogaju*. In the meantime, *shillaju* and nangnangju became the most popular alcoholic drinks in the Shilla Kingdom. According to legend, King Muyŏl, who was responsible for the unification of the Korean peninsula in the seventh century, ate two meals a day, consuming 6 bushels of rice, 6 gallons of wine and 10 pheasants.

Although the names of wines associated with Korea's ancient kingdoms have been found in historical records, no descriptions of their ingredients or fermentation techniques have been found.

Various grain wines were brewed during the Unified Shilla period, with refined grain wines gaining popularity among the aristocracy. One record describes such wines being served at a formal dinner hosted by King Shinmun (r. 681-692) in 683.

The brewing of grain wines was further diversified during the first half of the Koryŏ Dynasty to include *makkŏlli*, an unfiltered rice wine, and *ch'ŏngju*, refined makkŏlli. Multiple fermentation processes were developed during this period. Instead of simply fermenting steamed rice with yeast and water in a one-step process, more rice was added to the already fermented concoction to enhance the flavor and alcohol content.

It was also during this period that specialty wines were introduced. These were produced by adding herbs or fruits to the grain. Many wines were produced and sold by temples which often functioned as inns. An office was established in the royal palace to produce wines for state ceremonies, including royal

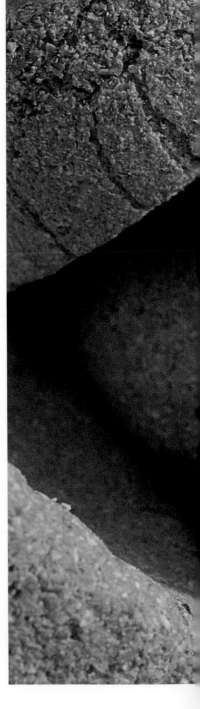

Nuruk, *a kind of malt, is used to start the fermentation process in most Korean alcoholic beverages.*

ancestral rites, which required libations of rice wine.

Makkŏlli was also called *t'akchu* ("turbid wine"), *pakchu* ("thin wine"), or *paekchu* ("white wine") for its appearance and consistency. A distilled liquor called *soju* was introduced to Korea in 1277 through trade with the Mongols and Yuan Chinese.

In addition to soju, which was produced in a one-step distillation process, stronger liquors such as *kamhongno*, which required two distillations, were produced. Soju, which was also known as *hongno, kiju, hwaju* and *aragilchu*, the last a name alluding to its Arabian origin, quickly gained such tremendous popularity among the upper class that many squandered their wealth on it. The government soon branded soju an extravagant commodity and banned it.

The names of most Korean liquors known today can be traced to the Koryŏ period. They were generally made with rice and wheat or rice malt. One of the more memorable names introduced at the time was *ihwaju* ("pear blossom wine"), a variety of makkŏlli so named because it was brewed with rice malt that had fermented during the pear blossom season.

In the latter part of the Koryŏ Dynasty more brewing and distilling techniques were introduced from Song and Yuan China, together with new kinds of liquor. *Mayuju* ("horse milk wine") came to be known in Korea as a result of contacts with Mongols. The grape wines of the Western world arrived through Yuan China. Chinese *shangzunjiu* and *baijiu* were favored by the privileged class.

Two distilling techniques were introduced to Korea from abroad around this period. One originated in the Middle East or India and was brought to Korea by the Mongols during the early Koryŏ period. The other, an indigenous Mongol technique, was introduced to Korea after the Mongols established themselves as China's Yuan Dynasty with which Koryŏ had frequent contact. Both techniques soon established themselves in Korea, and Koreans developed a new technique combining distillation with grain fermentation to produce *noju*, the result of a single distillation, and *hwalloju*, which required multiple distillations. Two major methods of alcohol production, grain fermentation and distillation, were thus firmly established in the Koryŏ period.

During the Chosŏn Dynasty, production of most Koryŏ-era beverages continued, and production techniques were refined. Plain rice was replaced with glutinous rice, and multiple

Officiants make an offering of food and makkŏlli rice wine before the opening of the Miryang Paekchung nori, a folk game in Kyŏngsangnam-do province (below). A traditional jar is still essential to the distillation of fine soju (opposite).

brewing came to be favored over single brewing. There was increased variety, and distilled liquors, in particular, improved so much that they were exported during the reign of King Sejong (1418-1450).

Sejong encouraged comparative studies of Korean and Chinese medicinal herbs. Information on the distribution of herbs was included in the *Geographical Description of the Eight Provinces* (*P'alto-chiriji*) compiled in 1432. Sejong also promoted the publication of medical works such as *Emergency Prescriptions of Native Medicine* (*Hyangyak kukŭppang*, 1417) and *Compilation of Native Korean Prescriptions* (*Hyangyak chipsŏngbang*, 1433). These texts had an important influence on the eating habits of the Korean people and encouraged a scientific approach to the Korean diet. The ingredients for medicine and food were often of the same origin; medicinal herbs, for example, were used in the making of cakes, porridge and drinks, including alcoholic beverages.

Many different herbs were used in wine production. Ginseng wine was made with ginseng. A variety of pine wines used pine needles, chrysanthemum leaves and pine needles, pine cones, pine sprouts, pine sap, young branches of pine, or pine pollen. "Lying pine wine" was stored for a set time in a cavity carved in a pine log. A variety of bamboo wines was made with water in which bamboo leaves were boiled with bamboo oil. These wines were stored in the hollows of bamboo stalks. Some wines used a single herb whereas others used a combination of many. In all, over 130 kinds of herbs were used to make more than 60 varieties of herbal wines.

Flowers were also added for fragrance. Wines enhanced with chrysanthemums, azaleas, lotus blossoms, shepherd's purse, plum blossoms, roses, cherry blossoms, camellia or apricot blossoms were especially popular. The flowers were usually placed in a gauze bag and soaked in wine at a ratio of approximately one gallon of blossoms to five gallons of wine. Wines were also made with fruits and nuts, such as pomegranates, citrons, mandarin oranges, crab apples, grapes, walnuts and pine nuts.

In a Confucian society where ancestral spirits were revered with the utmost formality, the making of wine needed for libations made during memorial rites was a regular undertaking in every household. Moreover, housewives had to maintain a generous stock of wines for each season because good wine and good food were indicative of their families' status.

Wines of regional origins thrived during the late Chosǒn period. It was at this time that Seoul's *yaksanch'un*, the Chǒlla region's *hosanch'un*, the Ch'ungch'ǒng region's *nosanch'un*, P'yǒng-an-do province's *pyǒkhyangju* and Kimch'ǒn's *ch'ǒngmyǒngju* became popular throughout the country.

A new brewing technique, which combined distillation and fermentation, was introduced during this period. Representative of the spirits produced from this process were *kwahaju* ("summer wine"), a mixture of soju and rice wine, and *songsunju* ("pine sprout wine").

After the opening of Korea's ports to international trade toward the end of the Chosǒn period, foreign liquors were imported in large quantities and quickly became popular with the upper class. Japanese sake and beer were introduced to Korea after the two countries signed the 1876 Treaty of Kanghwa, which opened Korea's ports and made way for Japan's eventual colonization of Korea in 1910. In 1907, when Korea was a protectorate of Japan, the Japanese government proclaimed a tax on liquor. This tax was a major source of revenue. Homemade wines were banned, and in each village a brewery was designated to produce taxed alcoholic beverages.

By 1930 traditional homemade wines had all but disappeared along with generations-old recipes. Public breweries, which felt the strain of heavy taxes, made little attempt to improve their products. In particular, no improvements were made on the traditional t'akchu, the main casualty as Japanese sake flooded the local market.

After liberation in 1945, liquor was taxed in much the same form as during the colonial period. Because of shortages of rice and other grains, numerous regulations were placed on the production of alcoholic beverages. In 1952, the government required molasses be substituted for grain. From 1962, sweet potatoes were generally used in the production of soju. Distilled soju was banned in 1965 and replaced with diluted soju. From 1974, tapioca was imported for use in the production of alcoholic beverages.

In the 1970s, Korean companies began the large-scale production of Western liquors, such as grape wine, whiskey, brandy, gin, vodka and rum. Domestic beer had a head start, beginning in 1934 when Japan's Kirin and Sapporo breweries established breweries in Korea.

The quality of traditional wines deteriorated in the meantime because of prohibitions on the use of rice in wine production. Flour and

other materials were substituted because of the chronic shortage of rice, Korea's main staple, which was largely imported at that time. The ban on rice wine was lifted in 1971, and rice makkǒlli was produced again.

In 1985, the government designated as cultural assets many traditional wines: soju from Andong, red *hongju* from Chindo, kwahaju from Kimch'ǒn, pear-ginger *igangju* from Iri, Seoul's *songchǒlchu* made from tender pine joints, songsunju from Kimje, *sogokchu* from Hansan, *tongdongju* from Kyǒnggi-do, and ch'ǒngmyǒngju from Chungwon.

In 1994, the Ministry of Agriculture and Fisheries designated experts in the making of *paegilchu* from Songhwa and Kyeryong and ginseng wine and *ok'yangju* from Kǔmsan in Ch'ungch'ǒngnam-do province as "masters of traditional wines" in an effort to preserve and promote traditional Korean wines. The government's new concern for traditional and regional wines reflects the Korean people's growing interest in traditional culture and their desire to preserve regional culture. ◆

Alcoholic beverages are an integral part of Korean cuisine. A bottle of wine and a few side dishes provide the perfect excuse for a party (above). Wine accompanies all ancestral rites (opposite top). Regional wines (opposite bottom) are enjoying a revival today.

Korea's Best-loved Wines

Yoo Tae-jong

Korean liquor and wine are rich in the fragrance and flavors of traditional culture. Azalea wine from Myŏnch'ŏn, crystal-clear *soju* from Andong, *sogokchu* from Hansan, smooth rice *makkŏlli*—they are all part of Korea's epicurean culture, slowly being forgotten in the bustle of modern society.

In traditional Korea, alcoholic beverages were made at home, from seasonal grains, flowers and herbs. They were served at ancestral rituals and when guests visited. From ancient times, Koreans also enjoyed a cup of wine with their meals.

The distillation or brewing of wine and alcoholic beverages continued to develop through the Chosŏn period. Today gourmands estimate that there are some 50 different traditional alcoholic drinks. Here we consider ten favorites.

Makkŏlli

Korea's oldest and most popular alcoholic beverage is makkŏlli. It is usually referred to as *nongju*, "farmer's wine," but farmers are not the only ones who have enjoyed it.

During the Koryŏ Dynasty, it was called *ihwaju*, "pear blossom wine," because the *nuruk*, malt or yeast used to start the fermentation process, was made when the pear trees were in bloom. It was also known as *t'akchu*, or "turbid wine," because the thick liquid which resulted from fermentation of the nuruk, water and steamed rice was not filtered prior to bottling.

The milky wine has a relatively low alcohol content of 6 to 8 percent and a somewhat sour yet refreshing taste because it is still in the process of fermenting. It also contains a good amount of carbon dioxide gas, due to the ongoing fermentation, which adds to its thirst-quenching quality. For this reason, makkŏlli was an important part of Korean life; it was enjoyed after a hard day's work and at special occasions, such as weddings and funerals.

Makkŏlli contains a relatively high level of rice protein, 1.9 percent, as well as vitamins thiamine, riboflavin and other B complexes such as inositol and choline. It contains approximately 0.8 percent organic acid, which contributes to its sour taste and thirst-quenching properties and stimulates the metabolism. Many Koreans who live to a healthy old age are makkŏlli drinkers.

Andong *Soju*

The soju from Andong, Kyŏngsang-buk-do, is a distilled liquor produced from fermented nuruk, steamed rice and water. It is said that Kublai Khan, grandson of Genghis Khan, created this liquor during his stay in Andong, while he prepared to invade Japan. Andong was known for its good water, which no doubt contributed to the quality of its soju. Soju was a valuable commodity in olden times. Historical records show that it was used for medicinal purposes as well. Even today people in the Andong area use soju to treat injuries and various digestive problems as well as to stimulate the appetite.

Andong soju has a high alcohol content of 45 percent, as it is aged in a storage tank for at least 100 days after fermenting for 20 days. Despite its potency, it is known for its smooth taste and rich flavor.

Traditionally the distilled liquor was aged in a jar placed underground in a cave at a temperature of under 15 degrees Celsius for 100 days. During that period

A bowl of creamy makkŏlli hits the spot during a hot summer folk festival (opposite). Cho Ok-hwa (left) has been designated an intangible cultural asset in the art of distilling Andong soju (above).

kyŏngje shimnyuk-chi), written by Sŏ Yu-gu (1764-1845) in 1827, and the *Encyclopedia of Herbs* (*Ponch'o kangmok*). Kŭmsan has long been known for the fine quality of its ginseng which has firm flesh and a high saponin content. (Saponin is the primary substance responsible for ginseng's medicinal benefits.)

Korean ginseng has been acclaimed as a multipurpose remedy for hundreds of years and its medicinal efficacy related to a wide range of health concerns has been scientifically proven. Ginseng helps relieve stress, fatigue and depression, and is effective in treating heart disease, high blood pressure, hardening of the arteries, anemia, diabetes and ulcers. It also improves skin quality by preventing dryness. In addition, some medical reports suggest that ginseng works as a cancer suppressant.

Many ancient records indicate that ginseng wine was first developed during the Paekche Kingdom. Kŭmsan ginseng wine is made using a unique method. Nuruk is made by mixing wheat and ginseng. Once the nuruk is ready, tiny ginseng roots, rice and water are added to

the jar was opened periodically and the froth skimmed off with a soft cloth or a sieve. According to the *History of Koryŏ* (*Koryŏsa*), while stationed in Andong, Koryŏ's General Kim Chin earned the nickname "soju disciple" for he neglected his duties because of drinking.

In the Andong area, almost every household used to make its own soju for guests, funerals and weddings, but this practice was all but stopped during the Japanese colonial period. Only recently has soju worthy of its old reputation

been produced again, using scientific methods of brewing, distillation and temperature control.

Kŭmsan Ginseng Wine

The ginseng wine (*insamju*) of Kŭmsan, Ch'ungch'ŏngnam-do province, and information about its manufacture and beneficial effects are mentioned frequently in publications from the Chosŏn Dynasty, notably *Sixteen Treatises on the Development of Nature and the Comforting of the People* (*Imwon*

make a wine starter. This is then fermented with a mixture of steamed rice, ginseng roots, pine needles and mugwort. The wine's unique flavor comes from the blending of pine needles, mugwort and ginseng.

It takes about 10 days to make the wine starter, 60 days to ferment, and 30 days to age. In other words, the whole process takes about 100 days. The longer the aging, the more flavorful the wine. The failure rate is low thanks to the ginseng nuruk, which is an ideal environment for the proliferation of the necessary microbes.

The ginseng wine of Kŭmsan is completely different from liqueur-type drinks made by immersing ginseng in alcohol. The latter is visually appealing, but lacks taste, not having undergone the fermentation process.

Hansan *Sogokchu*

Sogokchu is believed to have been produced in Hansan, Ch'ungch'ŏngnam-do, since the Paekche period. The water used to make the wine is drawn from a well in Poam-ri, Hansan-myŏn. Only a small amount of nuruk is added to a mixture of regular rice and glutinous rice to make the wine. Hence its name sogokchu, "small grain wine." Some brewers use malt, and others add ginger, wild chrysanthemums and peppers.

There are two types of sogokchu: one takes seven to eight days to prepare and can be made throughout the year, whereas the other variety is begun in February and completed in May or June.

Sogokchu is a clear wine with a clean taste. It is sometimes called the "sitter's wine" because long ago a scholar traveling to Seoul to sit for the state examinations stopped at a tavern in Hansan for a drink and enjoyed the sogokchu so much that he missed his examination altogether. Another tale tells of a thief who in the midst of a burglary stopped to taste some sogokchu. He enjoyed it so much that he kept on drinking and was finally caught in the tavern. Yet another story recalls a guest who so enjoyed the sogokchu his host served that he could not bring himself to leave.

Sogokchu has an alcohol content of 15 to 16 percent. The proportion of rice, nuruk and wheat flour is 10:1:1. The rice is washed, ground, cooked into porridge and fermented for seven days at a low temperature to make the nuruk. Then rice, twice the amount of the nuruk, is either steamed or cooked into porridge and added to the nuruk. This mixture is allowed to ferment for about three weeks at a low temperature.

Kamhongno

Kamhongno is a purplish pink wine from the northwestern region around P'yŏngyang. Its basic ingredients are rice, millet, sorghum and malt, to which herbs used in traditional medicine, such as perilla, longan, dried orange peel, cinnamon, dried clove buds and ginger, are added. Kamhongno is fermented, distilled three times and allowed to age for 120 days. It has an alcohol content of 41 percent, although a new variety with only 21 percent alcohol is now being developed. In *Sixteen Treatises on the Development of Nature and the Comforting of the People*, kamhongno is described as "red dew" and the best of all wines. In the *Korean Almanac* (*Tongguk seshigi*, 1805) kamhongno is described as one of three

Kŭmsan ginseng wine (above) has been famous for its medicinal effects since at least the 18th century.

Rice (top) and malt starter (above) are mixed to make sogokchu (left).

notable wines along with P'yŏngyang's *pyŏkhyangju* and *samhaeju*, a spring wine from Hanyang, today's Seoul.

Kamhongno is made by soaking millet, which accounts for 30 percent of the total ingredients, in water. The millet is then steamed. The resulting watery nuruk is combined with steamed sorghum, rice and more water and allowed to ferment. After eight days, the mixture is placed in a pot-still for distillation. The herbal ingredients are wrapped in silk and placed in the mixture during fermentation or during the distillation process. After the third distillation, the liquor is placed in a jar to age.

The blending of rice, millet and sorghum with perilla and longan extracts creates an excellent taste and color. The overall process is extremely complicated and requires painstaking attention. The resulting drink is believed to facilitate urination, cleanse the blood and cure frostbite and boils. Kamhongno aficionados say that it does not cause hangovers or the cotton mouth, headache or stomach ache associated with excessive drinking.

Munbaeju

This wine is thought to have been developed by an aristocratic family as a special gift to the king during the Koryŏ

231

Dynasty. It was the custom for families to offer a local speciality to the king in exchange for government appointments. The process by which *munbaeju* was made remained a family secret for generations and has been designated an important intangible cultural asset by the government in recent years.

Munbaeju is made by fermenting a mixture of nuruk and cooled steamed millet (cooled to 25 degrees Celsius) for about eight hours in a gauze wrapper. It is then mixed with water to produce a watery nuruk. After two days, cooled steamed sorghum is added, and after a day, more sorghum is added and the mixture is left to ferment. After ten days, a 16-proof spirit is obtained. It is then distilled in a pot-still and allowed to age in a storage jar. The final liquor has an alcohol content of over 40 percent.

Munbaeju has the flavor and fragrance of pear blossoms, from which its name is derived, although pears are not actually used in its making. It is similar to the Chinese spirits kaoliang and maotai but does not have the strong alcohol smell and flavor associated with them.

Igangju

Igangju is a high-quality distilled liquor that has been made in the Chŏlla-do and Hwanghae-do provinces since the mid-Chosŏn Dynasty. It is mentioned in many publications from the Chosŏn Dynasty including *Sixteen Treatises on the Development of Nature and the Comforting of the People* and the *Korean Almanac*. The name derives from the Chinese characters for the liquor's main ingredients: pear (*i*) and ginger (*gang*).

Cho Chŏng-hyŏng has been designated an intangible cultural asset of Chŏllabuk-do province for his skill in making igangju. The recipe has been handed down in his family for six generations.

To make igangju, the juice of five pears is mixed with extracts of ginger, cinnamon and turmeric. The ginger, cinnamon and turmeric extracts are obtained by soaking each in 96 proof soju for 30 days. The flavored mixture is added to 18 liters of 30 percent soju, which is then sweetened with honey. The soju must be distilled from fermented liquor, not diluted, because diluted soju does not mix well with ginger. Everything is mixed together, then filtered. It is aged for at least one month.

Traditionally much of Korea's ginger was grown around Chŏnju, Chŏllabuk-do, which may be one reason igangju developed in that region. In the old days, peeled pears were grated on roof tiles and filtered through a soft cloth to obtain the pear juice, which was then mixed with ginger extract, similarly obtained. In the *History of Chosŏn Winemaking* (*Chosŏn chujosa*), published in 1935, igangju is described as a sweet, pale brown alcoholic drink, mainly catering to high-class tastes.

Powerful munbaeju ***(top),*** igangju, ***a pear and ginger flavored liquor (above), and a traditional jar still used to distill*** Andong ***soju (right).***

The harmonious blending of soju, fragrant spices and pear gives a subtle aroma to this lemon-yellow drink. Turmeric, found in curries, is used in herbal medicines for treating mental and nervous conditions. Cho Chŏng-hyŏng, the maker of this wine, says that turmeric contributes to igangju's unique absence of hangover. Igangju goes down smoothly compared to ordinary soju. Records show that trade representatives from the United States drank this wine during the reign of Chosŏn's King Kojong (1864-1907), and South Korean representatives took 200 bottles to P'yŏngyang when they attended the Inter-Parliamentary Union in 1991.

Paegilchu

Paegilchu is a popular traditional wine produced in central south Korea. It is also known as *shinsŏnju*, the "wine of the immortals." The recipe for this wine was supposedly given to Yi Ch'ungjŏnggong, a high-ranking civil servant, by King Injo (r. 1623-1649). The recipe was handed down in the Yi family as a brew for ceremonies. Now, after 14 generations, it is kept alive by Chi Pok-nam, the wife of Yi Hwang, a descendant of Yi Ch'ungjŏnggong. Chi was designated an intangible cultural asset by the Ch'ungch'ŏngnam-do provincial government and a brewing expert by the Ministry of Agriculture and Forestry.

The main ingredients of paegilchu are glutinous rice and whole wheat, to

Intangible cultural asset Chi Pok-nam (opposite) collects chrysanthemum petals, pine needles, safflowers and other ingredients (above) for paegilchu (below).

which other minor ingredients, such as chrysanthemum, schisandra chinensis fruit, azalea flowers, safflower and pine needles, are added. The plants are cultivated by the wine maker herself, and the chrysanthemum is a native variety.

The most important ingredient is good water. Chi uses only water drawn from a well on a hill in Kongjŏng-dong, Kongju. The well never runs dry, even in times of drought, and provides excellent water for winemaking.

Paegilchu has an alcohol content of 16 to 18 percent, and is known for its smooth taste and aroma. In the old days, the first lunar month was considered the best time to brew paegilchu, but now that temperatures can be more easily controlled, it is brewed year-round. The fermented substance is distilled to obtain a 40 proof spirit.

Azalea Wine

In *Sixteen Treatises on the Development of Nature and the Comforting of the People*, wines made with flower petals and other aromatic materials are listed as aromatic wines. For aroma, medicinal herbs or other herbs are added to grain wine. Aromatic wines have been mentioned in written records since the Koryŏ Dynasty.

During the Koryŏ Dynasty, flower wine, including chrysanthemum wine, peach flower wine, pine pollen wine and azalea wine, was the most representative aromatic wine. Of these, azalea wine, *tugyŏnju*, is the most frequently mentioned.

Azalea wine from Myŏnch'ŏn, Tangjin-gun, Ch'ungch'ŏngnam-do, is by far the most famous. The wine starter is made by adding boiled water to washed, powdered rice on the first Pig Day of the first lunar month. The mixture is stirred well and left overnight to cool. Powdered nuruk and wheat flour are blended into the mixture. In advance, the nuruk powder is sifted through a silk-thread sieve and placed outside to gather dew. Azalea flowers, stamens removed, are added to the starter along with steamed regular rice or steamed glutinous rice. The flower petals and rice are not mixed together, but alternated in layers. Another method is to place a silk purse of dried azaleas in the wine when it has fermented for over a month. The winemaking process takes more than 100 days. The azaleas give the wine a lovely color and aroma. The alcohol content is over 18 percent.

In Myŏnch'ŏn, there is a legend about this wine and Pok Chi-gyŏng, a prominent figure in the founding of the Koryŏ Dynasty, who lived there. Pok fell ill and no medicine seemed to help him. His daughter, Yŏng-nan, climbed Mt. Amisan

to offer a 100-day prayer for her father. On the last day of her prayer, a god appeared in her dream and told her to make wine with well water, azalea flowers and sticky rice. After 100 days she was to start giving it to her father regularly for an extended period. Yŏng-nan did so and Pok recovered. The god also told her to plant a ginkgo tree. The ginkgo tree and the well from which the water for the wine was drawn still exist.

Wolfberry Wine

According to legend, a traveler once saw a young woman whipping a white-haired man who looked more than 80 years old. When he asked the woman why she was beating the old man, she said the old man was her son, but he looked much older because he had not drunk *kugijaju*, a liquor made with wolfberries. The woman was 395 years old. The traveler returned home, made the wolfberry wine and drank it himself. He too did not grow old for more than 300 years.

The ingredients for this wine are nuruk, rice, malt, water and the wolfberry plant, including its berries, roots and leaves. The mixture is stored in a cave for five to seven days for fermentation. When the wine is ready, it is filtered through a bamboo strainer. Kugijaju is a clear yellow-brown. It is a bit sticky, with a rich aroma and refreshing taste. The alcohol content is about 16 percent, which makes prolonged storage difficult. It can be stored for about a month at 15 degrees Celsius, and in a cool cave or refrigerator, it lasts longer. Clay jars maintain the original taste best. The wine tastes much smoother if it is warmed before serving.

According to documents from the Chosŏn Dynasty, wolfberries are good for all constitutions. The wolfberry has long been touted as a miracle longevity drug. The *Exemplar of Korean Medicine* (*Tongŭi pogam*, 1613) notes that wolfberry is not toxic and helps strengthen bones and muscles as well as relieve fatigue and bolster energy. It is also known as a good medicine for stomach, liver and heart ailments. Its components include rutin, which strengthens capillaries, betaine, which normalizes liver functions, and essential fatty and amino acids, vitamin B and vitamin C. ◆

Azalea wine, or tugyŏnju (*above*), is made by adding azalea blossoms and rice to the wine starter (*opposite, left*). Kugijaju, wolfberry wine, is made from the berries (*below*), roots and leaves of the wolfberry plant.

237

Drinking Customs

Choi Seung-beom

No one can be sure when Koreans discovered alcoholic beverages. There is no accurate record about the introduction of alcohol to Korea nor about Koreans developing alcoholic beverages themselves. However, Chinese historical documents tell of the Korean people enjoying alcohol before the Three Kingdoms period of Shilla, Paekche and Koguryŏ. Alcohol was an essential part of life, consumed during rites honoring the heavens, after planting and harvesting, and when families celebrated special occasions. Koreans drank, sang and danced. This was true throughout the Korean peninsula, in the north and south.

Other records indicate that the people in the northern part of Korea drank first, then reveled in singing and dancing. In the south, singing, then dancing were said to precede drinking. Who knows if this order was actually followed, but clearly when people drink, they get in the mood for singing and dancing. No doubt early Koreans drank to better enjoy themselves.

Certainly the origins of Korean literature, music and dance, indeed all art forms, shared a common link to the consumption of alcohol. Wine figured prominently in the *Song of Confucian Scholars (Hallim pyŏlgok)*, a late Koryŏ (1216) poem that tells of the escapades of gentlemen-scholars affiliated with the Hallim, an academy of letters. A variety of wines is mentioned: "golden" wine, pine nut wine, "sweet" wine, wine made from water filtered through bamboo leaves, pear blossom wine, wine made of the bark of roots, and so on. The poem tells of the gentlemen filling elegant cups and drinking in turns according to their age.

Yi Kyu-bo (1168-1241), a renowned Koryŏ poet and contemporary of these gentlemen, was fond of drinking. He loved poetry, the *kŏmun-go* (six-string zither) and wine so much that he was called "Mr. Three Pleasures," a nickname he seemed to encourage. Poetry, music and wine were both temptations and means of expression for Yi.

A drink shared with friends and family has been an important part of Korean culture since early times. At left, A Gathering of Friends by Yi Inmun (1745-1821) (National Museum of Korea).

There is hardly room here to tell of all the Korean poets and artists who enjoyed drinking. Instead I will focus on the role of wine in everyday life.

Throughout history, opinions about alcohol have been mixed. Some call it the best of all medicines, while others claim it is the worst of poisons. Both points of view say more about the drinker than the drink. The manner in which one drinks can determine alcohol's positive and negative effects. Wine can be medicinal, but it can also be harmful if consumed in excess.

Hŏ Chun, a famous practitioner of Korean medicine in the late 16th and early 17th centuries, noted the following in his *Exemplar of Korean Medicine* (*Tongŭi pogam*, 1610).

Alcohol is good for circulation. It helps gastric function, adds luster to the skin, reduces anxiety, and diffuses anger. It has a fierce character, however, and when imbibed in excess can cause yellowing of the liver and deterioration of the gall bladder. When drinking, men rage like heroes, but they regret their actions when they wake up the next morning. If one overdrinks, the liquor's poison gradually rots the heart, intestines and liver, causing mental derangement and loss of eyesight. One can even lose one's life.

As Hŏ suggests, the manner of the drinker and the amount he drinks determine which side of alcohol's dual character manifests itself. Each person has his or her own capacity for drink. Some people can drink a lot, others hardly a thimbleful. Still, no one is immune to the effects of alcohol. As the old saying goes "The person drinks the first cup of wine, the wine drinks the second, and with the third cup, the wine drinks the person."

Some 40 years ago the poet Cho Chi-hun (1920-1968) published an essay entitled "A Ranking System for Drinking." In it he established 18 ranks for alcoholic consumption. Since then his system has been frequently invoked by Korean drinkers.

The first rank is reserved for people who, while able to drink, choose not to. The second refers to people who drink but are afraid of alcohol. Third are those who can drink, are not afraid of drinking but are leery about getting drunk. Fourth are those who know how to drink, are not afraid to drink and will get drunk, but only by them-

Rice makkŏlli *(top)* and a depiction of a Chosŏn drinking party by Kim Hong-do (1745-?) (above)

selves because they do not like paying for other people's drinks. Fifth are mercenary drinkers who like to drink but only buy drinks for others when it serves their purposes. Sixth are those who drink to improve their sex lives. Seventh are those who drink because they cannot sleep. Eighth are gourmands who drink to whet their appetite.

Cho further ranked grades one through eight as go players are ranked. Grade eight drinkers were given second class ranking, grade seven was the equivalent to third class in go, grade one was ninth class, and anyone lower than that might as well be a member of the temperance league.

Cho dubbed grade nine drinkers "student drinkers" who were learning the true nature of wine. Tenth grade was for lovers of the true taste of alcoholic beverages. Eleventh was for those completely enamored with drink. Twelfth were masters of wine. Thirteenth were wine-lovers who had attained a complete grasp of drinking etiquette and customs. Fourteenth were known as "sons of Bacchus." Fifteenth were scrooges who rarely shared their alcohol or emotions with others. Sixteenth were otherworldly drinkers who could drink and did drink, unfettered by cares of the mundane world. Seventeenth were those who enjoyed seeing others drink but could no longer drink themselves. Eighteenth were "Nirvana drinkers" who had passed onto another drinking world because of their

drinking.

The latter nine grades referred to drinkers who, in Cho's view, had achieved "enlightenment" in that they understood the true nature of alcohol and were able to act according to their own will. Grade nine would correspond to the first class for go, drinkers in the tenth grade approached an understanding of the ways of drinking, and drinkers in each higher grade had achieved a higher level of understanding, until the eighteenth grade, which corresponded with the go master. Anyone surpassing these standards was superhuman and beyond Cho's, or anyone else's, categories.

Everyone who likes to drink should consider what class or grade they fall into. But remember the old saying: "If you drink wine like water, you're not worth the price of the wine." No matter how much one loves to drink, life is not something to be idled away in a drunken stupor. If one is going to drink, it is imperative that he understand the correct way to drink. It is no coincidence that the Korean term *chudo*, "drinking etiquette," contains the word *do*, "the way."

Lin Yu-tang (1895-1976), the Chinese writer renowned for his book *The Importance of Living* (1937), once described how drinking customs should change with the setting and season.

When drinking at formal occasions, one must imbibe in a slow and leisurely manner. In a familiar environment, one must drink vigorously but in a dignified manner. Sickly people should drink only small quantities, while it is imperative that those with sadness in their hearts drink themselves senseless. In spring, drink in the garden. In summer, leave the city and drink in the countryside. In autumn, drink aboard a ship, and in winter drink at home. When drinking at night, take the moon as your drinking companion.

I wonder where Lin would rank on Cho Chi-hun's drinking scale. I have seen a photo of Lin smoking a pipe, but never drinking, so I cannot say for sure, though I imagine he would be at least a 10 or 11 on Cho's scale.

My own acquaintance with alcohol is now in its 40th year, but I have never achieved the heights of Pyŏn Yŏng-no (1892-1961), the poet who wrote the famous *Forty Years of Drunkenness* (1953), and therefore cannot compare my philosophy of drinking to his. Still, I have found my drinking rules to be useful and take the liberty of introducing them.

— Take care to use the appropriate glass for each drink. Sake drunk from a glass made for whiskey tastes bland, and Korean soju from a beer glass is improper.
— Fill the glass or cup four-fifths full. People often say that a cup must be filled to the brim, but an overflowing drink wastes precious alcohol and can intimidate the drinker.
— Do not finish a drink in a single gulp. Take at least three swallows to finish. This is true of all drinks, whether whiskey, sake or *makkŏlli*. When drinking beer, an exception can be made for the first glass, but after that, there can be no more exceptions. After each sip, place the glass on the table and pick up an appetizer or converse with others.
— Do not drink during the daytime. Not even a glass of beer. Unless one wants to sleep the afternoon away, daytime drinking is forbidden.
— Regardless of the season, never drink before sunset. I agree with those who say that alcoholic beverages do not taste their best during the daylight hours. But what about summer when the days are long? No matter. Whatever the season, one must wait until dusk for drink to taste its best.
— Never drink on an empty stomach. Even beer requires some snacks or appetizers on the side. Three different kinds of snacks are good. Whether it is whiskey, *soju* or sake, even the toughest physique needs something to soak up the alcohol, if only kimchi.
— When drinking, two is definitely not enough company. You have to invite a third person, even your girlfriend, to have a good drinking party. It is not enough to have only two people talking back and forth.
— When drinking in a bar or beer hall, one must be careful not to listen to the conversations of others. And one must never exchange glasses with other parties. The spirit of conversation is a beautiful thing, but if one is not careful, small disagreements can escalate into big arguments.
— One should avoid the custom of going to a second and then third drinking venue, the Korean tradition of *ich'a* and *samch'a*. Mixing different types of drink doubles the effect of the alcohol.

A friend of mine ridicules my drinking rules. The whole idea makes him lose his appetite for drink. He says, "If I followed your rules, I'd never experience the true joys of drinking." People may accuse me of never "graduating" from Cho Chi-hun's "student drinker" category, but this is how I have imbibed in the past and how I will continue to enjoy my drink. I have my rules and I plan on obeying them for the rest of my life.

Koreans often talk about *p'ungnyu* when discussing the "art" of drinking. What is p'ungnyu? There is not enough space here for a detailed explanation, but in short p'ungnyu can be likened to the feeling of fresh wind and clear water.

In "The Fishermen's Song," an anonymous Koryŏ Dynasty poet offers some insight into the meaning of p'ungnyu. "As far as one can see, the mountain is illuminated by moonbeams. So why do we need [a beautiful woman] on our boat? This is p'ungnyu enough for us."

Must one have song, dance and women to have p'ungnyu? The dictionary defines p'ungnyu as "the rejection of the common or vulgar in favor of tasteful, elegant enjoyment." Of course, song, dance and women are sure to liven up any drinking party, but one should remember that our ancestors' devotion to p'ungnyu prevented such parties from descending into the vulgar.

In an essay, the poet Shin Hŭm (1566-1628) noted the delicate balancing act between good taste and vulgarity at the drinking table.

A drinking party can turn into drinking hell if human greed is allowed to take over. While entertaining a guest is acceptable, one must be careful not to let the party veer in a greedy or lustful direction for the intersection between happiness and tragedy lies in the realm of human greed.

Consider the following drinking party to which a lady was invited. The Chosŏn poet Im Che (1549-1587) once sat down to drink with the famous P'yŏngyang *kisaeng* Han-u (literally "Cold Rain"). After exchanging several cups of wine, Im passed a cup to Han-u and recited a poem using a pun to invoke the literal meaning of her name.

The northern sky clear
I left home without my raincoat.
Snow came to the mountains
and a cold rain to the fields.
Drenched by cold rain
it looks like I will freeze in bed tonight.

Im Che's poem was an attempt to enhance the atmosphere of their drinking party. Han-u must have known this for she poured Im another cup of wine and sang this song in which she continues the pun.

Freeze? Freeze? Why should you
freeze?
Where have you left
your nuptial pillow and quilt?
Drenched in cold rain
you will melt in bed tonight.

A bottle of wine is shared among relatives at an ancestral rite (below). Wine and nature enhance meditation and friendship as is apparent in A Gentleman Taking a Nap by Yi Kyŏng-yun (1545-1611) (opposite top) and the anonymous depiction of a summer drinking party (c. 1541) (opposite bottom).

Here it is not a question of whether the two were really attracted to each other or not. It is simply an example of the p'ungnyu of drinking.

In the history of Korean literature, Chŏng Ch'ŏl (1536-1593), a renowned poet of the mid-Chosŏn era, was probably the most prolific writer of drinking poems. If a friend had good wine at his house, Chŏng went right over to enjoy it.

Yesterday I heard that farmer Sŏng
from over the hill had new wine.
I kicked the ox to its feet,
threw on a saddle-blanket and rode up
here.
Boy, is your master home?
Tell him Chŏng Ch'ŏl has come to visit.
(Translated by Kevin O'Rourke)

Sharing the pleasures of drink was part of the traditional Korean concept of p'ungnyu. Only a vulgar cad would hoard good liquor for himself at home.

My friend, if you have some wine at home
be sure to invite me.
When the flowers at my house bloom
I will call you.
Let's discuss ways of forgetting
the worries of one hundred years.

This old *shijo* recalls the custom of sharing a bottle of wine and the experience of a beautiful pear blossom or orchid with a friend. Chŏng Ch'ŏl's "A Time to Drink" (*Changjinju-sa*) is an excellent example of poetry singing the praises of flowers and wine.

There is an interesting story regarding Shin Yong-gae (1463-1519) and drinking. Apparently Shin loved drinking so much that when his friends were gone and he had no one to drink with he sat down across from a pot of chrysanthemums and lifted his glass to the flowers. Gazing up at the moon he would

say, "One cup for you, one cup for me." After emptying his cup, he poured a cup for the chrysanthemum. "A cup for you, my dear, then another cup for me." And so on, until he slumped down next to the flower pot and fell asleep. The scene exemplifies the essence of p'ungnyu.

Chŏng Ch'ŏl wrote a poem that was really a dialogue with wine. In it, he sings to wine and wine responds with its own song. Certainly only a wine-loving poet would write this way. Chŏng was truly a model of traditional p'ungnyu. He also wrote an essay entitled "A Warning About Wine."

> I enjoy wine for four reasons: for washing away discontent, for recreation, for the entertainment of guests and because it is difficult to refuse wine when offered. When discontent is my reason for drinking, one could say it is a matter of fate. When I drink for recreation, it is much like whistling. When I drink to entertain visitors, you could say I do it with a sincere heart. But when my mind is made up, it is better that I not be shaken by the words of others, even if wine is urged upon me.

At the beginning of Chŏng's essay, he warns of the hazards of wine but the conclusion is clear: he cannot give up drinking. This observation never could have been made by someone who did not understand the true nature of wine.

I think it was Charles Baudelaire who said, "Wine and man are like two comradely warriors who fight and reconcile endlessly. The loser always embraces the victor."

Wine has been part of human life since ancient times. It has made humanity feel closer to its deities and individuals closer to one another. The warm feelings that bind people are not something that can be turned on and off as one pleases. No one can simply decide to stop drinking the wine they love. Like the old proverb—"A pan that heats easily cools just as easily"—one must learn to drink at the knee of respected elders if one is to drink responsibly in adulthood. In Korea, periodic ancestral memorial rites provide a natural opportunity to sample wine. And one must never force wine upon someone who does not want to drink.

Modern life is hectic, but when drinking we should remember p'ungnyu and the wisdom of our elders, savoring the taste of the drink and the atmosphere with a relaxed and unhurried mind. ◆

APPENDICES

Folk Villages

As Korean society gradually made the transition from a hunting and gathering culture to an agrarian culture, villages began to form in the valleys nestled among Korea's many mountains. The profusion of mountain villages is not simply a reflection of Korea's natural topography; it also reflects the Korean people's love of nature.

Villages conformed to the surrounding environment, dotting the valleys and nestling beside streams and springs. Some had only a dozen households; others were home to several thousand families. Large villages were surrounded by earthen or stone fortifications. Most of these embankments are gone today, but a few fortified villages remain. Several have been designated cultural assets or folklore monuments by the Korean government in recognition of their historical value and in an effort to preserve them for future generations.

Woe-am-ri Folk Village

The village of Woe-am-ri is located on a plain to the west of Sŏlhwasan Mountain in Song-ak-myŏn, Asan-gun in Ch'ungch'ŏngnam-do province. Most of its houses face southwest. A stream fed by waters flowing from Sŏlhwasan in the east and Kwangdŏksan Mountain in the south runs past the entrance to the village. It is the source of the residents' water supply and, according to traditional geomancy theory, serves to balance the strong fire element of nearby Sŏlhwasan.

Sixty-five households make up the village today. They are linked by twisting paths and sheltered by large trees. The traditional flavor of the village is carefully preserved.

Some 400 years ago the Yean Yi clan left the village, but many of the old houses have been maintained. The village was designated an official folk village by the provincial government of Ch'ungch'ŏngnam-do in 1978 and has been designated a preservation zone for traditional architecture by the central government.

Hahoe Village

The village of Hahoe in Andong, Kyŏngsang-buk-do province, is home to the P'ungsan Yu clan and boasts many well-preserved examples of traditional folk practices and architecture.

According to traditional geomancy theory, the village is in an ideal spot, protected by the Naktong River in the south and mountains in the north. Hahoe is famous throughout Korea for the

Hahoe Pyŏlshin-gut, a traditional village rite dating to the Koryŏ Dynasty, and the Hahoe masked dance, as well as for its architecture and proudly maintained clan traditions.

The village, Important Folklore Object No. 122, is divided into two sections: North Village and South Village. As of 1988, there were 188 households in both sections. The homes of well-established *yangban* elite families are substantial with sturdy gates and tile roofs. Yangjindang (Treasure No. 306) and Ch'unghyodang (Treasure No. 414) are two fine examples of elite architecture. The homes of commoner families were generally made of mud and covered with thatched roofs.

Nak-an Ŭpsŏng

Located near the southern coast of Chŏllanam-do province south of the city of Sunch'ŏn, Nak-an Ŭpsŏng is a traditional walled village that remains home to 108 households. Unlike the newer folk villages developed for exhibition, Nak-an Ŭpsŏng is a real village. Its

fortified walls were built in 1450 and several of its main pavilions and gates have been rebuilt in their original forms. The village has been designated Historical Site No. 302 by the Korean government.

On the first full moon of the Lunar New Year, Nak-an Ŭpsŏng holds a torchlight festival and other folk games. On holidays and weekends, traditional wedding ceremonies are often held in this picturesque setting. For a week in early October a food festival celebrates the delicious cuisine of the Chŏllanam-do region.

Yangdong Village

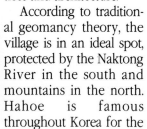

Yangdong Village in Wŏlsŏng is located on the banks of the Hyŏngsan-gang River, north of Kyŏngju, the ancient capital of the Shilla Kingdom. In the old days it was an important transportation center, linking

Kyŏngsang's inland region to the sea.

The village is still quite large today. The Son and Yi clans dominate the village population. More than 30 houses in the village date back some 200 years. All belong to members of the Yi or Son clans. Fifteen houses have been designated Treasures or Important Folklore Objects by the Korean government. The village itself has been designated Important Folklore Object No. 189.

Yangdong Village sponsors numerous folk festivals today. It is best known for its regular summer festivals marking the seven seasonal divisions of the summer according to the lunar calendar. In the fifth lunar month, a special festival of food, poetry and song is staged for elderly villagers.

Sŏngŭp Folk Village

The village of Sŏngŭp is located on the southeast slope of Mt. Hallasan, the principal mountain of Chejudo Island. For nearly five centuries, from the early Chosŏn Dynasty, it was the defensive headquarters of Chejudo. The site was protected by a stone wall and a handful of small "parasitic" volcanoes.

At the center of the village is a zelkova tree thought to be 1,000 years old. Twelve *tol harŭbang*, "stone grandfathers," watch over the village. Groups of four stand at the southern, eastern and western entrances to the village, much like the stone or wooden spirit posts that guard the entrances to villages on the Korean mainland.

Because the island winds are strong, Sŏngŭp's houses lay close to the ground and their thatched roofs are secured with ropes. The walls around the homes are made of black basalt and are seemingly impervious to the wind.

Folk belief remains a powerful force on the island. Regular rites are held to honor local spirits and deities. Traditional folk songs are also well preserved.

Wanggok Village

This village on the northern-most coast of Kangwon-do province is nestled in a basin surrounded by five mountain peaks. At the center of the village is Songchiho, a lake where heavenly fairies are said to have come to sing and dance. Today the village is home to 49 families who make their living at farming. The  windswept village is isolated by the elements and topography, so isolated that it suffered little or no damage during the Korean War.

Most of the homes are not surrounded by stone or earthen walls on all sides. Their front yards are open and shared for large village projects. The lack of boundaries may be the result of the long history of domination by just two clans, the Hams and Ch'oes.

Folk Museums

Agricultural Museum

75 Ch'ungchŏngno 1-ga, Chung-gu, Seoul 100-151
Tel: (02) 397-5673-7
Hours: 10 a.m.-5 p.m. (Closed Sundays and holidays)

Founded in 1987, this three-story museum houses some 1,600 articles related to agriculture. With the help of local farmers' cooperatives around the country, the museum staff took three years to collect, date and label each item, thus providing scholars with an important collection of primary resources on the history of Korean agriculture. The museum is divided into seven display areas: the Prehistory Room, the Three Kingdoms Room, the Koryŏ-Chosŏn Period Room, the Farmer's Almanac Room, the Implement Distribution Room, the Cooperative Farming Room and the Modern Agriculture Room.

Lotte World Museum of Korean Folklore

40-1 Chamshil-dong, Songp'a-gu, Seoul 138-220
Tel: (02) 411-4760-5
Hours: 9:30 a.m.-11 p.m. (Entrance closed at 10 p.m.)
(Open year round)

This museum was designed to help visitors better understand Korean history and culture through reproductions of artifacts and implements from everyday life. More than a simple display of objects, the museum uses advanced audio-video technology, dioramas and models to depict Korean life over the centuries.

Onggi Folk Museum and Institute

497-15, Ssangmun 1-dong, Tobong-gu, Seoul 132-031
Tel: (02) 900-0900, 0399
Hours: 10 a.m.-4 p.m. (Closed holidays)

This museum specializes in the dark-brown jars or *onggi* that Koreans use for food storage. With some 2,500 jars from around the country in its collection, including the work of several accomplished artisans designated Human Cultural Assets, the museum provides a valuable resource for scholars interested in everyday life in traditional Korean society. The museum also displays some 1,000 varieties of *tanch'ŏng*, the colorful painted motifs used to decorate palaces

and Buddhist temples, and offers classes in folk painting to the general public.

Museum of Korean Indigenous Straw and Plant Handicraft

97-9 Ch'ŏngdam-dong, Kangnam-gu, Seoul 135-100
Tel: (02) 516-5585
Hours: 10 a.m.-6 p.m. (Open for general admission on Wednesdays and Thursdays)

This museum, founded in 1993, is the only one of its kind in the world. Straw and thatch have been part of Korean culture since ancient times but with the influx of foreign influences over the last 100 years, their use has gradually declined. The museum is dedicated to perpetuating the use of straw and thatch in an effort to preserve long-cherished traditions and to protect the

environment. More than 3,500 artifacts, including straw shoes, floor mats and baskets, are in the museum's collection.

Pacific Museum

Pacific Technical Research Institute
314 Pora-ri, Kihŭng-ŭp, Yong-in, Kyŏnggi-do

Province 449-900
Tel: 0331) 285-7215
Hours: 9 a.m.-5 p.m. weekdays, 9 a.m.-1 p.m. Saturdays (Closed Sundays and company holidays)

The goal of this private museum, founded in 1979 after more than ten years of preparation by the Pacific Corporation, is the perpetuation and development of Korea's traditional culture and the promotion of research in the field of culture.

The museum is divided into two sections: the History of Cosmetics Hall, which exhibits some 800 items related to cosmetics and their use, and the Tea Hall, which displays items related to Korea's traditional tea culture.

Korean Furniture Museum

9-11 Sŏngbuk-dong, Sŏngbuk-gu, Seoul 136-020
Tel: 02) 766-0167-8
Hours: 1 p.m.-5 p.m. (Closed weekends and holidays)

This museum focuses on traditional Korean furniture and interior design. Conveniently located just ten minutes from Kwanghwamun in downtown Seoul, it is especially valuable for foreign visitors who do not have time to visit the Korean Folk Village in Yong-in, south of the capital. Furniture and household necessities are exhibited in traditional arrangements, with separate displays for the men's and women's quarters, kitchen and other parts of the Korean home.

The Museum of Korean Embroidery

89-4 Nonhyŏn-dong, Kangnam-gu, Seoul 135-010
Tel: 02) 515-5114
Hours: 10 a.m.-4 p.m.
(Closed weekends and holidays)

The collection consists of some 3,000 pieces of embroidery and other handicrafts created by women or used in the women's quarters of traditional Korea. The collection was assembled by Huh Dong-hwa, the museum's founder, over many years. Huh founded the museum with his own funds and collection in 1976.

Of special interest are the more than 1,000 *pojagi* wrapping cloths, which Huh began collecting in the early 1970s. The museum also displays several remarkable embroidered screens, one dating from the 13th or 14th century, embroidered and appliqued curtains, Buddhist embroidery, and personal ornaments, such as belts, tassels and hairpins.

Kŏndol Pa-u Museum

733-4 Taebong-dong, Chung-gu, Taegu, Kyŏngsangbuk-do Province, 700-430
Tel: 053) 421-6677
Hours: 10 a.m.-6 p.m. (Closed Mondays)

This museum specializes in Korea's folk religions. After more than a decade of preparation, the museum opened in 1989 with more than

1,500 items. The first-floor exhibition halls is dedicated to village beliefs, family beliefs and shamanism. The second-floor hall focuses on fortune-telling, sorcery, folk Buddhism and ancestor veneration. The third floor will soon house an audio-video facility, which will be used for educational programs and the screening of videotapes on folk religion.

Onyang Folklore Museum
403-1 Kwon-gok-dong, Asan City, Ch'ungch'ŏngnam-do Province, 336-030
Tel: 0418) 42-6001-4
Hours: 8:50 a.m.-6 p.m. (November-March 9 a.m.-5:30 p.m.)
(Open year round)

Korea's largest folk museum, the Onyang Folk Museum houses some 14,000 items related to traditional Korean lifestyles, handicrafts and industry, folk art, folk belief, entertainment, scholarly pursuits and government. The museum participates in exchanges with domestic and foreign museums and collectors to enhance its exhibitions. It features a large outdoor exhibition area and a special hall often used for traditional wedding ceremonies.

Dongjin Irrigation Folk Museum
105 Yoch'on-dong, Kimje City, Chŏllabuk-do Province 576-010
Tel: 0658) 547-3121
Hours: 10 a.m.-5:30 p.m. (Winter 10 a.m.-5 p.m., Saturdays 10 a.m.-noon)
(Closed Sundays and holidays)

This museum follows the history of Korean agriculture through the development of irrigation. The collection includes 1,243 artifacts of 481 kinds of items. Of these, 725 are on exhibit. Many are invaluable reminders of traditions that have been lost in Korea's rapid modernization.

Agricultural Museum of Chŏllanam-do
307 Nabul-li, Samho-myŏn, Yŏngam-gun, Chŏllanam-do Province 526-890
Tel: 0631) 78-2796, 78-7254
Hours: 9:30 a.m.-6 p.m. (November-March 9:30 a.m.-5 p.m.)

(Closed January 1 and 2, Mondays)
The Chŏlla region is known as an important agricultural center in Korea. The museum is home to a large collection of artifacts representing Korea's traditional agrarian culture. Outdoor and indoor exhibits allow visitors to experience rural life directly.

Andong Folk Museum
784-1 Sŏnggok-dong, Andong, Kyŏngsangbuk-do Province 760-360
Tel: 0571) 821-0649
Hours: 9 a.m.-6 p.m. (Winter 9:30 a.m.-5 p.m.)
(Closed Mondays, January 1, Ch'usŏk and the day after all national holidays)

This museum specializes in the unique features of Andong's regional culture, especially Confucian culture and customs and indigenous folk games and practices. The audio-video room and screening room are used for educational programs. Outside, traditional homes, which were moved prior to construction of Andong Dam, and a traditional icehouse have been erected to offer visitors a taste of traditional Korean life.

Yŏng-il Folk Museum
39-8 Sŏngnae-ri, Hŭnghae-ŭp, Yŏng-il-gun, Kyŏngsangbuk-do Province 791-940
Tel: 0562) 61-2798
Hours: 9 a.m.-6 p.m.
(Closed the day after national holidays)

This local museum, founded in 1983, is dedicated to the preservation of regional customs and artifacts. More than 2,300 artifacts collected by the P'ohang Cultural Center and P'ohang Municipal Government form the basis of the collection.

Cheju Folk and Natural History Museum

996-1 Ildo 2-dong, Cheju City, Cheju-do Province 690-012
Tel: 064) 53-8771, 22-2465
Hours: 9 a.m.-6 p.m. (Winter 9 a.m.-5 p.m.)
(Closed January 1, Lunar New Year's Day, May 24 and three days in June or December for fumigation)

This museum offers a cross-section of exhibits showing life on Chejudo Island, its cultural traditions and natural heritage. Chejudo's

rich marine resources, inland agriculture and mountainous topography are explored in detail with dioramas and display cases. The indigenous culture is portrayed in exhibition halls focusing on everyday life, the local economy and industry, customs and cuisine.

Cheju Folklore Museum

2505 Samyang 3-dong, Cheju City, Cheju-do Province 690-073
Tel: 064) 55-1976
Hours: 8 a.m.-8 p.m.
(Open year round)

Founded in 1964 by a local resident, this museum portrays the lives of the Cheju people through its 3,000-piece collection. Indoor and outdoor exhibitions, including an indigenous thatched cottage, show how the Cheju people have lived over the centuries.

Chungmun Folklore Museum

2563-1 Chungmun-dong, Sŏgwip'o City, Cheju-do Province 697-120
Tel: 064) 38-5511
(Closed Wednesdays)

Located in the southern port city of Sŏgwip'o, this museum portrays life in a traditional fishing port with 18 traditional homes and a myriad of indigenous fishing and farming implements. On exhibit are artifacts dating from prehistoric times that were unearthed in the Chungmun area. Each exhibit focuses on a particular element of traditional culture, helping modern visitors better understand life in traditional Korea.

Korean Folk Village

Kihŭng-myŏn, Yong-in City, Kyŏnggi-do Province 449-900
Tel: 0331) 283-2106-7
(Open year round)

A large-scale replica of a traditional village, the Korean Folk Village offers a slice of old Korea to visitors from around the world. Among its many structures are small thatched cottages from various regions around Korea, large estates in which the *yangban* elite once lived, government buildings, a real market and numerous workshops where artisans produce handicrafts as their forebears did for centuries before them. Special restaurants serve traditional Korean foods, and traditional wedding ceremonies and processions are held every Sunday and holiday during the spring and autumn.

ABOUT THE AUTHORS

Chang Chul-soo was born in Shihǔng, Kyǒnggi-do province in 1946. After studying Korean language education and archeology at Seoul National University, he studied in the graduate folklore program at Tüebingen University in Germany. He is presently Professor of Folklife Studies at the Academy of Korean Studies and a member of the Kyǒnggi-do Provincial Committee for the Preservation of Cultural Properties.

Cheon Wan-kil was born in 1943 and graduated from Sung Kyun Kwan University's Department of History. He is presently Curator of the Pacific Museum in Seoul and Director of the Human Resources Development Institute. He has published on a broad range of topics, from the philosophy of Korean movement to the history of Korean cosmetics.

Cho Hyo-soon received her B.A. from Myongji University, her M.A. from the Department of Education at Ewha Womans University and her Ph.D. from Sejong University. She is presently Professor of Home Economics at Myongji University and a clothing columnist at *Korean Clothing* (*Uri ot shinmun*).

Cho Woo-hyun received her B.A. and M.A. from Seoul National University and her Ph.D. in the history of Korean costumes from Sookmyung Women's University. She is presently Professor of Clothing and Textiles at Inha University and is actively involved in the Korean Clothing Society, the Korean Fashion Society, the Comparative Folklife Society and the Korean Home Economics Society.

Choi Chang-jo was born in Seoul in 1950. He graduated from the Department of Geography at Seoul National University and has taught at numerous universities around Korea. At present he works as a geographer and is a nationally recognized and widely published expert in traditional Korean geomancy.

Choi Seung-beom was born in 1931 in Namwon, Chǒllabuk-do province. He was educated at Chonbuk National University where he received his Ph.D. in Korean Language and Literature and Classic Literature. Choi is active in the literary field and is presently Professor Emeritus of Korean Literature at Chonbuk National University.

Choi Young-taik was born in 1931 in Myǒngch'ǒn, Hamgyǒngbuk-do province, and graduated from the Department of Architecture at Hanyang University. He has spent his life in the heating field, researching and developing heating systems, and holds 12 patents related to the *ondol* hypocaust, Korea's unique under-floor heating system.

Chung Seung-mo graduated from the Department of Anthropology at Seoul National University. He has taught at Seoul National University and Chonnam National University and is now Curator of Seoul City Museum and a member of the Kyǒnggi-do Provincial Committee for the Preservation of Cultural Properties.

Han Pok-jin graduated from the Department of Home Economics at Ewha Womans University and received her graduate degree in Food Science at Korea University. She has been designated an initiate in the court cuisine of the Chosǒn Dynasty by the Korean government and is presently Professor of Korean Traditional Cuisine at Hallym Junior College, as well as a nationally recognized instructor in court cuisine.

Huh Dong-hwa was born in Hwanghae-do province in 1926. He graduated from the Department of Law at Dongguk University and received his Masters degree in Public Administration. Since 1976 he has been the Director of the Museum of Korean Embroidery, now known as the Sachon Embroidery Museum, and has been instrumental in the preservation

and understanding of embroidery and textiles from traditional Korea.

Joo Nam-chull was born in Sǒngjin, Hamgyǒngbuk-do province in 1939. He received his B.A., M.A. and Ph.D. in Architecture from Seoul National University and studied the history of architecture at Rome University. Since 1981 he has been Professor of Architecture at Korea University and is active in the field of architecture in Korea.

Kang In-hee was born in Seoul in 1919 and has taught at numerous universities throughout Korea. Since 1984 she has been Professor Emeritus of Home Economics at Myongji University and Director of the Kang In-hee Korean Taste Institute. She has written extensively on Korean cuisine and food customs.

Kang Shin-pyo is a native of T'ongyǒng in Kyǒngsangnam-do province. He has taught and been active in research in cultural anthropology at numerous institutes around Korea and is currently Professor of Cultural Anthropology and Director of the Academy of Humanities and Social Science at Inje University.

Kim, Bong-ryol was born in Seoul in 1958. He graduated from the Department of Architecture at Seoul National University. He has worked in several architecture firms and is presently Professor of Architecture at Ulsan University. Among his publications are *Korean Architecture–Traditional Architecture* and *Pǒpchusa*.

Kim Kwang-hyun is a native of Seoul, born in 1953. He graduated from Seoul National University's Department of Architecture and received his Ph.D. in Architecture from Tokyo University in 1983. He is now Professor of Architecture at Seoul National University. In 1997, he received the Korean Institute of Architects' architecture award for his design of the Architectural Culture Building.

Kim Kwang-on was born in Seoul in 1939. He studied Korean Language Education and Archeology at Seoul Normal University and graduated from the graduate program at Tokyo University. The former director of the Inha University Museum, he is presently Professor of Social Education at Inha University. Among his many publications on traditional Korean culture are *The Korean Kitchen*, *Oh, Koguryŏ!* and *Geomancy: House and Village*.

Kim Manjo received her B.A. in Marine Food Chemistry from Pusan National University and a M.Sc. and Ph.D. in Food Technology and Food Microbiology from the University of Leeds, England. She has served as a lecturer at Yonsei University and Seoul Women's University and is now an independent food industry consultant in the United States, working on assignment in Indonesia.

Kim Yong-duk is a native of Muju in Chŏllabuk-do province, born in 1949. He graduated with a Ph.D. in Korean Literature from Hanyang University and is now Professor of Korean Language and Literature there. He has written extensively on the history of Korean customs and literature.

Kim Yoo-kyung was born in Seoul in 1947. She is a graduate in French Language and Literature from Seoul National University's School of Education and Ewha Womans University. For many years she worked as a reporter and Editorial Board Member for *Kyunghyang Shinmun*. She now is a freelance journalist.

Kum Ki-sook was born in Okch'ŏn, Ch'ungch'ŏngbuk-do province in 1952. She received her B.A., M.A. and Ph.D. from Ewha Womans University and did postdoctoral work at East Michigan State University in the United States. She is now Assistant Professor of Textile Art at Hong-ik University and is active in fashion circles.

Lee Hyo-gee was born in Seoul in 1940. She studied Home Economics at Sookmyung Women's University and received her Ph.D. from Chung-ang University. She is presently Professor of Home Economics at Hanyang University and author of numerous publications on cooking.

Lee Kwang-kyu was born in Inch'ŏn in 1932. He taught at Vienna University and since 1979 has been a Professor of Anthropology at Seoul National University. He is presently a member of the National Committee for the Preservation of Cultural Properties and is active in numerous cultural organizations.

Lee Sang-hae graduated from the Department of Architecture at Seoul National University and received a M.Arch. and a Ph.D. in the History of Architecture at Cornell University in the United States. Since 1986 he has been Professor of Architectural Engineering at Sung Kyun Kwan University. He has written extensively on Korea's traditional and modern architecture.

Lim Young-ju was born in Kaesŏng in 1943. He graduated with a Ph.D. in Art History from Hong-ik University. Formerly a researcher at the National Museum of Korea, he is presently Head of the Culture Research Division at the Korean Antique Fine Arts Association and a member of the Kyŏnggi-do Provincial Committee for the Preservation of Cultural Properties.

Park Hye-in was born in Inch'ŏn in 1952. She graduated from Seoul National University's Department of Home Economics and received her Ph.D. in Home Economics from Korea University. She has been a visiting scholar at the Research Institute for Japanese Culture at Tohoku University and a research scholar at the Center for Korean Studies at the University of California at Los Angeles. She presently is a Professor of Home Economics at Keimyung University.

Park Tae-sun graduated from the Department of Korean Language and Literature at Sung Kyun Kwan University and received his M.A. in History at Dankook University. After serving as Director of Exhibitions at the National Museum in Seoul, he moved to Kwangju where he is the Head of the Liberal Arts Research Department at Kwangju National Museum.

Yim Jae-hae is a native of Andong, Kyŏngsangbuk-do province, born in 1952. He graduated from the Department of Korean Literature at Yeungnam University and is now Professor of Folklore at Andong National University and active in the study of oral literature and folklore.

Yoo Byung-rim was educated at Seoul National and Harvard universities. He is presently Professor of Environmental Studies at Seoul National University as well as Chairman of the Korean Landscape Architecture Society and the Korean Landscape Architects Association. He has designed the landscaping for numerous parks and traditional gardens in Korea.

Yoo Tae-jong was born in 1924 in Kongju in Ch'ungch'ŏngnam-do province. He taught Food Science at Ch'ungbuk National University, Hanyang University and Korea University and is now Professor of Food Science at Konyang University and the Director of the university's Food Culture Institute. He has published widely on the nutritional value and traditions of Korean cuisine.

Yun Seo-seok is a native of Seoul, born in 1923. She taught Home Economics at Myongji University, and since 1961 has taught in the College of Home Economics at Chung-ang University. She has published numerous works on Korean food and the history of Korean cookery, including *A Dictionary of Korean Food Terms* and *Research into the History of Korean Food*.

WORLD CHRONOLOGICAL TABLE

	KOREA	CHINA	JAPAN	THE WEST
B.C.	Paleolithic Age			
5,000	Neolithic Age			
				Early Mesopotamia
2,000		Bronze Age	Jomon Period	Egyptian Kingdoms
		Shang Dynasty (1766-1122)		
1,000		Zhou (1122-256)		Greek Civilization
	Bronze Age	Spring and Autumn Era (770-476)		Founding of Rome (735)
500	Ancient Chosŏn	Iron Age		
	Iron Age	Warring States Era (475-221)	Bronze Age	Socrates (469-399)
	Puyŏ	Qin Dynasty (221-206)	Yayoi Period	Alexander the Great (356-323)
		Western Han Dynasty (206 B.C.-		First Punic War (264-241)
		A.D. 9)		Second Punic War (219-201)
200	Confederated Kingdoms of			
	Samhan (Three Han States)			
100	Three Kingdoms:			
	Shilla (57 B.C.-A.D. 935)			
	Koguryŏ (37 B.C.-A.D. 668)			
	Paekche (18 B.C.-A.D. 660)			Birth of Christ
A.D.	Kaya (42-562)			
200		Shin Dynasty (8-25)		
		Eastern Han Dynasty (26-221)		
300		Three Kingdoms (220-280)	Iron Age	
		Qin Dynasty (265-420)	Tumulus Period	Christianity adopted as the state
				religion of Roman Empire (392)
				Roman Empire divided (395)
400		Northern & Southern Dynasties		Anglo-Saxons established in
500		(420-581)		Britain (449)
600			Asuka Period (552-645)	Mohammed (570-632)
	Parhae Kingdom (669-928)	Sui Dynasty (581-618)	Nara Period (645-794)	Hegira (622) and beginning of
	Unified Shilla Kingdom (618-935)	Tang Dynasty (618-906)		Islamic era
700			Heian Period (794-1185)	
800				Charles the Great crowned first
				Holy Roman Emperor (800)
900	Koryŏ Kingdom (918-1392)			
1000		Five Dynasties (906-960)		
1100		Song Dynasty (960-1279)		First Crusade (1096-1099)
1200			Kamakura Period (1185-1392)	
				Magna Carta (1215)
		Yuan Dynasty (1279-1368)		Marco Polo (1254-1324)
1300	Chosŏn Kingdom (1392-1910)		Muromachi (Ashikaga) Period	The Hundred Years' War
		Ming Dynasty (1368-1644)	(1392-1568)	(1618-1648)
1400				Gutenberg's Press (1438)
				Columbus discovered America
				(1492)
1500			Momoyama Period (1568-1615)	Martin Luther launches reform
				of the church (1517)
1600			Tokugawa Period (1615-1867)	The Thirty Years' War (1618-1648)
1700		Qing Dynasty (1644-1911)		American Independence (1776)
				French Revolution (1789-1793)
1800	Taehan Empire Proclaimed (1897)		Meiji Period (1868-1912)	American Civil War (1861-1865)
1900	Annexation by Japan (1910)	Establishment of the ROC (1912)	Taisho Period (1912-1926)	World War I (1914-1918)
	Establishment of the ROK (1948)	Establishment of the PRC (1949)	Showa Period (1926-1988)	World War II (1939-1945)
	Korean War 1950-1953		Heisei Period (1989-)	

Koguryŏ (37 B.C.-668)		Paekche (18 B.C.-660)		Shilla (57 B.C.-618)		Unified Shilla (618-935)		Koryŏ (918-1392)		Chosŏn (1392-1910)	
Tongmyŏng		Onjo	18 B.C.- A.D. 28	**Pak Clan**		**Kim Clan**		T'aejo	918-943	T'aejo	1392-1398
	37 B.C.- 19 B.C.	Taru	28-77	Hyŏkkŏse	57 B.C.-A.D. 4	Munmu	661-681	Hyejong	943-945	Chŏngjong	1398-1400
Yuri	19 B.C.- A.D. 18	Kiru	77-128	Namhae	4-24	Shinmun	681-692	Chŏngjong	945-949	T'aejong	1400-1418
Taemushin	18-44	Kaeru	128-166	Yuri	24-57	Hyoso	692-702	Kwangjong	949-975	Sejong	1418-1450
Minjung	44-48	Ch'ogo	166-214	**Sŏk Clan**		Sŏngdŏk	702-737	Kyŏngjong	975-981	Munjong	1450-1452
Mobon	48-53	Kusu	214-234	T'arhae	57-80	Hyosŏng	737-742	Sŏngjong	981-997	Tanjong	1452-1455
T'aejo	53-146	Saban	234	**Pak Clan**		Kyŏngdŏk	742-765	Mokchong	997-1009	Sejo	1455-1468
Ch'adae	146-165	Koi	234-286	P'asa	80-112	Hyegong	765-780	Hyŏnjong	1009-1031	Yejong	1468-1469
Shindae	165-179	Ch'aekkye	286-298	Chima	112-134	Sŏndŏk	780-785	Tŏkchong	1031-1034	Sŏngjong	1469-1494
Kogukch'ŏn	179-197	Punsŏ	298-304	Ilsŏng	134-154	Wonsŏng	785-798	Chŏngjong	1034-1046	Yŏnsan	1494-1506
Sansang	197-227	Piryu	304-344	Adalla	154-184	Sosŏng	798-800	Munjong	1046-1083	Chungjong	1506-1544
Tongch'ŏn	227-248	Kye	344-346	**Sŏk Clan**		Aejang	800-809	Sunjong	1083	Injong	1544-1545
Chungch'ŏn	248-270	Kŭnch'ogo	346-375	Pŏrhyu	184-196	Hŏndŏk	809-826	Sŏnjong	1083-1094	Myŏngjong	1545-1567
Sŏch'ŏn	270-292	Kŭngusu	375-384	Naehae	196-230	Hŭngdŏk	826-836	Hŏnjong	1094-1095	Sŏnjo	1567-1608
Pongsang	292-300	Ch'imnyu	384-385	Chobun	230-247	Hŭigang	836-837	Sukchong	1095-1105	Kwanghae	1608-1623
Mich'ŏn	300-331	Chinsa	385-392	Ch'ŏmhae	247-261	Minae	838-839	Yejong	1105-1122	Injo	1623-1649
Kogugwon	331-371	Asin	392-405	**Kim Clan**		Shinmu	839	Injong	1122-1146	Hyojong	1649-1659
Susurim	371-384	Chŏnji	405-420	Mich'u	262-284	Munsŏng	839-857	Ŭijong	1146-1170	Hyŏnjong	1659-1674
Kogugyang	384-391	Kuishin	420-427	**Sŏk Clan**		Hŏn-an	857-861	Myŏngjong	1170-1197	Sukchong	1674-1720
Kwanggaet'o	391-413	Piyu	427-455	Yurye	284-297	Kyŏngmun	861-875	Shinjong	1197-1204	Kyŏngjong	1720 1724
Changsu	413-491	Kaero	455-475	Kirim	298-309	Hŏn-gang	875-886	Hŭijong	1204-1211	Yŏngjo	1724-1776
Munja	491-519	Munju	475-477	Hŭrhae	310-355	Chŏnggang	886-887	Kangjong	1211-1213	Chŏngjo	1776-1800
Anjang	519-531	Samgŭn	477-479	**Kim Clan**		Chinsŏng (Queen)	887-898	Kojong	1213-1259	Sunjo	1800-1834
Anwon	531-545	Tongsŏng	479-501	Naemul	356-402	Hyogong	898-912	Wonjong	1259-1274	Hŏnjong	1834-1849
Yangwon	545-559	Muryong	501-523	Shilsŏng	402-417	**Pak Clan**		Ch'ungyŏl	1274-1308	Ch'ŏlchong	1849-1864
P'yŏngwon	559-590	Sŏng	523-554	Nulchi	417-458	Shindŏk	913-917	Ch'ungsŏn	1308-1313	Kojong	1864-1907
Yŏngyang	590-618	Ŭidŏk	554-598	Chabi	458-479	Kyŏngmyŏng	917-924	Ch'ungsuk	1313-1330	Sunjong	1907-1910
Yŏngnyu	618-642	Hye	598	Soji	479-500	Kyŏngae	924-927	Ch'unghye	1330-1332		
Pojang	642-668	Pŏp	599-600	Chijŭng	500-514	**Kim Clan**		Ch'ungsuk	1332-1339		
		Mu	600-641	Pŏphŭng	514-540	Kyŏngsun	927-935	Ch'unghye	1339-1344		
		Ŭija	641-660	Chinhŭng	540-576			Ch'ungmok	1344-1348		
Parhae (698-926)				Chinji	576-579			Ch'ungjong	1348-1351		
Ko	698-719	Kan	817-818	Chinp'yŏng	579-632			Kongmin	1351-1374		
Mu	719-737	Sŏn	818-830	Sŏndŏk (Queen)	632-646			U	1374-1388		
Mun	737-794	Yijin	830-857	Chindŏk (Queen)	647-654			Ch'ang	1388-1389		
Wonŭi	794	Kŏnhwang	857-871	Muyŏl	654-661			Kongyang	1389-1392		
Sŏng	794	Kyŏng	871-893								
Kang	794-809	Wigye	893-906								
Chŏng	809-812	Ae	906-926								
Hŭi	812-817										

INDEX

256